# WOMEN, WORK, AND GENDER RELATIONS IN DEVELOPING COUNTRIES

Recent Titles in
Contributions in Sociology

For Democracy: The Noble Character and Tragic Flaws of the Middle Class
*Ronald M. Glassman, William H. Swatos, Jr., and Peter Kivisto*

Social Oppression
*Adam Podgórecki*

Eastern Europe in Transition: The Impact of Sociology
*Mike Forrest Keen and Janusz Mucha, editors*

Stepparenting: Issues in Theory, Research, and Practice
*Kay Pasley and Marilyn Ihinger-Tallman, editors*

The Temptation to Forget: Racism, Anti-Semitism, Neo-Nazism
*Franco Ferrarotti*

Critical Theory and Political Possibilities: Conceptions of Emancipatory Politics in the Works of Horkheimer, Adorno, Marcuse, and Habermas
*Joan Alway*

Demographic and Structural Change: The Effects of the 1980s on American Society
*Dennis L. Peck and J. Selwyn Hollingsworth, editors*

Family, Women, and Employment in Central-Eastern Europe
*Barbara Łobodzińska, editor*

Constructing the Nation-State: International Organization and Prescriptive Action
*Connie L. McNeely*

New Poverty: Families for Postmodern Society
*David Cheal*

Housing Privatization in Eastern Europe
*David Clapham, Jozsef Hegedus, Keith Kintrea, and Ivan Tosics, with Helen Kay, editors*

# Women, Work, and Gender Relations in Developing Countries

## *A Global Perspective*

EDITED BY
PARVIN GHORAYSHI AND CLAIRE BÉLANGER

Contributions in Sociology, Number 118
*Dan A. Chekki, Series Adviser*

Greenwood Press
Westport, Connecticut • London

Library of Congress Cataloging-in-Publication Data

Women, work, and gender relations in developing countries : a global
  perspective / edited by Parvin Ghorayshi, Claire Bélanger.
      p.  cm.—(Contributions in sociology, ISSN 0084–9278 ; no.
  118)
    Includes bibliographical references and index.
    ISBN 0–313–29797–5 (alk. paper)
    1. Women in development.  2. Women—Employment—Developing
  countries.  3. Women—Developing countries—Social conditions.
  I. Ghorayshi, Parvin.  II. Bélanger, Claire.  III. Series.
  HQ1240.W6659     1996
  305.4'09172'2—dc20        96–10741

British Library Cataloguing in Publication Data is available.

Library of Congress Catalog Card Number: 96–10741
ISBN: 0–313–29797–5
ISSN: 0084–9278

First published in 1996

Greenwood Press, 88 Post Road West, Westport, CT 06881
An imprint of Greenwood Publishing Group, Inc.

Printed in the United States of America

The paper used in this book complies with the
Permanent Paper Standard issued by the National
Information Standards Organization (Z39.48–1984).

10  9  8  7  6  5  4  3  2  1

# Contents

# Preface

Over the past decade, study of work has dealt with the most sensitive and important problems of social life. Considerable change in the nature of work has occurred, and this increasingly complex field of study has been covered by many theories and research, gradually building up an impressive body of knowledge. The growth of new intellectual approaches has provided fresh answers to the old questions and raised novel issues as legitimate areas of investigation. One of the most important additions as well as challenges to the study of work comes from the growing interest in women's work. Feminist scholars have shown that although women have always engaged in productive activities, women and women's work have long remained invisible. As well, the terms under which they participate in the labor force continue to be a considerable problem.

Feminist studies have demonstrated that women's invisibility and their unequal treatment are not limited to studies of the labor market, but exist in all areas of social science and society. Feminist scholars have criticized and reevaluated existing social science theories, discovered new concepts, established interdisciplinary linkages, and created new sociological paradigms. They criticized research and theories on work for ignoring the experience of women as women and for downplaying women's experience as workers. Academic disciplines were questioned, sometimes in their most basic self-conceptions and categories. The result has been a massive amount of literature and an increasing specialization within the field of women's studies itself, of which the area of women in developing countries is a strong component.

Feminist scholars studying women and development challenged the established male perspectives of development theories of the 1950s and the 1960s. Modernization, the dominant theory at the time, was criticized either for ignoring the social dimension of change in the developing countries or for simply asserting that economic modernization and Westernization would liberate women. Marxist literature was also criticized for ignoring the experience of women, and feminist analyses were questioned for downplaying women's experience as workers. Feminist scholars of the Third World and women of color, in particular, have argued that women's studies reflect mainly the privileged women who live at the center, whose perspective of reality excludes knowledge and awareness of those who live on the margin. They stressed that the concept of woman has become synonymous with white middle-class woman, whereas women of color and women of developing countries are seen as *other*. They agreed that women are oppressed, but stressed, as does Nawal El Saadawi in this book, that not all women are equally oppressed. Varying degrees of oppression based on nationality, class, ethnicity, and other factors have to be recognized. In short, they drew our attention to the complexity and diversity of women's experiences and questioned the universal notion of woman.

Feminist scholars set out to fill the void they saw, making women visible and women's questions a central issue of debate, nationally and internationally. During the past two or three decades, in particular, we have witnessed an impressive volume of research focusing attention on the condition, lives, and experiences of women in developing countries. The inauguration of the United Nations' decade for women in 1975 was a high point in the evolution of women's studies in developing countries. Various UN agencies, the World Bank, many Western institutions for international development, private voluntary groups, women academics, and even multinational corporations identified with the field. At present, governments in different parts of the world have established ministries and institutions to deal with women's issues. Whatever their limitations and successes, their very formation shows the recognition of the need to involve women.

By 1990, our knowledge of women's lives and experiences had substantially improved. We know that women, compared to men, in developing countries work longer, receive less money, have more responsibilities, have less schooling, and even absorb less calories. The growing number of empirical studies on women's work in developing countries has made it impossible to deny the centrality of women to economic life. This literature has shown that women in developing countries are heavily concentrated in the rural sector and the so-called informal economy and that much of their work is not only undervalued, but omitted from the calculation of national and international products.

More recent studies on women and international development have benefited from past achievements and the growing amount of information and research on women. In these writings, the complexity of women's experiences is acknowledged, and there is a shift of focus in women's studies. By emphasizing the complexity and diversity of women's lives, feminists drew our attention to the importance of social relations between the sexes. They argued rightly that gender relations have to be located within the hierarchical relations of domination both at the micro- and macrolevels of analysis. As Marie France Labrecque discusses in her chapter, we need to talk about hierarchical relations and identify a series of domination relations, not necessarily all masculine, which impede women in the effort to be equal partners in their societies. This focus on social relations allows us to look at gender relations both at the structural level and at the level of everyday life. This also enables us to see how changes do and can take place.

Scholars of international development have, again and again, discussed the interdependence among national economies and the central role of women both locally and internationally. Les Levidow's chapter on Malaysian women who make the chips makes the important point that women of developing countries not only contribute to their own individual societies, but also produce for the international market and are linked to the global economy. Therefore, understanding the nature of the global economy and women's place in this economy is essential.

It is important to note that the global economy or the new world order is but the latest stage of development of the world capitalist system. This new onus entails a shift away from the international division of labor that emerged after World War II and toward a more encompassing historical context. With the global economy, capital has now reached a new stage of development that bypasses the nation state and the national market in favor of what geographers have named "production sites." The division of labor is no longer solely geographical, between the North and the South, but reflects the separation, within a transnational firm, of the managerial and research functions from the productive sphere. Management and research are concentrated in urban service centers, while production is found in economically marginalized areas in both the North and the South where an abundant supply of cheap labor is available. This new order has been labeled, by some researchers, as post-Fordism.

In light of these changes, what we have to keep in mind in addressing women's issues in the developing countries is that development and underdevelopment are interrelated and are two sides of the same coin. Women are part of this reality. Awareness of this global perspective, as Lynne Phillips argues, is critical for all those interested in the study of development issues.

Parallel to this broader structural outlook, we need to understand social relations at the microlevel. Everyday life is a place of multiple contradictions and it allows us to document the experience of individuals and how they interpret, understand, and define their world. Most notably, the study of everyday life lays bare the ideological representations pertaining to women that have so long been taken for granted, women's assumptions, and also what women find problematic about their lives.

Studying gender relations at the microlevel signifies that whatever roles women assume in a given society, they are devoid, in most social formations, of socially entrenched value. Women's roles change across time and space, but their subordination does not. The gender relations are sanctioned by social institutions, especially the state, as well as other institutions in the civil society. Women are socialized to internalize these gender relations. The relations of domination shape women's destinies and their psyches. The French anthropologists have coined the phrase of *dominated consciousness* to describe the mental state of these women who consent to gender relations of domination and who identify with the power relations.

By focusing on gender relations we are able to see the social construction of the subject. Case studies, in this collection, unfold at the local level and arrive at the diversity of socially constructed gender relations. In this way, these chapters question the universal notion of women and recognize that there are differences of class, ethnicity, and other important factors among women. Being a woman means different things, for example, for various economic groups, as well as for women from different countries and regions. In fact, the notion of woman can even vary within the same culture, yet similarities do exist.

Study of everyday life also makes it clear that women, as individuals and as agents, are social subjects who actively build their universe and are aware of the structural constraints within which they operate. Chapters by Gisèle Simard and Gertrude Mianda make these points very clear. Women are subjects—agents who make choices, have critical perspectives on their own situations, and who link and organize collectively against their oppressors. Each individual, man or woman, within his or her limits, has the power to change the conditions of daily life. To the extent that individuals organize, change occurs.

Within this perspective, as reflected in Suzan M. Ilcan's research, we see that social change results from a complex interrelationship between structure and everyday life, in a dynamic and nonlinear fashion. By understanding the links between structure and individuals, we will recognize that social change takes different forms. In this way, we avoid determinism, acknowledge the multiplicity of social relations, and admit that systems of domination operate through the setting up of particular, historically specific "relations of ruling." It is through the understanding of the intersections that we can attempt to explore questions of consciousness and agency without naturalizing either individual or structure. It is only by grasping the contradictions inherent in women's locations within various structures that effective political action and challenges can be devised. It is on the basis of such context-specific differentiated analysis that effective political strategies can be generated.

In this book, we aim to contribute to the recent feminist scholarship. We look at the complexity and diversity of women's lives both at the micro- and macrolevels. We also attempt to find out how social relations link structure and individuals, and how social change takes place. This intention explains the way in which we have organized the chapter. Part I broaches theoretical and methodological considerations. The three chapters in this part serve to situate the debate in gender studies today and reflect the focus of this book.

Labrecque's chapter is based on her many years of field work experience and recommends a framework that helps us to understand the complexity of social relations at three distinct, but interrelated levels: the structure, the individual, and the group. The concept of hierarchy allows us to grasp the multiple dimensions of social relations and the working of inequality at all three levels. This framework calls for the necessity of linking the macro- and microlevels of analysis in order to effect social change. Phillips draws our attention to the postcolonial criticism of development and discusses methodological problems in the development literature. She provides us with explicit guidelines for a methodology that is accountable and makes a conscious attempt to avoid generalizations that Western development demands. Within this framework, the aim of the research, whom it serves, and its context must be made explicit. She reminds us of the power of the researchers and stresses that placing women in the center is not sufficient. In chapter 3, Tiffany R. Patterson and Angela M. Gilliam interview El Saadawi, the Egyptian doctor, novelist, and activist, who discusses how Western feminism can construct and has indeed constructed the other woman. El Saadawi questions the relations of hierarchy between Western and non-Western women, and she stresses that Western women should listen to the voices of Third World women and cease talking for them. She draws our attention to the necessity of using culture-specific studies in the discussion of inequality and of developing strategies for change.

Part II links the global perspective to women's daily lives. The first three chapters illustrate what takes place on the macrolevel. Levidow studies how women are integrated into the global capitalist economy. Third World women, in this case study, are the chip makers who provide the cheapest labor for the international market. In Southeast Asia, governments court multinationals using gender ideology to control and suppress women. Christiana E. E. Okojie shows that women's economic activities are central to rural Nigeria, but that there are major constraints on their productivity. She calls for policies that acknowledge women's contribution, target women, and aim to promote their access to resources. Collette Suda focuses on Kenya and shows both differences and similarities in women's working lives in rural and urban settings. Women's work experiences vary by class, region, and ethnicity. As a whole, Kenyan women have made major gains, but barriers continue to exist.

In chapters 7 through 10, the authors provide us with a detailed understanding of daily life and establish linkages with global change. Mianda's analysis of the organization of garden production as the space of power relations shows first, the dynamics of social construction of gender, and second, how women manipulate the sexual division of labor to change the power relations that impede their access and control over production. The social construction of gender cannot be understood, in this case, without taking into account colonial policy, kinship, and lineage systems in Zaire. Tuula Heinonen discusses how gender ideology under postcolonialism constructs women as being economically inactive and contributes to their invisibility. However, this case study of rural Philippine women shows how the ideal of men as breadwinners and women as homemakers was challenged by the exigencies of household needs. Suzan M. Ilcan employs Foucault's notion of power and argues that tradition and morality are discourses of power. She shows, in her case study of rural Turkey, that migrant labor resulting from proletarianization was seen in moral terms, challenging the traditional landlord-peasant relationships. She analyzes how class and gender relations resulted in the feminization of agriculture and the masculinization of cash relations. She also broaches the resistance of women and how this form of challenge differs across generations. Delia D. Aguilar's research demonstrates that the experience of mothering in the Philippines differs from that of Western women, and also that there are important class differences among Filipino women themselves. Overall, Filipino women see marriage as the most natural state of their lives and internalize the ideology of the self-sacrificing, natural mother. Thus, while the specific role of women in reproduction varies in time and space, the author highlights how the discourse on society and nature defines women in terms of biological reproduction, legitimizing a construction of gender that serves, along with class, to subordinate women.

Parts III and IV show that changes can and do take place. Chapters 11 and 12 present an alternative as well as a challenge to capitalist development. The last two contributions show how women can and do empower themselves, bringing about change through self-organization. Gisèle Simard questions the adequacy of the economic model for grasping the reality of women entrepreneurs in Mauritania. Urban enterprises are a way of life for African women. This study emphasizes the dynamics of cultural rationality and its importance, as opposed to economic rationality, for understanding women's productive activities in urban Mauritania. Veronika Bennholdt-Thomsen's study of Juchitán contradicts the established notion that industrialization and globalization are necessary for development to occur. In her study of a peasant subsistence economy, she discusses how trade and subsistence are not mutually exclusive. Here, women are the main acting participants in an economy that is centered around use-value. They are also the main social actors in ensuring, through the marketing of food, that wealth is spent through collective consumption.

Dina Abbott's chapter on the Annapurna women of Bombay shows how women, by coming together, were able to assist each other and start their own cooperative credit. Credit has to be understood both within the context of poverty and of power relationship. Women, through their self-organization, challenged negative images and changed both poverty and relations of power. This case study illustrates how women bring about social change when they are given access and control over their production and the capital it generates. Mary Morgan uses popular education techniques to develop curriculum based on women's experiences. This educational methodology encourages self-development and can be a premise for social change.

# Acknowledgments

Special thanks go to Dan Chekki, Naomi Guilbert, Nancy Lehr, Lou Lépine, Elizabeth Soto, Carol and Joe Szekely, all the contributors to this book and the editors at Greenwood Publishing Group, in particular, Arlene Belzer; each, in their own way, made this book possible. We are grateful to the Social Sciences and Humanities Research Council of Canada for providing financial support.

# PART I

# Theoretical and Methodological Considerations

# 1

# The Study of Gender and Generational Hierarchies in the Context of Development: Methodological Aspects

*Marie France Labrecque*

One of the main problems currently confronting those who reflect on the social dimensions of change in the context of international development stems from the fact that relevant models and theories were conceived for understanding structural processes referred to, by some, as macrosociological. When the particular situation of women and children within these processes of change constitutes one's main interest, as it does mine, these theoretical models appear to have no direct significance. The same problem presents itself with approaches that focus to a greater extent on individuals and actors: They seem to lose all meaning when we attempt to understand the structural integration of the latter.

The discussion presented here deals with the methodological alternatives available for studies that take into account all of the dimensions of social change in general, and of social relations between various significant social categories. Throughout this discussion two main influences will be apparent: that of feminist thought and that of political economy in anthropology, as described by William Roseberry in an important article published in 1988 in which he shows to what extent Marxist anthropology of the 1970s has undergone a mutation, making it more sensitive to the practices of daily life.

This chapter comprises three main parts. In the first, I will present the general context of my reflection, which is that of a research project I carried out in the La Cocha region of Colombia. I will briefly describe the main characteristics of the region and of its population, especially since the introduction of income-generating projects for women in the mid-1980s. In the second part, I will describe what research guidelines were used in La Cocha in order to understand the effects of the development projects, and I will expose the problems that rapidly arose in this study of social change. In the third part, I will explain what I mean by *hierarchy*, and particularly by *gender* and *generational hierarchies*. I will also specify, beyond the political economy approach, which influences most directly have affected the development of my thinking on this subject. I will end this chapter with a discussion of some of my research results in light of the methodological approach I have adopted.

## THE STUDY REGION

The La Cocha region is located in the Colombian Andes, more precisely in the province of Narino. My first contact with the people of this region goes back to 1988. I was sent there to evaluate a small development project funded since 1985 by the Canadian International Development Agency (CIDA) through one of its executing agencies, the Société de développement international Desjardins (SDID). One aspect of the project was the creation of small income-generating projects for women, mainly raising guinea pigs and dairy cows, and secondarily growing blackberries and fish farming. The approach generally referred to as "women and development" therefore constituted the context for the research project that I subsequently carried out in the region, funded by the Social Sciences and Humanities Research Council of Canada (SSHRC). Some of our findings have been published in Côté (1993a, 1993b), Labrecque (1994a, 1994b), Lopez Arellano (1993), and Ménard (1993a, 1993b).

The La Cocha region derives its name from a lake also known as Lake Guamuez. At 14 km long and 3 to 5 km wide, La Cocha is one of the largest lakes in Colombia. Located at an altitude slightly under 3,000 meters, the lake drains an area covering approximately 22,500 hectares. The source of the Guamuez River is south of the lake and joins the Putumayo River, which is itself a tributary of the Amazon River.

The climate is cool (average of 14° C) and rainy (200 mm per month). The land is hilly and the vegetation is lush, although the virgin forest has been decimated and replaced by second growth forest. The slopes around the lake have been eroded, and occasionally there are landslides.

Seventeen hamlets (or *veredas*), whose houses are quite dispersed, surround the lake. The population, mostly from other regions of the province of Narino, was about 4,500 in 1984 (SDID 1984). The slopes around the lake were settled only about fifty years ago by peasants who were expelled from communities devastated by minifundismo and political violence.

Although they define themselves as farmers, the inhabitants of La Cocha practice a wide range of activities, some of which, for example the making of charcoal, are as important as agriculture, with men, women, and children all actively involved in its production. While certain tasks are exclusively carried out by adult men, all social categories of the population are acquainted with all of the production processes.

The La Cocha peasantry is integrated into wider commercial networks through local merchants in a context of clientele relations that could be qualified as "classical." Merchants provide the people with subsistence items in exchange, most often, for their charcoal production. In fact, there is a hierarchy of intermediaries between the communities, the nearest town, and the capital, Pasto. In the communities, there are peasants who usually have a means of transportation (a small motorboat) and some cash and who can act as intermediaries for the less fortunate. In an environment that is characterized by an absence of roads, the control over transportation can constitute the basis for a certain accumulation. Since the price of charcoal tends to remain stagnant while that of consumer goods continually rises, the vast majority of peasant families have been indebted for years to the merchants in town or in the city, who are in fact moneylenders, or in the local language, *gamonales*.

Several governmental or paragovernmental entities are present in La Cocha, some of whom deal with the protection and development of the environment. The La Cocha region in fact constitutes a significant tourist resource for the country. The Colombian state is represented in every hamlet by the Junta de Accion Comunal, an entity that was set up in the context of a rise in guerrilla activity in the 1970s in order to better control the population. The president of the junta has very limited power, but nonetheless constitutes the first link in the administrative chain.

The people of La Cocha share several cultural traits distinctive to the Andean region. Since there have never been any ethnographic studies of the region, it is difficult to say to what extent the people, while not indigenous, have integrated certain aspects of the heritage of the native Indians of the neighboring valley of Sibundoy. Several elements of indigenous material culture can be observed, such as brewing *chicha*, a fermented drink made of corn. Certain beliefs and representations that are not directly related to native culture as such, but rather to the blend that ensued from the confrontation between dominant colonial society and native peoples over the past centuries, also persist.

Of the traits that have their origin in the broader Andean culture and that are practices of the people of La Cocha, the *minga* is a good example. It consists of occasional community work carried out to solve practical problems such as making trails, draining riverbanks, or building a school or a chapel. Because it constitutes an obvious opportunity for mobilizing people and is part of the cultural background of the population, the *minga* has been used by various political and community groups for a variety of purposes. It is currently one of the main tools used by the Association for Peasant Development. This association was the SDID's partner in its development work in the region. Through its promotion of income-generating projects for women from the mid-1980s on, it contributed to spreading a particular conception of social change, which explains why it occupies a special place in this research.

## THE RESEARCH QUESTIONS

One of the initial questions of the La Cocha research concerned the changes likely to take place within the division of labor and their effects on gender relations. However, given the relatively limited time between the initiation of income-generating projects and the beginning of our research, the difficulty in measuring the changes and bearing witness to their effects very quickly became apparent. This methodological difficulty prompted me to broaden the research beyond the study of development projects and to reflect on the anthropological approach to change and its relevance to understanding gender relations. Having realized that La Cocha constituted one of the rare recently colonized regions of the Andes, I expanded the definition of development in order to take into account the changes that had taken place since the beginning of the settlement, about fifty years ago. This made it possible to incorporate all of the socioeconomic and political measures the population had been subject to, particularly in the context of integrated rural development policies in Colombia.

Pinpointing these measures in the structural arena and identifying their general effects on Colombian peasant communities was relatively easy due to paradigms developed on the basis of political economy both by Colombian researchers and by foreign researchers interested in Colombia (Edwards 1980; Machado 1986; Galli 1981; Gros and Le Bot 1980). Difficulties in interpretation arose when I attempted to focus on the specific dynamic of development and social change in the immediate study region, as well as on the integration of the various categories, particularly women, within the population.

It must be admitted that the approaches and models used for studying development and social change in general are more concerned with the social structure than with individuals and their daily lives. As feminists have demonstrated, concentrating on the study of structure rather than on that of daily life or individuals has detrimental consequences for social categories such as women who are particularly invisible within structures. The question that arose out of this research is therefore the following: *How, in a study on social change, can we take into account both structures and daily life while acknowledging the complexity of social relations, in particular, those involving women?*

Thus formulated, the question appears to be resolved through a combined study of both macrosociological and microsociological factors. Since the mid-1980s, while political economy approaches have become somewhat less popular, and we have been witness to a "return of the social actor," it is considered good form to propose a structural study of the socioeconomic context followed by an ethnographic study of the community.

One of the methodological problems of this approach lies in the fact that the dimensions and categories selected for the analysis of each of these arenas, that is, the structure and the daily life of individuals, do not coincide. Such studies generally show that social changes in the areas of structure and daily life have their own separate dynamics that meet only during special, spectacular moments such as revolutions or concrete protest movements. Social change is still generally viewed as a mechanical variation of enumerable features. However, thanks to researchers like Georges Balandier, for instance, we know that social change is far from being mechanical and that its study cannot be limited to such special moments. He considers social change to be a complex phenomenon with *multiple dimensions* (Balandier 1993). Its study must simultaneously take into account a great number of factors. Among these factors, social relations certainly constitute a valuable object of analysis.

It is therefore less a question of studying social change in a way that takes into account structures, daily life, and individuals, but rather that considers the *continuity* between structures and individuals. From a methodological point of view, the problem is one of studying social processes without reifying them and interpreting them in an effort to finally understand the dynamic of social change. We can then, along with the people concerned, help orient social change in a given direction.

In light of the few descriptive elements provided above on the region and taking into account the preceding critical remarks, the objective of the next section is to share some elements of the methodological approach used in the research in La Cocha and in the analysis of the findings. Beyond the specific case of this region, I would like to emphasize the interest of an approach to social change based on the study of social relations rather than on that of the structure, of daily life, or of individuals as such. By focusing on social relations, research is better able to reveal the dynamic of the multiple connections between the various arenas of social life.

More specifically, we need an approach that recognizes that social relations, most notably gender and generational relations, cross the whole social fabric, thus connecting the structure, daily life, and individuals. In the following section, the discussion will focus on the notion of hierarchy, enabling us to deal with social relations in all their dimensions. We could, of course, examine several types of hierarchies. However, we will limit the discussion to gender and generational hierarchies because they are both based on physical differences. While corresponding intimately to the global structure of society, these hierarchies influence the daily practice of all individuals without exception. Examining these hierarchies constitutes a basic step for those who wish to understand social change as a dynamic process connecting the structure with individuals. The argument I will develop, based on the contributions of feminist scholars, is that it is equally as important to study the relationships between categories as it is to study the categories themselves.

## THE STUDY OF HIERARCHIES AND SOCIAL RELATIONS

In the study of gender and generational relations, the use of the word *hierarchy* seems to impose itself. However, in social anthropology, the contribution of Louis Dumont obliges us to move beyond the common meaning of the term and to contemplate its multiple dimensions.

In its most simple form, hierarchy can be considered a relationship between two adjacent levels of experience (Dumont 1992: 17). In the case of gender relations, Dumont states that the fact of being a man or of being a woman corresponds to these "two adjacent levels of experience." From a certain point of view, there is therefore *identity*. Experience, placed in its historic and social context, shows however that one category has been incorporated into the other. Thus, the category "Woman" is included in the general category "Man." From another point of view there is also *difference*. The two adjacent levels of experience are, in fact, different levels. As Dumont says: "Thus the hierarchical relationship, or incorporation, can be analyzed in simple logical terms whose contradiction is avoided by implementing two different levels" (Dumont 1992: 18).

The notion of hierarchy therefore constitutes an interesting contribution to the study of social relations in that it obliges us to consider dimensions other than those of the real or assumed inequality of these relations according to the level at which we are placed. We may well point out that social relations are unequal in a given context and that certain individuals are excluded because of this inequality. However, this exclusion is far from absolute. It may prove to be true at one level while at another it may be totally absent. It is not a case of affirming that inequality is relative but rather of proposing an approach that makes it possible to refine the study of gender relations. As Tcherkézoff states: "Both inequality and equality establish a single level of practices: those with the required qualities are equal, the others are in a situation of inequality; the hierarchy therefore establishes several levels of practices" (1993: 146). In other words, the notion of inequality (or of equality) makes only a very minor contribution to our understanding of the complexity of social relations. The notion of hierarchy, on the other hand, enables us to consider these social relations on several levels.

A certain convergence seems to emerge from this free interpretation of hierarchy according to Dumont and from French feminists, in particular.

Of the few authors I have selected, Christine Delphy is probably the one who deals most directly with the notion of hierarchy. In an article published in 1991, she points out that most authors are interested in the (equal-unequal) type of classification generated by the relationship between sex and gender. She proposes that we ask ourselves instead why sex should give rise to any classification at all. It is in the paradigm of hierarchy that she sees the driving force behind division (Delphy 1991: 98). She considers hierarchy to be a component of gender (Delphy 1991: 94).

Like Delphy, authors such as Anne-Marie Daune-Richard and Anne-Marie Devreux are concerned by the fact that sex is a "socially constructed category" and not, as French sociology of the 1970s claimed, "a classification variable" (Daune-Richard and Devreux 1985: 44). Gender categories "are in fact constructed in and through the social relationship that both unites and opposes them: unites them because it refers to the same system of social division (based on sex); opposes them because the relationship is profoundly antagonistic" (ibid.: 45).

The study of the construction of social categories therefore necessarily implies that of the gender relation and the processes that determine its transformation "through its own specific dynamic" (Combes, Daune-Richard, and Devreux 1991: 62). These authors go one step further, affirming that this relation crosses the whole of society according to a single logic that "assumes different forms in various arenas (of social life)" (Daune-Richard and Devreux 1992: 12). Here, of course, they are referring to social reproduction as not simply a "duplication, but a continuous and complex process which produces the conditions necessary for the continued existence of a system" (ibid.: 19). The process is therefore a dynamic one:

The question of reproduction is therefore that of the conditions necessary for the preservation or evolution of the system which is constituted by the reciprocal relationship between genders. The object of analysis will therefore be to identify, characterize and qualify the elements that contribute to its preservation and/or transformation: are there breaks, thresholds, shifts, reinforcements/consolidation? (Combes, Daune-Richard, and Devreux 1991: 63)

In light of these contributions, it appears that it is not the terms of the relationship that should most interest us, but rather the relationship itself, the dynamic interaction between categories. Along the same lines, Marie Claude Hurtig and Marie-France Pichevin write:

when dealing with hierarchical social categories (White/Black, French/Immigrant, men/women), the categorization process, aside from its role in differentiating, in distinguishing similar from different, acquires a discriminatory function which is social, not just cognitive. What influences the way information is processed is the hierarchy between the categories which constitute the classification system, undoubtedly more than the specific characteristics of any given system (race, sex, etc.). (Hurtig and Pichevin 1991: 171)

While this comment lies within the domain of perceptions, it undoubtedly is intended as an invitation to adopt a hierarchical approach to social categories rather than a contradictory and dual approach. In fact, it is not only the social categories themselves that are at issue here, but also the relationships between these categories. Monique Haicault, for example, reiterates the complexity of social relations, particularly gender relations, while maintaining that this complexity "is related to the availability of *several forms of relations between their two terms*" (Haicault 1993: 7).

This approach to the relationship between terms makes the study of social change possible. Obviously it is not the genders that are changing, but rather the relationship between them. Thus, "the gender relation changes, going from one state to another or from one degree to another, through its own specific dynamic" (Combes, Daune-Richard, and Devreux 1991: 62).

As presented and interpreted by these authors, the notion of hierarchy encourages us to focus on connections and relationships more than on the constituent elements of these relations. The notion of hierarchy invites us to move beyond static and unsophisticated approaches that simplistically oppose men and women, adults and children, and even social classes in a model of inequality based on exclusion. The notion of hierarchy allows for the possibility of apprehending situations in which the relationship between the terms is neither entirely antagonistic nor entirely complementary. It is true that the system in which we live tends to lead us to perceive events and social relations in a binary and contradictory manner and, in reality, that may often be the case. As Mary Douglas affirms:

Individualistic thinking, like the political experience of hierarchy, is structured by analogy to the production and distribution process. . . . Women are at a disadvantage in such a system not only because they are likely to be treated as commodities . . . but because they have no other way of thinking of themselves as women than in terms of commodities, of producers or purchasers in a system of marketing and trade. (Douglas 1992: 53)

Thus, without the possibility of thinking of the system differently from what it is in reality, any perspective of social change would be impossible. Eventually, reconsidering our environment according to a hierarchical system could favor "distinguishing differentiated categories of people and the awareness of their singularity" (Douglas 1992: 44).

The notion of hierarchy encourages us to consider social changes in a dynamic, nonlinear manner. The authors reviewed in this research conceive of social change as a modification of social relations. Although their focus is on gender relations, it does not exclude the possibility of simultaneously studying other relations. Daune-Richard and Devreux point out the importance of "combining, for analytical purposes, social class relations and gender relations, to which social relations between generations should undoubtedly be added" (Daune-Richard and Devreux 1985: 51). This is precisely the path I set out upon: taking into account a multiplicity of social relations that consider, in a non-deterministic fashion, that gender and generational relations cross the whole range of "social arenas."

## DISCUSSION AND CONCLUSION

The methodological choices regarding the approach to social change and social relations impose a treatment of the data that moves away from the dichotomy between the macro- and microsocial levels. Class, gender, and generational relations within social arenas or spheres constitute the elements that structure the analysis.

In the case of Colombia, the analysis is based on the fact that, as a country, it is tied to international development policies, including Canada's via CIDA's presence in the study region through income-generating projects for women. A study of the composition of these projects reveals that structural elements distinctive to Canadian society have direct and tangible repercussions on La Cocha women and on their interactions with men. In particular, gender relations in Canada and the ability of certain women to promote a specific conception of gender in development, whether or not one agrees with that conception, have been projected into a region of which most Canadian taxpayers have no knowledge. Examining these social relations in the *structural arena* therefore constitutes a *first level of analysis.* This examination makes it possible to draw connections between contexts that, at first glance, are unrelated. The process, as a whole, sheds a particular light on the constraints to social change in a given environment.

It is also important to show that while individuals or the social relations between them lie within the structural arena, the structure in turn can be detected in the arena of the individual and her-his daily life. In La Cocha, for example, social change in a development context has taken on completely different connotations depending on the hierarchical relations involving the various social categories; in other words, depending on whether one belongs to the poor or the rich peasantry, whether one is a woman or a man, a child, an adult, or whether one is a member of a community association.

Individuals and their daily lives therefore constitute a *second level of analysis.* Using life histories can prove to be extremely relevant for dealing with this aspect of research, in that one can focus on the gender relations that define women's and men's productive and reproductive activities. In the majority of studies on development as context for social change, when the subject of women is dealt with at all, it is handled as though women constituted a homogeneous social category whose members all share the same characteristics. Practice and experience, however, clearly show that such is not the case. Taking into account a factor such as age is sufficient to challenge this presumed homogeneity. Studies that focus on demonstrating the internal heterogeneity of social categories as defined by social scientists in general and by feminists in particular, when the social category is women, remain hard to come by.

In the research presented in this chapter, I wanted to demonstrate that the effects of development, whether capitalist development in general or development programs and projects in particular—which at any rate work along the same lines—are felt differently by men and women, by youth and elders. It appears that women's development, especially in the case of women in the middle of their reproductive lives, implies not a lightening, but an intensification of their productive activities. Even when their participation in agricultural work increases, women are more and more confined to tasks that require patience, meticulousness, and dexterity but that bring them no prestige. It is therefore to be expected that small income-generating projects for women will be abandoned or that they will be taken over by other social categories, most notably, men. This is precisely what has happened in La Cocha where male dominance and the weight of the patriarchal structures of the Colombian state have been confirmed.

Elucidating the connections between the social arena of the individual and that of the structure called for studying a *third level* that is neither exactly that of individuals nor exactly that of structures, but rather the social arena of *associations and organizations*. Studying the global structure of society and that of women's daily lives is unquestionably very important. However, without studying a "hinge" between them, such as associations, the connections between the first two social arenas would remain difficult to understand. In fact, change is likely to take on a more significant and more lasting social dimension only insofar as individuals are able to group together. The study of one of these associations, the Association for Peasant Development, has enabled us to take all hierarchical relations into consideration, particularly gender and generational hierarchies. The advantage of studying associations lies in the fact that their contours are quite clearly defined and that concrete signs of change are easily observable.

This third arena of study has shown that while it is true that income-generating projects for women have not fundamentally changed their living conditions, the fact that some women and youth have wanted and sought out positions within the various committees of the peasant associations has shaken up people's view of gender and generational relations. Social change does not in fact necessarily take place exactly as planners have foreseen in the structural arena. Sometimes, people, through their own organizations, must impose their own views. Studying this kind of social change brings other social relations into play that were neither in the structural arena nor in that of individuals.

In summary, the process I propose places the problem of social change in three different social arenas: global structure, daily life and individuals, and associations. Because all of these arenas are interwoven it is difficult to assume that any one takes precedence over the others. In fact, a knowledge of the historical, economic, and social structure is essential to understanding phenomena involving local populations and especially various categories of people within these populations. The weight of the structure can have more or less impact on individuals depending on how present the state and institutions (to give but an example) are in people's daily lives. However, if we assumed that individuals are completely at the mercy of transcendent factors, we could not speak of social change. Therefore, in the structural arena, social change can be defined as the result of the combination of historical, political, and social factors favored by the shift in the relative weight of hierarchical relations and which has been reflected in the general configuration of society.

Social change is not, however, only structural. In their more or less organized actions, individuals enter into a dynamic that constitutes both the outcome of and the basis for broader social change. Thus, social change can also be defined as the result of individual or group practices that modify the social relations in which they are involved. Thus defined, social change is therefore an ongoing process that cannot be measured in terms of the degree of success achieved by various categories of the population in their actions. That is why it is important to examine their practices independently of the more general scope of their actions. In La Cocha, the striking thing is how the pace of change varies depending on the social relations that connect various social categories to the surrounding structures of society. The kind of hierarchies involved in these social relations, to a large extent, define social change. In a word, social change must be approached in connection to social relations, keeping in mind that it is a process with multiple dimensions that varies depending on the social arena of the research.

## NOTE

This chapter, including all of the quotations, has been translated by Mary Richardson from French to English. This is a revised version of a paper presented at the 21st Annual Conference of the Canadian Anthropology Society in Vancouver in May 1994.

# 2
# Toward Postcolonial Methodologies
*Lynne Phillips*

## INTRODUCTION

In this chapter I consider some of the methodological problems of approaches in the emerging development literature that center on women's voices and women's interests. Speaking as a feminist anthropologist, with all the contradictions that this identity contains (Cole and Phillips, 1995), I focus on three assumptions that often underlie these approaches. These assumptions are that (1) women's words are raw data existing outside our ways of knowing them, (2) women's voices are data sources that are pure, somehow uncontaminated by patriarchal and capitalist and/or other ways of knowing the world and, (3) the retrieval of voices *for* development is a neutral, disinterested process. Taking issue with these assumptions, I argue that the methodologies of doing development with women, and the knowledge that these methodologies produce, cannot be understood independently of existing global theories of and for development. My research with rural women in coastal Ecuador provides a context for unraveling the practices of hearing, contextualizing, analyzing, and representing what women's interests might be—and for questioning why we want to "know" them. What I hear women saying today about their interests is different from what I heard in 1980 when I first came to Ecuador, but then my voice too has changed, as have the contexts that have shaped all of our voices and our political understanding of them.

## QUESTIONING DEVELOPMENT

Emerging postcolonial theories have shown Western notions of development to be an all-encompassing discourse of modernity, developed to explain and control the world (Apffel-Marglin and Marglin 1990; Sunder Rajan 1993; Williams and Chrisman 1994). These critiques have prompted a questioning of what we mean by development and how our use of the term silences other ways of knowing. As the contributors to *The Development Dictionary* (Sachs 1992) have made very clear, the development discourse is so saturated with Eurocentric modernist thinking that even concepts such as helping, participation, and equality become part of the problem. Such perspectives have led some analysts to dissect development as a disciplinary process for policing the world in the name of modernity (Escobar 1984, 1988). It has led others to reject development entirely, considering it a "threat" to humanity (Esteva 1987).

These critiques have been important for revealing the modernist assumptions of women and development, especially in the area of research/practice known as Women in Development (WID). Mohanty's (1991) analysis of the concept of the Third World Woman, integrated into Western development discourse as a homogeneous category, a victim who is in need of help, has been particularly important for showing how the modernity/tradition dichotomy in development thinking overlays how we come to understand global gender relations. Feminism of course has not remained unscathed by these new developments. Concepts of global sisterhood and international feminism are also revealed to be a kind of metadiscourse that swallows up or creates difference in the interests of Western feminists, a kind of "imperial" feminism (Amos and Parmar 1984). Apffel-Marglin and Simon (1994) talk about WID as "Feminist Orientalism" with its colonialist mission of eliminating tradition to increase women's economic productivity; WID experts, they argue, know what's good for women even if those "other" women don't say it.

Such arguments indicate the extremely difficult position in which those who are interested in development with women place themselves. It becomes necessary not only to rethink basic analytical categories such as "women" and "development," and transform the modernist foundation in which many feminist theories are rooted, but also to constantly question our role as researchers, our methods of doing research, and our political intentions and practices.

Within this context, it might seem preferable simply to discontinue doing research, but I think that such a solution only reinforces the current mystification of contemporary social relations and ultimately leaves intact many oppressive relations.[1] Giving up on critical research ensures, on the one hand, that racism, imperialism, and sexism remain unchanged and, on the other, that narrow, economistic interpretations of development continue to thrive. With the Ecuadorian women I have met over the last fifteen years reminding me of my reciprocal obligations to them, suspending research is not an ethical option for me, but neither is doing research that is blind to the postcolonial criticisms of development.

Perhaps because the contradiction of doing a postcolonial development *for* women is too great to ignore, one alternative has involved a shift to listening to women's voices, placing their interests at the center, and redefining social change from their perspective. This approach is meant not only to permit women's words to be heard but also to have women's interests provide the basis for undercutting existing paradigms of development. This approach, centering on social change from women's point of view, has been considered a kind of development *with* women rather than for them.

Yet the critiques outlined above make it clear that "placing women at the center" may not be sufficient to dismantle the productionist, modernist orientation of development. Indeed it is not uncommon to find that such an approach is not at odds with the promotion of greater productivity for basic human needs—what might be considered the cornerstone of Western development (cf. Young, Samarasinghe, and Kusterer 1993). Thus, to think uncritically of development with women as the alternative methodology that miraculously resolves the criticisms levied against the WID literature is to seriously underestimate the power of Northern interests on researchers, on development goals, and on women's interests everywhere.[2]

Underlying my argument is a concern about the implications of the increasing pressures of global capitalism for research collaboration with women. Given the successful push from the North for structural adjustment, trade liberalization, and entrepreneurship, should researchers from the North be concerned about a disappearing line between development with women and development in the interests of the North? In cases where women from the South have been convinced of the value of neoliberal solutions, what is the role of the (unconvinced) researcher who is doing development with women? In other words, how do those doing development with women come to terms with Northern hegemony? Is there a way of doing development with women that provides a critique of these solutions without slipping into another kind of feminist colonialism?

## QUESTIONING METHODOLOGIES

My focus here will be on how researchers might usefully work through (though not necessarily resolve) some of the assumptions that are contained within the methodology of placing women's voices at the center of development. My argument is that leaving these assumptions hidden and undiscussed permits this methodology to work with current ideas of development, when the objective, from a feminist perspective, must be to expose these current ideas for how they may work against women.

The process that interests me here is how women are "given voice" and for what purposes. There are three interrelated questions that I think need to be addressed, all of which involve some discussion of power and power differentials. They are (1) the epistemological question of how we know women's voices, (2) the translation question of how we make sense of those voices and, (3) the accountability question of for whom we do this kind of research. I discuss each of these in turn, by drawing on the following account of my own research with women in rural coastal Ecuador in 1992.[3]

## CONVERSATIONS IN RURAL ECUADOR

I had arrived at Amanda's house early in the morning. We talked about the encroaching "winter" (rainy season), the family's medical problems, her children growing up. I wondered if my comadre would want to talk about the changes that I saw in the area since my last visit, six years ago, but I hesitated to ask. The topic of social change is one that I had come to view with some trepidation. I had long given up asking women, "Do you think things have changed here?" or "How do you think your life has changed?" because they invariably said "no" and "it hasn't," respectively. Today I was going to try a different approach with Amanda.

"Is it okay with you if I ask you a big question?" My comadre looked suspicious, but nodded.

"When do you think was the most important event in your life?" I asked. Amanda laughed. "Another question like that?" After a pause, she said, "Well, I guess I have to say when I married."

"Why was that important?" I asked, surprised that Amanda had answered my question at all.

"Because my life changed so abruptly. One minute I was out dancing and going to parties. The next I was in the house and couldn't go out. When I was free (*libre*), I used to love dancing, I'd love to go out with my friends. But that all changed when I became compremetido."

"You say 'free' as though it was a kind of slavery after you were married," I ventured.

"But that's the way it was! That's the way it is. Exactly like slavery. I couldn't go anywhere. He was very jealous. He didn't want me to go out. I didn't like it at all. But little by little I got used to it. Now I don't like to go out much."

I had never heard my comadre talk like this before. I had many times asked her why she did not go to local parties or attend the Union of Working Women (UMT) meetings[4] and she had always told me simply that she did not "like to go out." I had come to take her position at face value, assuming simply that that is how she defined her interests—as the home and her family. I was prompted to ask a different sort of question.

"Did you have dreams of doing something different before you got married?"[5]

"I never had an education you know. I never went to school. I taught myself to read—but never once went to school. But you need to go to school to have a profession. That's what I tell my daughter. She needs to have something. Things aren't the way they used to be. Women have to have a profession. What I wanted to do before I married was go to the city and get a job, be a domestic (*empleada*) in Guayaquil, that's what I secretly wanted. But I never told anyone—most of all my mother. She would have beat me if she'd known that's what I wanted to do."

"Why?"

"Because in those days parents didn't think about their children contributing money to the house. All they thought about was controlling them. They would *never* have let me go to the city." (Pause.) "And then I got married and that was that."

That same day, Amanda's neighbors, Eva and her two sisters-in-law, Marisol and Marta, were preparing the midday meal when I arrived. It seemed like an ideal opportunity for initiating a group discussion on some of Amanda's observations. I asked them if getting married had changed their dreams.

"Yes," said Eva immediately. "I dreamed of marrying someone young and I married an old man!" (Everyone laughed; Eva and Marisol are married to men twenty years older than themselves.)

"It depends on what your dreams are," said Marta, more philosophically. "Some people don't hope for much, others hope for too much." (This inspired a general hum of agreement.)

Two of their spouses came in just as I was asking, "Do you think the relations between men and women here have changed? Have things changed in the home?"

"Of course," said Marisol. "Now that women are working more, in banana packing and in INNFA,[6] where my comrade works, there are more jobs for women."

"But has that changed relations *between* men and women? Does it give women more power in the home?" I asked.

"No," said Eva and Marisol in unison, looking at me (I felt) as though I had just grown a second head. "It's just that now there are jobs for them, and they can bring in some money."

"But what the man says is still the rule?" I asked, feeling brave despite the mixed company.

"Depends on what he's insisting on!" said Eva provocatively. "Of course women don't do everything men say."

"Well, if the man says you can't go out of the house . . ." I ventured.

"Oh, you mean women's liberation . . ." Eva's brother began with a smile.

"No!" Marisol interrupted him. "Women have equal rights to men. If men can go out, women can go out too. That is what is fair. Men and women are equal."

I was surprised by Marisol's bold comment. I looked at her partner, Alberto, and asked: "And what do the men say?"

"Depends," said Alberto. "The woman has to be trustworthy. Men don't start getting jealous and controlling women unless there is a reason. If the woman is walking around here and there as though she's not married, then the men don't like them to go out." (Pause.) "Now let me ask you a question. Does your partner get jealous about you being here by yourself?"

"My partner? No . . . ," I said hesitantly.

"Of course not," said Alberto confidently. "That's because he knows that you are a serious person. He can trust you."

I remembered then that several years ago Alberto had found Marisol with another man, or so I was told. I suddenly felt uncomfortable. Had my questions been played for a morality lesson? Was my presence here being used to discipline other women?

At the end of the day, exhausted from a long day of thinking in Spanish, I saw a woman washing clothes near the roadside. She stopped me. "You don't remember me?" she asked. (I didn't.) She wanted to talk, asking me, "Has my face changed? Do I look old to you?" We ended up considering the topic of dreams.

"My dreams? I never dreamed my life would turn out like this! Abandoned by my compromiso, living in this [bamboo] house with three families [her family, her sister's, and her mother] and no work. I had hoped that I would have had my own house by now, with my children, but it doesn't look like that is going to happen. This is my daughter," she said, putting her arm around a small girl. "This is the one my spouse abandoned. He's with another woman downriver now."

"Do you want to find another mate?" I asked her.

"No. Not now. What I want is work. But there isn't any. I work one day a week for the banana companies for 5,000 sucres. But they only need you for the one day. I used to cook and wash clothes for the gringos upriver but they're gone now. Ooh, they wanted to eat such strange things!. . . . And I'll wash clothes, but there is no one who needs someone permanently." (Pause.) "All I can hope for is that my daughter gets an education so she can better herself. They beat me in school so I was never too interested in going past primary school. I never did. I believe in curing. My mother does some. I could learn to do it but people wouldn't believe that I could really heal so it wouldn't be much of a business for me."

That night, sharing the cab of a pickup truck with two daughters of a local landowner, I was told that one of them would be going to university.

Following up on my comadre's comment, I indicated to the young woman that I thought it was good that rural women have professions now too. "Yes," she said to me quietly. "But there are some that are very critical of it. They're much happier if we stay at home and wash."

## Epistemology

In research, reciprocity is integral to the construction of knowledge. We cannot know anything about women's lives without their consent to participate in our research, but neither can readers understand these women's lives outside of a researcher's apprehension of them. This epistemological dilemma is not resolved by focusing on women's voices; we do not hear those voices outside the researcher's technique, context, and rationale for "giving" them to us. Neither is there some sort of natural connection between women that allows the shared gender of a researcher and her collaborators to account for how we know what we know. This means that in order for readers to appreciate the nature of the researcher's participation in those voices, it is essential for researchers to self-consciously document precisely how they have "taken" women's voices.[7]

My suggestion here is that researchers explore and make explicit their *theory of listening*. Listening should not be taken for granted as a nonjudgmental process;[8] it is, like any social activity, a process steeped in ideologies that need to be explicitly examined if we are to avoid the old development traps. A theory of listening would tell us what researchers think is important, why they might think so, and how they have played a role in ensuring that the reader will agree with them when they make women's voices central to their projects.

The above account, for example, is based on oral exchanges in which I was involved through participant observation in a region where I have done research for over a decade. The account is written in a way that makes it clear that I am there participating, asking questions, and instigating women's analyses of situations. Would they have analyzed their lives in this way if I had not been there to ask these questions? This of course is a question that is impossible for me to answer. What is more important is that I clarify the context in which I am giving these women a voice. Though I have tried to write this account in a way that makes multiple readings possible, my interest in social change is made explicit, and it is within this context that we hear these voices. Thus, not *every* conversation is documented; what we might call "small talk" is not here, for example, though other readers might have found it very informative in terms of their interests.

However, what is still absent from the above account are my reasons for being interested in social change. What are the assumptions that underlie my view that social change is necessary? An interest in social change could be, for example, because of an implicit belief in the value of modernity or because women's increased empowerment is viewed as imperative, two common assumptions in the development literature that are criticized by postcolonial orientations. My concern here is the impact that neoliberalism (Latin America's most recent definition of "development") has had on women's lives. Rural Ecuadorians have experienced several governments defending the need for structural adjustment, a reformed state, and more free trade, policies that are closely tied to changes in the global political economy over the last decade. Nongovernmental organizations (NGOs) in Ecuador have mushroomed over that period of time; a number of them are interested in improving rural women's "profitability." In the region where I have undertaken research, an organization of peasant women, the UMT, had been granted a small project through an NGO and the Ministry of Agriculture (MAG), where women are given access to credit so that they can grow their own rice. Each woman receives 400,000 sucres, which they must repay within a year with a lower interest than the current rate. This project interested me because rice growing is generally thought of as men's work in this area. I was curious about the impact of this attempt to, according to one ministry official, "give women experience in accounting, managing money, figuring out how to balance expenses and income in order to make a little profit [utilidad], to give them experience with this sort of thing so that ultimately they can operate through private banks."

Projects such as these gave people like Marisol the impression that there were more opportunities for rural women today to make money, but this money was in fact distributed to only a small group of women, most of whom either had someone else (a male) plant and harvest the rice for them or did not invest in rice production at all. I talked to one woman who had spent her rice credit money on starting (unsuccessfully) a small chicken-raising business. Also, within the group of women who did receive credit, there were important differences in life circumstances and ability to repay.

When I arrived in the area I was immediately asked if I would meet with the UMT to see if there were more projects of this kind that could be obtained. I agreed, but was surprised to find only the secretary (who dominated the conversation), the president, and the treasurer at the meeting. I asked them how things were working out with the current project. "Oh, it is a great help," said the secretary. "Let's face it, everything the woman does goes towards the home and so men are happy that more money is coming in, especially now when they have problems finding work or getting good prices for the products." I asked, "Do you ever worry that there are never any projects for women themselves, as women, not as mothers?" The women exchanged glances. Then the secretary said, "That's what [the NGO] had wanted too—that only women could be involved in these projects so that only they would get benefits. But it's not like that here. In any project that women do here men will be somewhat involved. It's all work together for the family as a whole."

I left the meeting with the specifications about the kinds of credit arrangements that the UMT was hoping to arrange, and I promised to meet with an organization in Quito on their behalf. But I felt uneasy about the meeting; the silence of the other two women in particular made me wonder about the extent to which I was being drawn into something that I did not entirely understand. It is *this* context that prompted my discussions with nonactivist rural women about social change.

An elaboration of this context, as part of my own theory of listening, permits readers to hear women's voices as part of—though not reduced to—the processes of global capitalism. Of course, there are limitations as to how much any of us are able to recover our own theories (Escobar 1992). But the point here is to detail what I can see from the privileged position of someone who can travel to do research, of someone who has the means to "locate" women's voices and write about them, of someone who has the power to identify global change as an important marker for women's lives, even when they may not want to put it in those terms. But the power of the researcher can also be overstated; I was not in control many, many times of the situations in which I found myself, as the conversations with Alberto and the secretary of the UMT indicate. The account above is meant to reveal both my privilege (to direct conversations, for example) and my inability to "know" (and thereby control) all that goes on around me.

I would summarize the above account by saying that it is a portrait of one small fragment of women's lives, as I inadequately understand it. My intention here, since development experts do not take kindly to such a summary, is that by making explicit one's theory of listening, and the limitations inherent in dismantling one's own position, women's words are not so easily devoured by development, a point I take up in the next section.

### Translation

The above conversational account involves translation in a number of senses. In the more usual sense, women's words are translated by me from Spanish into English, and the reader does not see the kinds of decisions I have made in this process. There is also the translation involved in transforming oral conversations into text: I have turned women's spoken words into sentences, inserting commas, paragraphs, and exclamation marks in places where the women themselves of course do not specify. In turning prose into flat text, I also have the privilege (and the responsibility, I think) to contextualize our conversations by saying how women might speak provocatively, look suspiciously, and so forth, giving their voices additional meaning that otherwise might not be forthcoming with words alone. And then there is the larger issue of translating women's voices into women's interests, a process that equally demands a documentation of our power as analysts. On what basis do women's interests get constructed from these voices? What is the process involved in making sense of women's words?

It is now generally recognized that essentialist arguments (i.e., that certain interests are naturally the lot of women) are misguided. Ecofeminist arguments that assume that women "mother" the earth, for example, only obfuscate the issue of women's interests. Much more fruitful are analyses focusing on specific situations that may shape women's interests, the creative role of women in (re)constructing these interests, and the role of researchers in translating what different women say about what is important to them.

I recognize that my understanding of women's lives in Ecuador over time has implicitly pivoted on the category of women's "interests." This category has developed, and constantly changes, through my relationship with the UMT and my conversations with women in the countryside who do not belong to this organization. One can extract from the above account that women have key interests in having greater access to money and in better education for their daughters. But I am wary to say categorically that these are women's interests in rural Ecuador. First, these are context-dependent interests. They are best understood within the specific positions from which rural women are speaking. One of those positions is that most households can no longer easily make ends meet in the increasingly impoverished countryside. The countryside is not impoverished because it is mired in tradition but because of global pressures for Ecuador to place all its efforts into paying back its debt, privatizing, and shrinking social services. It is not misguided to narrow women's interests in a way that eclipses this context? Second, these interests feed into neoliberal approaches that like to fund projects making women more profitable and upgrading the skills of young women for the emerging global economy. Income-generating projects and skills training are interests that are easily translatable as the kind of "needs" that Western development can manage, and thereby justify its existence (Illich 1992). Therefore, giving primacy to these two needs might well have more to do with Northern interests than with the interests of Ecuadorian women, who do not see their "needs" and their "lives" as synonymous.

I have tried to write the above account in a way that makes it difficult to decontextualize and sanitize women's interests in this way. In this particular case, I think that listening to women talk about their dreams works against simple translations of their interests as needs. Dreams provide the context of women's changing interests without victimizing them, without representing them in a way that rationalizes intervention with easy solutions. On the one hand, talking about one's dreams and the impossibility of pursuing them in the world as it is presently structured keeps in check any image that the researcher might have of the purity of women's voice. Men and their power are *there* in women's voices; my comadre's comments in particular make this clear. On the other hand, talk of one's dreams gives women the opportunity to incorporate their own agency. My comadre's admission that she taught herself to read without going to school (no small feat) is not an idle boast. In talking about this accomplishment within a general discussion about the considerable constraints under which she has had to live, Amanda does not romanticize her resistance (something that researchers are more likely to do) but neither does she allow anyone to see her only as a victim of patriarchy.

In this respect, though translation involves a process whereby researchers have a considerable amount of power to ensure that we hear the voices we want to hear and that we hear them in the way we want to hear them, women's collaboration in these projects always offers the potential to disrupt researchers' intentions. For example, Marisol's talk of equality very much took me by surprise; it was tempting to delete her interruption from the above account because it didn't seem to "fit." However, I think that allowing these disruptions to enter our translations is a potential way to undercut old stereotypes (stereotypes about modern cultures versus backward cultures, liberated women versus traditional women, etc.) as representations of the "goodness" of modernity that we might unwittingly be reproducing in our accounts. Perhaps if our accounts permit easy generalizations about women's lives, it should be viewed as an indication that we have not remained astute to the possibility of such interventions.

Yet easy generalizations are almost always what Western development demands. The question must be raised at this point: For whom is this thing called development with women really being undertaken?

## Accountability

The issue of accountability has been particularly important for feminist researchers since it has become clear that there is no easy answer to the question: For whom do we do research? While it was once assumed that the answer was "For women, of course!" it is now evident that simply because researchers working with women may define themselves as feminist does not necessarily mean that research is *for* women (Acker, Barry, and Esseveld 1983; Maynard and Purvis 1994).

The question of accountability is crucial because it forces us to be more explicit about our intentions in producing knowledge and about the potential for our intentions to be compromised. Issues of power once again enter the discussion. Researchers need funding and funding is usually based on the ability of researchers to undertake research that is useful. One might legitimately ask, useful to whom? One's answer to this question depends on the funding agency, as some are more closely linked to development agencies than others. Development agencies have their own agendas about having access to research that can be done quickly and is easily translatable into policy. Researchers usually also work within universities that have their own agendas concerning productivity in the publishing industry (Douma, Van den Hombergh, and Wieberdink 1994). The increasing pressure for the social sciences to meet the needs of policymakers indicates how easily our research may become part of reproducing the power relations that marginalize women in the first place.

Moreover one's accountability as a researcher doing development with women may be subtly compromised by the structures within which one must work. The onslaught of neoliberalism and its impact on agencies of development often *appears* to work to the benefit of women. For example, Canadian development agencies now claim to be interested in women's "empowerment," but what they mean by this, it seems, is improving women's ability to make money. That Western development now draws on older WID notions about the need to integrate women into production, making this synonymous with empowerment, indicates that feminist researchers need to be much more cautious about how we analyze social change for women and what language we use to describe such changes. As Kelly, Burton, and Regan note: "Some of the glib ways in which 'empowerment' is used in discussions of feminist research with women concern us greatly. They reflect either an arrogance of viewpoint or a failure to think through what our 'power' consists of" (Kelly, Burton, and Regan 1994: 36–37).

I have already made it clear that in order for research to be for women a full account of how we listen and how we make sense of what women say as researchers needs to be provided. But undertaking projects for women must also mean providing women with our "situated knowledge" (Haraway 1988) about how power is structured and reproduced and how it operates to marginalize them. This means documenting arenas of power relations such as the subtle (sometimes not-so-subtle) role of men and some women in marshalling women's consent to particular world views; the emergence of new class and ethnic differences among women within the context of neoliberalism; and identifying the larger political, economic, and cultural contexts that set the parameters for how women's words can be used.

Documenting these arenas, which may coincide with more traditional discussions of households, communities, regions, nation-states, and the world market (though this may not always be the case), helps to clarify how different hegemonies may shape the identity and interests of the women with whom research and development is being undertaken. However, there is a proviso that accompanies this kind of work: this situated knowledge is useful *for* women only if it does not reproduce representations of women as victims. It must be analyzed and elicited in a way that can be used *by* women if they so choose (Skeggs 1994).

In my own work I constantly grapple with my intentions in doing research. Am I doing research for the UMT? For my comadre? For you, dear reader, whom I imagine as someone who is also struggling with such concerns? Or perhaps for globalization, despite myself? As a researcher I have been largely concerned with documenting the gap between rural women's experiences and how rural development is taking place. In the current context of economic crisis and free trade, however, I am quite skeptical of the idea that "documenting the gap" constitutes research *for* women. Increasingly I feel that such research becomes fodder instead for imposed development models. Surely if we find that our desire to "know" women's lives is being compromised by the global relations in which we must undertake research, then such resistance—the refusal to translate women's interests in order to oblige Western development—is part of our responsibility to the women with whom we work. But perhaps it is here where the contradictions for the researcher who is both shedding layers of training in modernity and still doing something called development with women are the greatest: The UMT, an organization that I have always felt anchored me in my work, clearly has members who want to strengthen this kind of liaison with development agencies. I have dealt with this contradiction by responding to requests for medical supplies and looking into other potential NGO connections for these women at the same time that I argue with them about the drawbacks of maquiladoras and express my grave concerns about the divisions that I see emerging in the countryside. This is the uncomfortable space in which I now do research, always hovering between the knowledge that I am doing too little and the fear that I may be doing too much.

## CONCLUDING REMARKS

In the women and development literature there has been an important shift from a WID perspective, with its colonialist tones of dictating what women in the South need, to a more collaborative perspective that places women's voices and concerns at the center of social change. This perspective ostensibly represents a methodological shift away from fitting women into Northern notions of development and toward "putting the last first." While this kind of approach often assumes itself to be working outside the prevailing paradigms so that we may "really" hear what women have to say, what I have emphasized in this chapter is how research, which focuses on giving women a voice, is also a political process, informed by global relations and power. This argument has a number of implications regarding the responsibilities of researchers who intend to work toward a kind of development with women that does not carry the overtones of feminist colonialism and does not promote modernity at the cost of destroying other possible futures.

I have pointed to the need for researchers to develop a reflexivity about our own views, categories, and contexts. This means recognizing that there is no such thing as a "perspective-free voice" from which we can draw and that, although our accounts are not based on invented conversations, they are *our* inventions. It means that we make our research goals explicit (as contradictory as they may be) and analyze our role in reproducing and/or undermining representations of Third World Women in our research. It may also mean not offering information about women's lives if that information only serves to empower the development that we are trying to dismantle.[9]

Development with women requires accountable representations on the part of researchers. But it also needs to thrive on the uncertainties of a world where there are no global solutions and no all-encompassing theories that resolve the problem of power between development agencies and women, or between researchers and their collaborators. In a world hungry for easy solutions to accommodate "interests," this is the nomadic position (Escobar 1992) that we must inhabit if, as we claim, we really value women's *lives*.

## NOTES

1. In taking this position, I am disclosing a degree of feminist cynicism about the alternative antidevelopment "spaces" that some claim are now being generated by peoples in the South (Esteva 1987; Escobar 1992).

2. Majid Rahnema (1990) has made a similar argument regarding something as seemingly "empowering" as participatory action research (PAR).

3. Readers may want to compare this account with other representations that I have drawn of rural Ecuadorian women (Phillips 1987, 1989, 1990, 1993), where more background information on the coastal region is provided.

4. A few of the women in the area where she lives are actively involved in the UMT, the Union of Working Women, the peasant women's organization that I discuss briefly in the next section.

5. Caroline Moser suggested that I ask rural women about their aspirations, and I would like to thank her for this suggestion. I asked the women about their dreams (*suenos*) rather than their desires (*deseos*), though neither are perfect translations of the English notion of aspiration. The word *suenos*, admittedly, draws on the women's notions of romance, which are nurtured in part by the television soap operas.

6. INNFA refers to childcare centers in the countryside sponsored by the Ministry of Health. In this area the center is run by a wealthy rural family with two peasant women (one of whom is Marisol's comadre) as employees. The center is supported by poorer women because it provides a meal for children, though it is viewed with disdain by those who argue that only "lazy women" use it.

7. I am playing here on Ivan Illich's observation that we should be calling our data "capta," for they are indeed "taken" rather than "given."

8. For example, Kelly, Burton, and Regan (1994: 39) argue that "one version of feminist practice recommends listening, recording and a non-judgemental stance" in contrast to their approach of suggesting to women different ways of understanding experience during the research process itself. I think this sets up a false dichotomy of approaches, since all research involves a negotiation of knowledge

construction between two parties. What they identify in the former practice is simply a case of keeping your theory of listening a secret.

9. Yes, I do wonder if my critical examination of methodology, which has depended on exposing women's dreams to scrutiny in this chapter, is sufficiently unstable to escape notice.

# 3

# Out of Egypt: A Talk with Nawal El Saadawi

## Tiffany R. Patterson and Angela M. Gilliam

On April 9-13, 1983, a conference entitled "Common Differences: Third World Women and Feminist Perspectives" was held at the University of Illinois in Urbana-Champaign. The meeting brought together women from many countries in Africa, Asia, and the Middle East with women of color from the United States. In the course of the proceedings, it became apparent that "sisterhood" and "solidarity" are elusive goals that will require long and diligent struggle to attain. A particularly important aspect of that struggle has to do with the striving for political clarity of women of color in the United States. The following dialogue occurred involving Dr. Nawal El Saadawi, an Egyptian psychiatrist, scholar, novelist, and keynote speaker at the conference, and Tiffany R. Patterson and Angela M. Gilliam, Afro-American scholarly activists. Dr. Saadawi is the author of novels, short stories and plays, and of several nonfiction works including *Female Is the Origin*, *Women and Neurosis*, *Man and Sex* (in Arabic) and *The Hidden Face of Eve* (in English and Arabic). Subjected to persecution, including imprisonment, because of her views on Arab women's problems, she was dismissed from her position as Egypt's Director of Public Health when her first nonfiction work, *Woman and Sex*, appeared in 1972. In response to censorship of her books by Egyptian political and religious authorities, she shifted publications to Beirut and has continued to write and publish despite many pressures.

*Patterson*: In the preface to your book, *The Hidden Face of Eve*, which was deleted from the American edition, you made some interesting criticisms of the Western feminist approach to the oppression of women in Middle Eastern, African, and Asian countries. Would you comment on that further?

*Saadawi*: This issue came up at the Copenhagen conference in the summer of 1980. Usually when women from the so-called Third World meet with women from the United States and Europe, the latter (though not all of them) tend to be rather paternalistic—or, I should say, maternalistic. They want to teach us about our problems. At a conference at Wellesley, I found myself sitting in the audience listening to an American woman speak about Egypt. She had spent three months in Egypt. She wrote a book, and there she was preaching and teaching about Egypt. I had this experience several times, the last time in Vienna, where the feminist Germaine Greer, who had spent a few months in India, was speaking about Indian problems while Indian women sat there listening to her. This is sort of academic exploitation of Third World women. Some Western women like to build and promote their careers by going to the Third World and doing research work and becoming scholars. We feel as if we are guinea pigs or something to be researched by women from the First World, and we refuse to accept it. In Copenhagen, I raised this issue and said that, at these international conferences, you listen to us because we know about our problems and how to diagnose them and you speak about your own problems in your own countries, and don't speak about my problems. This sort of neocolonialism in the name of feminism has to go. It's like foreign aid, and it results in you increasing your debts. Of course, I mustn't generalize because there is a second group of women in the First World who are very good feminists, who believe in an equal exchange and who really want to help. They understand the meaning of solidarity among women, international solidarity on equal grounds, etc. And they are political; they know how to combine the personal with the political, not to divorce these things as is happening in some countries. Then, there are those women who are for sexual liberation and sexual identity, as evidenced by some of the panels at this conference. They're caught up in a new type of slavery—where we become obsessed with sex, all the time speaking about sexual preferences, about whether you are heterosexual, homosexual, a lesbian. As a psychiatrist, I believe everyone has a right to be whatever they want. I am not saying this or that sexuality is normal or not normal, but to be obsessed and to think that just by identifying yourself sexually you are political and liberated—this is not right. So these are the three categories. In the Third World, there are some women who are completely unaware and completely apolitical, and they think that they have come here to be taught—they have this sense of inferiority. They are not yet aware that they are more knowledgeable about their problems than women in the West. Anyhow, meeting in such conferences is quite useful when there is an exchange of information.

*Patterson*: After the "Politics of Sexuality" session yesterday, some of us were talking and the point was made that for an international feminist movement to have any basis, and to be legitimate, Third World women would have to lead that movement. It can't be led by women in this country. What's your response to that idea?

*Saadawi*: I have a certain conception in regard to leadership. I think who is going to lead is not very important. Of course, some people can lead better than others, but leadership should not be considered a privilege or a sign of greater knowledge. Rather, it's a way of working together. So we have a problem because the mentality of a patriarchal system is leadership, somebody is leading the other. It's a sort of hierarchy that I feel uncomfortable with. I think that leadership should be combined between First World and Third World. Leadership is also not static, it changes; it is not permanent. You lead and someone else leads. Which gives the chance for training. For example, who should lead a conference depends on the topic, it depends on the aims of the groups coming together, on the objectives. But generally speaking, if we're going to have an international feminist movement, there must be equal exchange, equal leadership.

*Gilliam*: Let me explain the context in which I made this assertion last night. Ever since the development of the International Year of Women in Mexico, which was followed by the meeting in Copenhagen—and the next meeting will be in Nairobi in 1985—there have been struggles over the theoretical formulation of the woman question. In the United States, our obsession with sex, which permeates everything from commercials to "liberation," has dictated a certain focus and that's the context in which I was speaking about leadership. I feel that if theories are being developed that serve to reproduce or reinforce capitalism, and if we go along with that in the name of international feminism, then we're helping to actually recreate the conditions for extending women's oppression.

*Saadawi*: I understand. I agree totally with what you say. But there is another face of the card because I think that capitalist oppression really created a more sophisticated awareness of how to resist in the United States and in other Western countries. You know, when you are exposed to oppression, you develop methods of resistance—mental, physical, psychological, and intellectual resistance. That's why some women in the Third World aren't aware, because they were not exposed to such a degree of oppression. So we have to make the best of everything, and that's what I mean by equal exchange. I am not with Third World women just because I'm from the Third World, and I am not against First World women just because they are in the First World. I am not with a black man just because he is black—he may be against me.

We had Sadat. He was Egyptian, black, my color, my everything, but he was against me, against my life, against my freedom. So I am ready to fight with people who are fighting my battle, whether they are black, white, women, men, whether they are in the First World or in the Third World. That's my conception of fighting.

*Patterson*: In our discussion, Angela and I were responding to the session on the "Politics of Sexuality," where it was almost impossible to move the discussion to a level of focusing on the concrete conditions of women of color. Instead, it bogged down in personal declarations of sexual preferences and how awful it was for privileged white women, and every attempt by a woman of color—whether she was from the United States, Morocco, or India—to address the realities of the masses of women in the United States and the Third World was dismissed. Therefore, we concluded that it's critical that leadership not come from the First or Third World necessarily but that the leadership's perspective be correct, that the leaders be those people who grasp the nature of oppression and understand the enemy. Throughout this conference, we've been stressing the need to identify the enemy.

*Saadawi*: A correct diagnosis of the enemy. What happened yesterday revealed some of the major problems of the feminist movement in the United States. The majority of the audience were those who really separate the personal from the political even though they are proclaiming all the time that the personal is political. It was very revealing. Fortunately, they are not the majority of women but they were the majority attending this panel. The majority of the women at the conference have a global view of the problems; they're not obsessed with their sexuality.

*Patterson*: I would like to ask a question that I think is very important to Afro-Americans—it was raised by someone yesterday after your keynote address. A friend of mine was saying that he rarely hears an Arab intellectual speak to the issue of solidarity with sub-Saharan Africa. We discussed this issue of whether or not what we get in the United States from Arabs is really reflective of the masses of people in, let's say, your country, Egypt, or North Africa.

*Saadawi*: During the Sadat regime, there was a feeling that his policies led to the isolation of Egypt from African and Middle Eastern countries, and some people came to me from sub-Sahara and asked if I agreed that Egypt was a part of Africa, and do I agree with the pan-African movement and the move to have solidarity between Egypt and other African countries. I said, of course. The majority of people in Egypt feel they are African. This notion that Egyptians are white and not part of Africa is a divide-and-rule tactic of colonial and neocolonial forces. They divide Africa and divide the Arab countries in order to control people. And they use the indigenous ruling elite and ruling classes as they used Sadat—to divide Egypt. Sadat adopted the colonial policy and isolated Egypt from the African continent. But the majority of men and women in Egypt are for Arab unity and pan-African unity.

*Gilliam*: There's another issue that I think is very important for Americans, particularly Afro-Americans. That is how your views were misrepresented by *MS* [*sic*] magazine. Would you comment on how people have tried to manipulate your intellectual production to serve their own interest?

*Saadawi*: Yes, and here is a very subtle form of exploitation practiced, unfortunately, by feminists—so-called progressive feminists. Gloria Steinem of *Ms.* magazine writes me a letter in Cairo and asks me for an article about clitoridectomy. So I write her an article setting forth the political, social, and historical analyses, along with comments about my personal experience. She cuts the political, social, and historical analyses and publishes only the personal statements, which put me in a very awkward position. People asked, how could Nawal write such a thing? She has such a global perspective on clitoridectomy, how could she write such a thing? They didn't know Steinem had cut the article. The second example is Beacon Press in Boston. I gave my book, *The Hidden Face of Eve*, to the publisher in London; he published all of the book—the preface, introduction, everything. The preface, which is a long preface, is crucial and important to the book. Beacon Press cut it without my permission, making me feel that I have been exploited and my ideas distorted. Without the preface, it appears that I am separating the sexual from the political, which I never do. To me, women who think they are liberated but who are obsessed with sexuality are not liberated. They are living a new slavery. They are obsessed by not having men around just as they were obsessed with having them around. It is the other side of the same coin.

*Patterson*: Let's turn to the Fran Hoskens report. At the African Studies Association meeting last fall, there were a number of Africanists who were upset with Hoskens for using clitoridectomy as the only point for defining women's oppression in Africa and the Middle East. I have read the report. She totally dismisses the issue of underdevelopment; she doesn't tolerate any criticism of her position by women from those countries she writes about, even those who are actively opposed to genital mutilation of women. Yet she is being characterized in this country as "the authority" on this subject.

*Saadawi*: Fran Hoskens came to my home in Cairo. I didn't agree with her approach. She was collecting information, and I gave her information regarding the political and historical aspects, and she didn't use it. Intentionally, she wants to say in her work that clitoridectomy is African, it is related to certain people, it's barbaric because those people are barbaric, etc. She is not taking a scientific approach to the problem. She is considered an authority here perhaps because people want to discredit Africa. That's the way colonialism works. The colonial system wants to find justification to colonize and exploit Africa so they can say, "How barbaric! We must

colonize them to modernize them." In Copenhagen, we had a lot of disagreement, we women from Africa and the Third World, with her. In our
workshop, we argued that clitoridectomy has nothing to do with Africa or
with any religion, Islam or Christianity. It is known in history that it was
performed in Europe and America, Asia, and Africa. It has to do with
patriarchy and monogamy. When patriarchy was established, monogamy
was forced on women so that fatherhood could be known. Women's sexuality was attenuated so as to fit within the monogamous system. But she
doesn't want to hear any of this.

*Patterson*: You mention in *The Hidden Face of Eve* that you struggled
against genital mutilation in your country, and I think I'm correct in saying
that as a result of the publication of your book, you lost a position in
Egypt. So you are not, as some African women have done when they've
come to this country because of the way they've been taught, defending
clitoridectomy—genital mutilation. Your position is that how one opposes
the practices determines whether or not there will be legitimate solutions.

*Saadawi*: Exactly. I raised the issue in my first book, *Women and Sex*
[*sic*], published in 1972. It was the first book in Arabic attacking clitoridectomy, and when I was a member of the medical syndicate I wrote them
and said that this was unhealthy and must be stopped. I was editing a
health magazine in which we were writing about clitoridectomy. But we
were tackling it as one problem among a number of problems, as a sexual
issue but one that is related to many political, economic, and historical
situations and circumstances. We were not taking it as an item and blowing
it up like Fran Hoskens does.

*Patterson*: Yesterday, you spoke about your readings in ancient history
and how the perceptions of what woman is and is not have been reversed.
Would you comment on this again?

*Saadawi*: First of all, there was a notion that female goddesses represented fertility, mother earth. But when I was reading on ancient civilization
in regard to Egypt, Iraq, and Palestine, I discovered that the female goddesses represented heaven and not the earth, the sun and not the moon.
Take Isis, our female goddess in Egypt. Even the word Isis means knowledge, brain. Eve represented the body. So a sort of role reversal took place
in the transition from the matriarchal to the patriarchal system. Women
were the heaven, the sun, the brain, knowledge. Then we were dropped
from heaven to represent earth, moon (you know the moon takes light from
the sun, it is not the original light-fertility), and reproductive power, and
not the intellect.

*Gilliam*: When we were discussing the relationship between class and
patriarchy, we mentioned that one of the responses by feminists to patriarchy in this country is to call for a matriarchy as the answer to the patri-
archal/class state. How do you see class and the organization of society,
particularly the relationship between authority and responsibility?

*Saadawi*: The problem with patriarchy and religion, especially monotheistic religion is this split between authority and responsibility. God has authority over humanity but no responsibility. The father has the power in the family but he is not responsible for the family, the woman is responsible. A husband can divorce his wife, he has the right to be polygamous and have three wives, while monogamy is forced on women. In other words, he can disintegrate the family and nobody blames him because he is not responsible. Who is responsible? The woman, even though he has the power. This idea of a split between power and responsibility created the idea of dictatorship, because a dictator is a man who has power but is not responsible. Nobody can ask him, why did you make this or that mistake? As for this question of matriarchy, of course, I am not saying that if we are going to abolish patriarchy we should have matriarchy. I am against authority in that sense. We do need authority if we're going to have an orderly society, but this authority should not be divorced from responsibility. And this brings me back to the matter of leadership. Leadership means that you lead, and that you are responsible and accountable. Furthermore, this leadership should be temporary, not permanent. In our country, a leader is lifelong. Sadat was elected to be a leader for life. How can this happen? Leadership must always be linked with responsibility.

*Gilliam*: You were also saying that, between men and women, there emerged this dichotomy of person-versus-thing and the flesh-versus-mind. Could you go over that again?

*Saadawi*: This dichotomy relates to the evolution of class and patriarchy in history because in Egyptian civilization before the Pharaonic period, before the slave society, the human being was whole. There was no separation between mind and body, no separation between men and women; they were more or less equal. But when man started to possess the land and wanted to inherit it, then the society was divided into people who owned and slaves who had nothing. This is reflected in philosophy. Aristotle, for example, divided society into two parts: Persons, human beings—the owners, and things—slaves, women, and cattle. This division was part of the knowledge inherited from the Greek philosophers and nobody questioned it. Western civilization is based on this dichotomy in that we are still living in a slave society but one of different shapes. The ancient slave society gave birth to feudalism, and then capitalism, and then colonialism, imperialism, zionism, neo-colonialism, etc., and we are still living with the dichotomy of those who own and have power and those who own nothing but their labor and sweat.

*Gilliam*: So that "sin" and "body" and "primitive" are on one side, and the technical, the scientific, the mind, the "civilized" are on the other side.

*Saadawi*: Yes, and one sees that in regard to women in Africa. Women represented sin, instinct, the body, emotion. Africa was also looked upon by Europeans as the body, flesh, instincts. I was reading how Europeans interpreted writings in a very sensual way, viewing Europe as the mind and Africa as the body.

*Patterson*: The dichotomy is reflected in how women are portrayed in the United States. They're irrational, nurturing, emotional; men are rational, capable of leadership, and direct.

*Saadawi*: This split we're talking about also led to the split between science and art because art was considered as if it was coming from emotion, from the body, from sexuality, as if it was irrational and had nothing to do with the brain. Actually, art is superconsciousness. I am a scientist, a medical doctor and an artist too, a writer. People are always saying to me, "You are a medical doctor, why are you writing novels, what is the relationship between scientific work and writing fiction?" Well, I say that fiction is part of the brain, it is not outside the brain. So this split between the mind and body, the master and the slave, female and male, was reflected in the separation between science and art.

*Patterson*: You've written seven novels, *The Hidden Face of Eve* and *Woman and Sex* . . .

*Saadawi*: Seven novels and five books on women, five collections of short stories, and three plays.

*Patterson*: How is your work received in Egypt?

*Saadawi*: It is received very well by ordinary people—students, women, professionals—people who want to read something about their lives. But the religious and political authorities don't like my books, and I know why. Because I link, scientifically, sexual oppression and political oppression and then don't like that. They want pornographic books. We have a lot of books on sex, but they separate sex from the political and economic situation. If you go to any Arab country—Saudi Arabia, Kuwait, Egypt—you find very exciting books on sex; you see belly dancing, etc.; no censor is bothering it, but when you link sexual oppression with economic and political oppression, then you are touching the untouchable. You are shaking the society and the system.

*Patterson*: What's interesting about that is that right here at this conference women who claim to be discussing the liberation of women are, in a sense, doing exactly what the society at large does—that is, separating the sexuality of women from their political reality. Therefore, their solution is not a political solution but a social and a personal solution. There's an incredible resistance to discuss the question of capitalism and the role of capitalism in a sexist/racist state and its impact on women in the Third World.

*Saadawi*: It's much safer not to get into that. It is safer to say, "I am a lesbian." Nobody will put you in jail. But if you start to link sexual oppression with capitalism and imperialism, then you endanger your security and your freedom and maybe even your life. We have a lot of women speaking about sex in Egypt and nobody touches them. We have a lot of prostitutes, nobody touches them. But a scientific woman like me who is straightforward and writes about the links, I go to jail. That's it.

*Patterson*: When were you in jail and under what conditions?

*Saadawi*: Well, I went to jail by order of Sadat on September 6, 1981, in spite of the fact that I have never had any political affiliation with any party ever in my life. (I should explain that I am not against belonging to a party, but with my temperament I cannot fit in because I feel I do not want any ceiling over my mind. A party imposes a sort of ceiling; you have to work within the framework. I very much respect people who are members of parties, but I feel limited intellectually in parties.) I am an independent, creative, and political writer, and I think Sadat put me in jail because of my articles, because I was linking democracy to women. How can you have a democracy when half of the people of a society are oppressed? I am not a politician, I was not directly attacking the political system, but I was trying to link the problems of women to the problems of the society.

*Gilliam*: You're a psychiatrist, and you mentioned that Western women don't acknowledge how they suffer from the Freudian theory of the clitoris. Could you go into that?

*Saadawi*: I mentioned this in my preface to *The Hidden Face of Eve*, which was cut from the American edition. Many women like Fran Hoskens think they have the clitoris and that African women don't. But, in fact, she has a clitoris that is not functioning. Because what Freud did was to say that the clitoris is a male organ in a female body. He said that because in childhood a girl has a clitoral orgasm. But to be a mature woman, the clitoral orgasm should become a vaginal orgasm. So, in fact, he completely abolished the function of the clitoris in a mature woman. This is psychological amputation, clitoridectomy. If you have an arm where the muscle and nerves are not functioning, it is the same as not having the arm. So the problem with Freudian theory is that he amputated the clitoris psychologically, causing a lot of frigidity in women because they thought that to be mature is to have vaginal instead of clitoral orgasms.

*Patterson*: In a sense, then, the current research going on in the United States and the workshops to help women reinstate the function of their clitoris are nothing more than a response to clitoridectomy. We can end on that note.

## NOTE

Reprinted, with permission, from *Freedomways* (Special Middle East Issue), Part 2, Vol. 23, no. 3, 1983.

# PART II

# The Link Between Structure, Global Economy, and the Everyday Life

# 4

# Women Who Make the Chips

## *Les Levidow*

The phrase "Chips with everything" was originally coined by Arnold Wesker to entitle his 1962 play. The phrase was taken up again in the late 1970s by promoters of a grander spectacle, the Information Technology Revolution. In this new era, potentially all human endeavors were to be computerized by using devices containing ever-cheaper integrated circuits etched on to tiny silicon chips. *Time* magazine has given away free calculator-watches in that spirit of media hype around chips as cheap, fun toys.

The chips certainly do come cheap to the Western and Japanese manufacturers who incorporate them into industrial equipment or mass-produced consumer items. Although the heralds of the electronic paradise dub them "labor-saving devices," many users are discovering the ways in which the clerical and industrial applications increase drudgery rather than reduce it. This effect is even more true for those who make the chips. Doing the most labor-intensive jobs in the microelectronics industry, these chip makers are prime targets for each firm's attempts to minimize its labor costs in a highly competitive market. As a result, they bear a great human cost that remains hidden to all who use microelectronic devices.

Even in affluent Silicon Valley, California, the chip makers form the lower part of a two-tier labor force. They are mostly Hispanic or Asian women, many of them illegal (or undocumented) immigrants who live in constant fear of being sacked or even deported. They work for the same firms as highly paid computer professionals but might just as well be living in a different world (Hayes 1987, 1989).

## HEART AND SOUL

On a global scale, most chips are made by workers who do live in a different world: Southeast Asian countries, whose governments impose severe restrictions on workers' right to organize, while imposing few health and safety requirements on the Western multinationals who run the plants there, most of them U.S.-based. Each government actively courts these firms by offering special competitive advantages in Export Processing Zones (EPZs). Such is the logic of export-orientated industrialization, by which each Third World country will supposedly prosper by finding its niche in the international division of labor.

Yet the resulting investment uses no local products and generates little extra employment beyond the chip makers themselves. It leaves behind only polluted environments and damaged workers. In the United States or Japan, microcircuits are photochemically printed on silicon wafers; with other materials, these are then flown in to each EPZ for slicing into tiny chips and bonding to circuit boards, which are then incorporated into microelectronic devices for export.

In Penang, one of Malaysia's states, there is one such place conveniently located near the Bayan Lepas airport. On the main road just outside the airport, numerous microelectronics firms—each protected by high-security fences—occupy both sides of a veritable "Silicon Highway." With no trace of irony, a National Semiconductors building bears the slogan, "Heart, Soul and Microelectronics." This slogan aptly expresses the diligent performance demanded by such firms, which offer little compensation for rapidly exhausting the hearts, souls, and bodies of their workforce.

A similar message comes even from the government. As Malaysia's deputy prime minister said in 1978, "Workers must uphold their dignity and not cause problems that would scare away foreign investors. They should instead be more productive so that government efforts to attract investors would be successful." In this way, politicians try to win support for their efforts toward creating a better investment climate.

## IMMIGRANTS OF THE EPZ

Like their counterparts in Silicon Valley, Penang's chip makers are immigrants, too. Roughly three-quarters are Malay women who were brought up with traditional Islamic values in other parts of the country, then recruited from their villages to Penang's EPZ. There such a woman gets her first experience of factory work, of Western dress, and cosmetics available in the shops, and of independence from her village elders. Her parents usually resent this independence, while at the same time appreciating the daughter's much-needed contribution to the family income, often amounting to one-third of her factory wages.

Despite local unemployment, the firms have the least skilled work done by these immigrant women rather than by Penang's unemployed men. Local people, especially Chinese, are employed mainly as skilled laborers and managers. In contrast to the Malays, they would be less willing to do the unskilled work under such unpleasant conditions at such low wages, at least not without protest. And Malay men remain unwilling to do such work, once it has been defined as "female."

Electronics firms claim that they prefer to employ women because they are naturally better suited to the routinized work of the electronics assembly line: nimble fingers, acute eyesight, greater patience. During Britain's Industrial Revolution, factory owners gave similar explanations for why they replaced well-paid, skilled male workers with women and children. In the case of the microelectronics revolution in Malaysia, the employers' real reasons are as transparent as they were in nineteenth-century Britain. As Intel's personnel officer has admitted, "We hire girls because they have less energy, are more disciplined and are easier to control."

Malays, especially those from rural areas, are seen as happy-go-lucky people accustomed to living simply, if only because the fertile land yields plentiful fruits and vegetables in return for little work. Although real-life Malays don't fit such a simple stereotype, they certainly have had little to prepare them for the rigors of working for a Western multinational, especially the new health hazards involved—including dizziness, headaches, and worsening eyesight, as well as respiratory diseases. These hazards may not be unique to the microelectronics industry but they are more easily imposed upon workers unfamiliar with the chemicals and conditions that cause the hazards, especially where governments oppose any legal safeguards that would damage the climate for foreign investment.

Overt mass protests have been rare in Penang's EPZ. In 1980, workers at numerous electronics firms struck for higher wages; after returning to work, they received a much smaller wage increase than they had been promised. Demonstrations occurred with the closure of three microelectronics firms in 1985, when all 1,500 workers from one plant took to the streets, though without winning anything. The firms have averted much potential protest by learning how to manipulate both the women's traditional submissiveness and their newfound consumerism. As an extra safety measure, the government set up the EPZs with restrictions on trade unionism; in 1970 it also exempted firms there from the law protecting women from night-shift work.

Long-term workers' organization has been made more difficult by the legal restriction preventing the electrical workers' union from organizing electronics workers. Trade union organizers face the sort of antiunion mea-

sures that typify Southeast Asian EPZs. They must also beware of a pe-
culiarly Malaysian phenomenon known as "religious police" who keep on
the lookout for any Muslim people committing the Islamic sin of *khalwat*,
or "association" (close proximity in private) between a man and woman,
a sin for which, under Sharia law, a court will impose the penalty of a fine
or jail; for *zina*, or adultery, the penalty is whipping.

## DOWN SILICON HIGHWAY

The predicament of these microelectronic workers first became widely
known in the West through Rachel Grossman's now-classic 1978 exposé,
based on a ten-week trip around Southeast Asia. Although more recent
publications have elaborated on her argument, they have provided little
update on her findings. The rest of this chapter, based on a very brief but
more recent trip to Penang in 1986, will emphasize changes there since she
made her report.

In my interview with a group of microelectronics workers in Penang, the
translation back and forth between English and Malay was done by Bala,
a staff member at Sahabat Alam Malaysia (SAM) or Friends of the Earth
Malaysia. (The fact that my interpreter and I were both men unfortunately
must have affected the responses to my questions and limited what the
women were willing to tell us.) For many years Bala has worked behind
the scenes to help microelectronics workers organize themselves and demand what few rights they have under Malaysian employment law. In a
country where the trade unions have made little effort to help empower
these workers, the need has been filled by SAM, which defines its environ-
mentalist brief to include all health and safety hazards, as well as those
forms of modern development that threaten the livelihood of peasants, fishermen, forest dwellers, and others.

The interview took place at one of the many shared houses rented by
women microelectronics workers; this house was also being used for classes
in cooking, dressmaking, and so on. While we were speaking with some
workers there, others were cutting cloth on the floor and then putting the
pieces together on sewing machines. The walls were adorned with posters
in the Malay language warning the women about health and safety problems and telling them their employment rights.

## BLINDED BY BONDING

All three women had held "bonding" jobs, among others; that is, they
had been soldering hair-thin wires on to each microchip and its lead frame
while peering through a microscope. Despite their traditional Islamic up-
bringing, two of these three women—Rachel and Jane—were wearing
modern, colorful dress and cosmetics, and had flamboyantly permed hair.

Their replies were often cryptic and accompanied by giggling, even when about the most serious matters. (Here I have given them pseudonyms corresponding somewhat to their differences of appearance and cultural identity.) Rachel had been a bonding operator for ten years, since she was seventeen, at Advanced Micro Devices (AMD). As a student she had needed glasses, but even if she hadn't, "after one year or so our eyesight becomes blurred, so we have to get glasses." In her case, she has had to get stronger and stronger ones. At Intel, Jane had complained about the difficulty of bonding work and eventually got herself transferred to the packaging section and so avoided having to get glasses. Many women, less fortunate or insistent than she, have allowed the bonding work to ruin their eyes and then found themselves made redundant.

Like Rachel, Aziza too was wearing glasses, but her clothing was simple, entirely black and white, with a headscarf much like a chador. While most of Penang's immigrant workers have taken up Western-style dress, encouraged by their new employers, recently there has been a return to traditional Islamic dress, encouraged by religious and political leaders. As I was to realize, Aziza's conservative dress did not indicate her more recent arrival from rural Malaysia; nor did it symbolize a return to Islamic fundamentalism. Rather, it seemed part of a cultural resistance to the microelectronics firms' psychological control over their women workers. As compared to the other women, her comments were far more articulate, serious, and critical of the industry.

Aziza had to get glasses seven years after she started her bonding work at age twenty at National Semiconductors. At that point she became one of the few workers to complain that she couldn't go on working with the microscope. "For seven years I had to put up with those conditions before being transferred to another section. And I had to pay for the glasses myself."

## "HYSTERIA"

In the 1970s these factories were renowned for outbreaks of mass "hysteria" (called by its English name), in which women would mysteriously start weeping, shouting, writhing, or fainting. It might begin with one woman seeing a spirit (*hantu*) while peering through the microscope. Then the hysteria would spread to dozens of women. Some would scream that they hated being there and wanted to go back to their mother; many believed they were possessed by spirits.

As women first arrived in Penang from a relaxed village life, Bala said, they initially couldn't meet the firms' production quotas and couldn't stand the pressure; moreover, they weren't allowed to leave the assembly line when they wanted breaks. They were unable to protest openly. When one of them reached her limit of endurance she would break into the hysteria and then others would join in.

As Bala explained, nowadays the hysteria happens only a few times a year because most of the women were able to meet the quotas: they've become "good workers." Originally the women were working all week long and were even asked to come in to work on their rest days, while nowadays they are on short working weeks, only three or four days per week, so they have more time to rest. Management benefits twice: It pays the workers only for the three days and gets more production for that pay. Moreover, the workers are able to release their tension through the consultative committees set up by management. As one American manager once said so touchingly, "If people believe management cares, there are no problems. Hysteria doesn't happen."

When I asked the three women about the hysteria, and whether they believed in possession by spirits, they replied with mock groaning and then burst out laughing. Apparently these women were now far enough removed from the hysteria for it to be a laughing matter. Yet the change since the 1970s seemed less about improved working conditions than about the women's acculturation to the factory's work discipline.

Jane thought that at Intel the hysteria had occurred for lack of proper food and because lack of adequate cooling had allowed the equipment to overheat the air, which of course was full of chemicals. "People go in and come out on an empty stomach. Sometimes they feel like vomiting." On one recent occasion, a worker on the line had fainted and fallen down, apparently because of the heat. The die attachment department must be kept hot for the production process, so the management reduces the air-conditioning there. So the heat is not simply a by-product, but an essential condition of production to which the workers must adapt themselves.

According to Aziza, at National Semiconductors the hysteria still happens a few times per year:

The workers' health is affected right from the beginning. There are psychological effects because the section demands that each worker meets a fixed quota. If a worker can't meet it, she goes to work with an in-built fear. People can't stand it, they scream, fall down, then get taken to the nurse.

The hysteria was frequent in the early days but not any more because now the workers are used to the working conditions. It usually happens in the afternoon because they have been travelling in hot, humid weather, then go into the air-conditioned factory, then into warm parts or the canteen, and back and forth. But people still don't understand the exact cause.

Apparently most of the workers now affected come from the same dormitory or hostel. "If one worker gets the hysteria, it can spread to the others, so they can believe that it comes from the house. But it really comes from their working conditions."

From Rachel's experience at AMD, the hysteria happens only a few times per year and at most to two or three people at a time. Yet the psychological strain now seems to be transferring from work to home. As she described one episode, "A friend of mine, living in a company-provided dormitory, dreamt that a friend came to visit her. In the dream she tells her friend not to disturb her. She wakes up, discovers the friend is not there, then screams and faints. The next day another friend had the same dream. The next day the hostel supervisor brought in the *bomoh* [village spiritual healer]."

On one level the dream might be understood as an Islamic villager's reaction to the fast pace and enforced social isolation of assembly-line work. It is peculiar to an Eastern culture, though? As distant as all this may seem from Western psychiatric problems, on reflection the story could parallel the way that tensions from our work invade our most private selves, and even construct our nightmares. When we fail to deal with those tensions collectively, we too bring them home to haunt us.

Anthropologist Aihwa Ong (1987) found much evidence to warrant interpreting spirit possession as a moral protest. Spirit invasions of factory toilets and prayer rooms suggest the distress of moral violation, by virtue of village women being subjected both to factory discipline and to the sexual attentions of male supervisors, particularly non-Islamic ones. As the women are often reminded that their honor is at stake, it is understandable that resistance to factory conditions would sometimes take the form of spirit possession by the *datuk*, the male ancestor.

## BEAUTY CONTESTS

In the 1970s many microelectronics firms invited cosmetics vendors to sell their wares during the lunch break on the women's pay day. They encouraged a competitive ethos around Western fashion, just as they did around productivity targets. The firms also held beauty contests, whose winners would get all-expenses-paid holidays, sometimes even to the United States. "I will try my best to take part in this contest hoping to bring back joy and glory to the number one company," as one beauty queen was quoted in National Semiconductors' employee newspaper.

When I asked about these contests, the women laughed, as they're not held anymore. The last was in 1983, on the tenth anniversary of the establishment of AMD in Penang. At National Semiconductors the last one was held in 1980; since then, there have been only competitions for singing pop music.

Why the change? Perhaps because many workers rebelled against the contests? No, because the Malaysian government asked the firms to stop, as part of its promotion of Islamic morality—one of the few examples that seems to have benefited women.

What had the workers thought of these contests? Like many of the Malay women, these three felt that it would have degraded them to participate. As Aziza explained, "It is the traditional Malay culture. We have been brought up not to expose our beauty to others. Of course, we don't all follow this tradition. Of every ten women, perhaps three didn't like the beauty contests, while the other seven took part."

When she stated that the Chinese women liked the contests far more, I asked why. "Because of the reward they expected to get by winning. Unlike the Malays, they want to earn more, to win prizes and promotion." Did the firm really use the beauty contests to decide promotions? At this point Rachel interjected: "No, at AMD, 'bonder bonder.'" All three women laughed, and Bala had to explain her quip: "If you're a bonder, you'll always be a bonder." I found Rachel's comment ironic, given that Chinese people often look down on Malays for showing little interest in competition and success. Here a Malay was ridiculing the inflated expectations of the competitive Chinese.

## DURHAKA

In addition to encouraging a competitive ethos, both within and between plants, the microelectronics firms' managements have attempted to manipulate *durhaka*, the traditional Malay injunction against women's disobedience to authority, especially to that of older males. How smoothly is this deference transferred from communal village life to a modern factory? Even apart from *durhaka*, fear of being sacked has certainly deterred potential protest. Yet the women's vulnerability also arises from an individual and collective deference that is cleverly structured by the firm.

As Rachel described *durhaka*, "one should not disobey the elders or disagree with them," though Aziza hastened to add a novel escape clause, "except when there is something bad done to us." All three women agreed that disobedience is against God's teaching but denied its relevance to their factory situation. They insisted that *durhaka* applied only to the family and so didn't stop them from complaining about their working conditions.

Yet these complaints are always made to a committee, elected by the workers but set up by management. They rarely protest directly to the managers, whose replies tend to put the women back on to the defensive. As Rachel recounted, "When there's no work for us to do and we are pushed around, we are given such answers that we cannot fight back such as, that there are no materials available. By moving around, you can learn more jobs. Sometimes in the same day."

Didn't they sometimes get so angry that they wanted to complain directly to the manager? I asked. Jane replied, "Yes, but we wouldn't succeed. And we wouldn't want to create problems and be out of our jobs. Sometimes we are very vocal about it and want to fight with them. But after hearing their explanation, we are convinced by them. Sometimes we believe it is our fault."

For example, the equipment is supposedly designed for the workers to make defectless products and also to check them, but, "if you come out with defects in spite of that, then you have to accept the punishment for careless work." Such carelessness should come as little surprise, given that their work is so boring that they tend to doze off, especially on the night-shift, and even while standing up.

"At National Semiconductors," says Aziza, "some of the microscope work has been replaced by machines, with the result that the machine can do four workers' jobs at the same time. Because of the automation, we look through a Visual Display Unit (VDU) at eight different machines, checking the integrated circuits. Sometimes we still get defective products with the automated process—usually the workers are not blamed, though the technicians may be questioned."

## HOME AWAY FROM HOME?

When women leave their village to work in Penang's EPZ, at first the only shared aspiration is to earn a living and send money back home to help support their families. Most of the women soon find financial and cultural independence an incentive to make the most of their new lives in Penang, as something more than a temporary detour from their village life. The term *kampung*, originally meaning "village," has come to describe a type of house run differently than the company-sponsored one.

As Rachel explained,

I chose the *kampung* house because at the company-provided house we would have to fill in forms saying when we are going out and coming back. The restrictions are very inconvenient, so I left the company house. The *kampung* house is the best, because the couple who run it are like mother and father to us, like adopted parents. About three-quarters of the women live in the *kampung* house and the rest live in the company-provided one.

Compared to Penang, she considers life better in her old village, in the northern state of Kedah. As the only woman to have left the place, she once made a return visit and told the others not to leave too, because "village life is better." She explained, "Urban life isn't bad, but your parents will suffer in their old age. And you'll end up on the night-shift." Then why doesn't she return? "I have adapted myself to the urban life."

Aziza, who clearly has not adapted herself as much, gave a more positive portrayal of the rural alternative: "In my village the women are more active, industrious, work on the farm and in the paddy fields." She didn't see herself as choosing Penang over the village: "I didn't make that kind of choice. I came here because there was work here. If the factory closes, then I'll go back to my village. There won't be any problem." Having resisted Western consumerism, she apparently has little to lose but her income as such, while Rachel or Jane would lose a whole new identity.

## REDUNDANCIES

For the microelectronics firms, a key attraction of Southeast Asian EPZs is their minimal workers' rights that permit them to reduce their workforces with little compensation in return. The firms may consider mass redundancies necessary because many of the women have lost their optimum eyesight after a few years of microscope work or because the international market has a reduced demand for chips.

In recent years AMD has had a voluntary redundancy offer, taken up by hundreds of workers. Says Rachel, "I myself won't accept it, but others may. If the offer is good, they take the money." Apparently a good offer means twenty day's pay for every year of service, if they've worked for five years or more. Why do they accept such low compensation? Says Aziza, "Now the market situation is very bad, and we are forced to go on a reduced working week, so it can seem better to take the redundancy offer instead of working only three days per week."

Even Aziza, the most suspicious of the three women, believed that the workers could count on the basic payment as in past years. Yet, as Bala later explained, organizations like his have already had to take microelectronics firms to court to force them to pay the amount provided by law, plus three months *ex gratia* payment. And for some time now the firms have been openly complaining that they can't afford redundancies because the statutory payment is too high. They propose to reduce it, as well as to abolish the requirements for the time-and-a-half rate for overtime and for wage increases in the first three years. Taking pity on the downtrodden multinationals, the government has agreed with their arguments, though the necessary statutory change has been delayed by divisions within the Malay-dominated ruling party United Malay National Organization (UMNO).

Why, then, did Aziza believe that the government will protect the workers? Along with UMNO's officially nonsectarian approach, the party claims to protect Malays from the ambitious Chinese through its ethnic quota system for state employment and university entrance. Says Bala, "The term *durhaka* could be applied to the present prime minister. Ordinary Malay people say that the government will do good for the people." Belief in this protection makes the workers even less inclined to take the risk of organizing to save their jobs.

When redundancies do come, many of the women return to their villages or get married, but those who refuse such options don't easily find alternative jobs, apart from working in bars or as prostitutes. Why don't they go back home instead? Bala paraphrased a typical answer that they give: "I am ashamed to go back home. Before, I was able to send money home, not I'm not able. Before, when I went back to the village, I was so well dressed. Now if I go back, I have nothing to show for myself. The village people will look down on me." Having learned to associate independence and social status with Western clothes and cosmetics, they dread facing the material and symbolic loss involved in returning to their poor village life.

And this is not the only way in which their independence from Malay tradition has become a new form of dependence and even control. While many of them choose to wear jeans and high-heeled shoes, at National Semiconductors they were actually told they had to wear a certain kind of miniskirt. So they did wear it, except for the fundamentalist Muslim women, many of whom quit their jobs in disgust. Says Bala, "There is a lot of sexual harassment, with supervisors using their authority to demand the girls go out with them. When a woman applies to go on leave, often it's not granted, and then the supervisor uses threats and blackmail with her. Things have improved a bit because of some pressure, especially protests from the Muslim fundamentalists."

## WORKERS' EDUCATION

In the face of such obstacles, how can outsiders help strengthen the workers' hand? In the education programs set up by SAM, seminars deal with health and safety, basic needs, leadership, and workers' rights. They also take up economics, politics, and current issues. Although SAM cooperates with local trade unions, Bala feels that they "aim at training only the up-and-coming official leaders." He says, "SAM aims to train grassroots people to make demands and to provide a potential leadership of their own."

How does SAM try to build up the necessary self-confidence? Bala describes a typical frustrating episode:

The first session will be arranged through informal contacts, who pass the word very secretly to people whom they trust and who will come. Many do come to the first session, where we give an introduction about their basic needs in the factory. They ask questions, recommend what we should do, and agree to bring more people the next week. But the next week not a single one will turn up. Why? Perhaps because we are men. Also, someone who attends these group discussions will leak the information that so-and-so was leading a group discussion and that certain workers were there. The management then warns the workers that they must not attend such discussions or else they will be dismissed immediately.

In response to the firms' obstruction, SAM decided to open up a resource center near the workers' dormitory. By the mid-1980s there were three such centers—one by the Malaysian Trade Union Congress, one headed by the electrical workers' union, and the Young Workers' Centre by a university lecturer. However, when the centers opened, the electronics employers' federation gave instructions that no workers may attend them; if found there, they would be dismissed. Bala said: "To enforce this rule, the firms brought in a top-ranking officer to live in a house by one center, to stay there and watch. He needn't watch all day because the workers can't come during working hours anyway. Outside of working hours he or someone else will be there watching. So most workers are too frightened to visit the place." Had the women thought of forming a trade union in the factory? Said Aziza, "I have always thought of it, but until now I thought I couldn't do anything. There is no support from my friends because they are afraid of losing their jobs if found out." These are just some of the obstacles that SAM faces, simply in getting the most interested workers to attend meetings in their free time.

Despite the obstacles, the centers have had sufficient success to attract repression. Their activists were among those detained without trial in late 1987, when the government invoked the Internal Security Act (a legacy of British counterinsurgency) to arrest dozens of key political figures as supposed threats to "national security" and/or "racial harmony." If we substitute the term "investment climate," we have a clearer view of the government's motives.

## STYLISH FREEDOM

The government has also attempted to portray the microelectronics firms (particularly the Japanese ones) as respecting traditional values, amidst public concern about a supposed moral threat to female purity. In Penang's EPZ, dominated by U.S.–owned firms, the women workers have acquired factory-specific nicknames such as *micro-syaitan* (microsystems "micro-devils"). They are more generally dubbed *minah lektrik* ("hot stuff"), whose several connotations include the lure of the bright city lights. Academics have attributed the moral threat to rural-urban migration, Western culture, and economic freedom for women seen as less religious or having loose morals. Newspapers have even spread scandal stories about the factory women servicing soldiers and tourists. Such stories displace the real problem of prostitution, which arises not from the women's new economic independence but from its loss when their failing eyesight or ill health results in their being made redundant.

A more general displacement of the women's problems is described by Aihwa Ong (1987): "Greater public control came to be exerted over their 'leisure' time (which in actuality was very limited), while simultaneously diverting attention from the harsh realities of their 'working' time." This control includes guidance and surveillance by Islamic fundamentalist groups that denounce consumer culture; yet they divert attention from the women's grievances by supporting some firms' claims to respect traditional Malay values. Many factory women accept Islamic guidance in order to defend themselves from suspicion of immoral behavior.

Many other women resist such control. They assert their independence through dress styles and *sosial*, evening socializing between men and women. That exploration has gone farthest around the Bayan Lepas EPZ, which also has the distinction of being located in a somewhat urbanized and multicultural island; Malaysia's other EPZs are mostly located in the mainland's rural areas, more imbued with Malay rural traditions.

What does this new way of life mean for Malay women in Penang's EPZ? Their first experience of wage labor frees them from their village elders' authority, which is then replaced by an economic and even psychological dependence upon the firm, often to the extent of accepting blame for their failure to adapt to degrading working conditions. The women are free to enjoy Western goods and fashion, yet the consumption and even the styles are structured by advertising and the electronics firms themselves, sometimes to the extent of being made a job requirement.

Although the women have nominal sexual freedom, it is their managers who directly or indirectly manipulate their sexuality. Moral sanctions discourage liaisons between Malay women and non-Malay supervisors, partly as a way of protesting unequal treatment of workers. However, Islamic law doesn't reliably protect the women from sexual harassment at work. At the same time the Islamic revival itself, especially its personal austerity, can perhaps be understood as a response to a new, more subtle kind of Western imperialism: one that colonizes the mind with stylish images of freedom, images that mask the economic and sexual vulnerability of the new female consumer.

Although the chip makers live and work together in close proximity, their presence doesn't compromise even the beginnings of a new urban working class (unlike, for example, in Britain's Industrial Revolution). As part of the global assembly line, their work is closely linked with that of others in a similar predicament throughout Southeast Asia and beyond, yet the firms are protected from potential worker solidarity by the weapons of company blackmail, multiple sourcing, and easy capital mobility. Obliging governments provide competitive bargains in cheap, flexible labor obviously preferable to investing in more highly automated equipment that would tie a firm down to a particular place. Having profited from this manipulation, the firms easily get rid of "redundant" workers—they are sent away to get married, to return to their villages, or to become prostitutes. Such is the price paid for cheap chips.

## NOTE

Reprinted, by author's permission, from *Science as Culture*, 2(1) (1991).

# 5

# Women in the Rural Economy in Nigeria

*Christiana E. E. Okojie*

## INTRODUCTION

In recent times, rural development and the role of women in rural development have received a lot of attention at seminars and conferences, and more recently in policy making in Nigeria. It is being increasingly recognized that women play important roles in the rural economy and that the neglect of the rural sector must be corrected if rural dwellers, especially rural women, are to take their rightful places in the development process.

The inferior status of women in general and rural women in particular has also been widely discussed. Women in many societies constitute an underprivileged group compared to men. Customs and norms of behavior condition women, especially rural women, to think of themselves as inferior beings. Special measures are therefore required to change these attitudes and to create an awareness in rural women of their important roles in the development of the rural economy.

Why is it necessary to discuss women's roles in the rural economy? It is important because the participation of rural women in rural development is essential if some of the more serious problems are to be solved—for example, the lack of adequate food production, health, and nutrition. As women represent about half of the human resources in Nigeria, their potential cannot be neglected. Although in principle there is nothing to prevent women from participating in economic, social, and other activities, there are several constraints on women's effective participation in the economy, especially for rural women.

Women participate in the economy as members of the labor force. It should be pointed out that women's participation in the economy is only one dimension of their participation in the country's development. This chapter is concerned with the economic activities of rural women, that is, with their participation in productive activities in the rural economy. How do rural women contribute to the country's national product? They do this directly through their activities as members of the labor force.

Neglect of women's contributions to the economy has led to their marginalization in the nation's planning process in the past. This neglect was partly due to the assumption that women benefit via the trickle down effect from their husbands. Rural women in particular were neglected because of the erroneous belief that only men were farmers while women, as farmers' wives, merely assisted with farm work (Patel and Anthonio 1973). Such beliefs were due to lack of reliable data about women's work.

In many countries, national labor force surveys and, consequently, economists' models, planners' designs, and agricultural programs based on these figures, continuously ignored women's contributions to the economy (Oppong 1987). Inadequate data on women's work was partly due to issues of determining who are members of the labor force or who is employed. Most employment statistics in many countries tended to omit informal sector activities and home-based production—areas of economic activity in which women in developing countries tend to concentrate. This is especially so in West Africa. Efforts have therefore been made to improve definitions of labor force status (Oppong 1987). At its 1982 Conference, the International Labor Organization (ILO) recommended that labor force participation should include: "All persons of either sex who furnish the supply of labour for the production of economic goods and services as defined by the UN system of national accounts and balances" (Oppong 1987).

Economic activities should therefore include production and processing of primary products whether for the market or for home consumption. Noninclusion of these activities in which women predominate has led to the underestimation of women's economic activities, their invisibility, and the consequent underallocation of resources and opportunities to women and programs that affect women (Oppong 1987).

African delegates at the Nairobi Conference noted the widespread failure of planning agencies to incorporate women on an equal basis with men into macroeconomic planning both as decisionmakers and as foci of concern, and the fact that women are often treated as peripheral and marginal (Oppong 1987). As will be shown presently, rural women in Nigeria perform many economic roles in the rural economy that qualify them to be targets of macroeconomic planning in their own right. This is necessary if their productivity is to be enhanced so as to maximize their contributions to the nation's economic development.

This chapter discusses women's activities in the rural economy in Nigeria. What are the economic opportunities open to rural women and what are the constraints on their higher productivity? Section two of the chapter discusses women's economic roles in the rural economy. Section three highlights some of the constraints on rural women's productivity. Section four reviews the impact of some of the current programs with women as a target group. Section five suggests ways of enhancing rural women's productivity while section six concludes the chapter.


## WOMEN'S ECONOMIC ROLES IN THE RURAL ECONOMY

Increasingly available data suggests that it is in the agricultural sector that women make their greatest contribution to the economy. Nigeria's rural women, as in many other African countries, play important roles in food production and processing activities (Ezumah 1988; Longe 1988; Okojie 1991, 1992). However, one should not make generalizations, as there are variations in the nature and intensity of women's participation in agricultural activities between regions of the country depending on vegetation, religion, and other sociocultural practices (Okojie 1991). Rural women engage in different economic activities in Nigeria, including food production (farming, fishing, animal-rearing), cottage industries such as food processing, preservation, and storage, crafts, and distributive trades.

Apart from these general activities, there are trades and industries that are specific to some areas. The variation is due to ecological and sociocultural differences. Why are so many women engaged in economic activities in Nigeria? Financial motivation is the strongest factor. Most women in both urban and rural areas work in order to earn separate incomes from their husbands. Women spend their incomes on the maintenance of themselves, their children (including school fees), and their homes (Simmons 1975; Okojie 1985, 1993). Given widespread polygamy, especially in rural areas, many women are largely responsible for the maintenance of their children. Apart from financial reasons, in many parts of Nigeria social norms dictate that every responsible female adult should have an occupation (*Sana' a among the Hausas*). Thus, most women are involved in some economic activity or other.

The discussion of women's activities will show regional variations and present as much information as is available on individual states. The country will be zoned into four regions: Northern Nigeria, Western Nigeria, Midwestern Nigeria, and Eastern Nigeria, following the original division of the country into four regions.

### Northern Nigeria

Northern Nigeria comprises states that made up the former Nonhem Region. There are wide variations in women's participation in farming activities in this region—the proportion ranges from 2 percent in Katsina/ Kaduna States to 84 percent in Benue State. Generally, predominantly Muslim states in which female seclusion is widespread have smaller proportions of women engaged in farming. However, Muslim women are actively engaged in food processing in these states (Olayiwole 1985; Simmons 1975). Crops grown by women in the northern states include grains (maize, millet, wheat, guinea-corn, rice), legumes (soya beans, beans, groundnuts), vegetables (tomatoes, peppers, carrots, and cotton). Women are also engaged in fishing and livestock rearing. In many states, women are actively involved in bush clearing, planting, weeding, harvesting, and transportation.

### Western Nigeria

Western Nigeria comprises the states inhabited by the Yorubas. The proportion of women engaged in farming ranges from 7 percent in Lagos State to 53 percent in Ondo State. Rural women participate in planting, weeding, harvesting, and transportation. The major crops grown by women are maize, rice, tubers (yams and cassava), and vegetables. Fishing takes place in the riverine areas of Ondo State. In Ogun State, women grow cowpeas and plantain (Patel and Anthonio 1973; Oshuntogun 1976).

### Midwestern Nigeria

Midwestern Nigeria comprises Edo and Delta States. Farming is a major occupation among most ethnic groups in this region (Binis, Ishans, Urhobos, Westem Ibos, and Akoko-Edos). The Ijaws and Itsekiris are engaged mainly in bush clearing and tilling, as well as in planting, weeding, harvesting, and transporting. The major crops grown by women are: rice, cassava, maize, cocoyams, peppers, beans, melon, plantain, and okro (Okojie 1983, 1985; Igben 1980). Forty-three percent of rural women are engaged in agricultural activities.

### Eastern Nigeria

Eastern Nigeria is inhabited by the Igbos, Efiks, Ibibios, and so forth. Rural women are actively involved in farming activities, with the proportion engaged in farming ranging from 58 percent in Rivers State to 86 percent in Anambra State (now Anambra and Enugu States). Igbo women participate in the more arduous tasks of land clearing and tilling. Tubers (cassava, yams, and cocoyam) are widely grown. Most women grow vegetables such as greens, peppers, tomatoes, and okro (Ezumah 1988).

## Rural Women in Food Production

Available studies of rural women in food production show that:

- women actively participate in planting and weeding
- most harvesting is done by women
- while women often perform heavy work such as bush clearing, family and hired labor are also utilized
- women spend six to eight hours daily on the farm and divide their time between their own farms and their husband's farms
- the average size of women's farms is very small
- while women generally grow food crops (such as cassava, yam, maize, and vegetables), men grow commercial crops such as cocoa, oil palm, and rubber (Tewe 1978).

## Rural Women's Cottage Industry Activities

Women's cottage industry activities can be classified into two main groups (Akande and Awosika 1994). These are (1) food processing, preservation, and storage and (2) crafts and other production. Activities involved in the first group are: dehusking, drying, fermenting, milling of roots, tubers, and grains; oil extraction from palm fruit, coconut, palm kernel, groundnuts, melon, and so forth; smoking of fish, prawns, and fingerlings; production of milk, butter, cheese, and yoghurt; and brewing from grains, fruits, and so forth. The second group of women's cottage industry activities include tasks such as: textile weaving, tie and dye; pottery and ceramics; raffia and cane work (baskets, mats, ropes); soaps, pomades, oils, and other cosmetics; herbal products; and other crafts and decorations such as seashells and seeds.

## Women in Food Processing

All over Nigeria, food processing and preservation activities are handled mainly by rural women using traditional methods that are often inefficient. In many parts of Nigeria, rural women engage in food production (farming) as a primary activity and food processing as a secondary (postharvest) activity. It has been estimated that Nigerian rural women spend about 35 percent of their time on farm work and 40 percent on home-related activities. Of the time spent on home activities, 47 percent is spent on food processing activities (ILO/UNDP/FDRD 1987). The rest of their time (25

Table 5.1
Distribution of Women's Craft Activities by Region

| Region | Major Craft Activities |
|---|---|
| Western Nigeria | spinning and weaving, tie and dye, batik pottery, and mat-weaving |
| Midwestern Nigeria | cloth-weaving, pottery, basket and mat-weaving |
| Eastern Nigeria | cane and raffia works, soap-making, cloth-weaving |
| Northern Nigeria | cloth-weaving, pottery, salt mining, dyeing |

Source: J. Akande and K. Awosika, Women in Trade and Industry in Nigeria. A Study Report Submitted to UNIFEM, Nigeria, 1994.

percent) is spent on other income-generating activities such as the marketing of processed foods.

Generally, women are responsible for the processing and preservation of food crops grown in their respective regions. Most crops are either dried or dried and milled into flour, and processed for sale and consumption (Okojie 1991).

## Women in Craft Activities

Women engage in various craft work in different regions of the country. Table 5.1 shows craft activities by region.

In many parts of Nigeria rural women engage in craft activities either as a primary or secondary occupation. In a 1983 study of rural women in six communities in Edo and Delta States, craftwork was the primary occupation of 26.7 percent of the respondents (Okojie 1992).

Yoruba women (Western Nigeria) are well known for their tie and dye activities. In Eastern Nigeria, the weaving of akwete cloth is well known while the okene cloth is also famous (Northern Nigeria). Pottery is also a common craft activity in all regions.

### Rural Women in Distributive Trade

In Nigeria, labor force studies show that the majority of employed females are sales workers (Federal Office of Statistics 1985). While trade is the primary occupation of the majority of women in the urban informal sector, in the rural economy trade is mainly a secondary occupation of women engaged primarily in food production, processing, or craft activities. Rural women sell their surplus products, such as foodstuffs, handicrafts, and so forth, in the market.

Women constitute the majority of participants in rural market activities. Participants have been categorized as primary, secondary, and tertiary traders (Akande and Awosika 1994). Primary traders are farmers who bring their produce to markets or women who bring traditional homemade goods to the market. Secondary traders come from neighboring villages, while tertiary traders (mainly urban women) come from distant urban centers to buy on a periodic basis. Most rural markets are periodic markets, that is, they are held every five, seven, or nine days. Women's trading activities are largely informal. Much of their trading activities are also classified as "petty" to characterize their small size, low capital base, and low technological content (Akande and Awosika 1994). The low level of capitalization that permits ease of entry into trading is at the same time a major constraint on women's trading activities.

The preceding discussion has shown that women play vital roles in the rural economy. They produce a substantial proportion of the nation's food. They are responsible for the processing and preservation of our food crops. They are engaged in distributive trade (of both domestic and foreign products). Of importance, therefore, are rural women's rights of ownership or use and control of the means of production—land, machinery, finance, and so forth, and of their end products such as agricultural produce and income (Oppong 1980). Access to the means of production affects their productivity and income.

## CONSTRAINTS ON RURAL WOMEN'S PRODUCTIVITY

The constraints on rural women will be classified into two groups: (1) access to resources and (2) sociocultural constraints.

### Access to Resources

*Education.* Lack of formal education is a major constraint on women, especially rural women in Nigeria. Illiterate women are tradition-bound and are surrounded by various taboos and restrictions on their behavior. Most rural women are illiterate. In 1980, only 16.3 percent of adult females were literate. This figure increased to 17.3 percent by 1984. In 1983/84 only 6.1 percent of women over 30 years old were literate (Federal Office of Statistics 1985). It is easier to target new technologies (agricultural or food-processing technology) at the educated who are usually more willing to adopt new ideas. Lack of education creates other constraints on women's economic activities when they cannot read bank regulations or statements, pamphlets, and so forth.

*Credit.* The majority of rural women have limited capital for their economic activities. Credit is required as initial capital and working capital to purchase raw materials (seedlings, cane, raffia), equipment, spare parts, and so forth. Traditionally, credit needs were met largely by husbands as well as by other family members, savings and loan schemes, or personal savings. Very few rural women have had access to bank loans. Partly due to lack of information about availability and sources of credit, their access to credit has been limited. Women also lack collateral such as land or other property to support loan applications. The Peoples Bank is helping in this area, but relatively few rural women have been reached (Okojie 1987, 1991; Akande and Awosika 1994).

*Technology.* The technology requirements of rural women in Nigeria have been identified to include:

*Food Production*

Improved methods or equipment for land clearing

Simple design planters for grains, legumes, and tubers

Better design hoes or equipment for tilling and ridging

Simple fertilizer applicators/dispensers and rotary weeders for use by rural women, and simple design row harvesters for grains and tubers

*Food Processing and Packaging Technology*

Simple, inexpensive threshers for grains and legumes

Simple dehulling machines for village use

Sorting/cleaning machines

Oil mills for extracting oil from groundnuts and palm kernels

Kerosene or diesel fuelled-dryers for crops

Better storage facilities

Better packaging methods

New and improved preservation methods such as canning, pickling, bottling, and juice extraction at cottage industry levels

Improved transportation methods, especially of farm produce to the house and market, such as wheelbarrows and bicycle carts (ILO/UNDP/FDRD 1987)

Currently, most food production and processing techniques are manual. They involve drudgery, low productivity, and wastage (crop losses). In recent years, efforts have been made to provide improved technologies. Some of the technology introduced has been criticized on the following grounds:

- it is designed for men and ends up displacing women from their traditional tasks, for example, cassava graters and oil mills
- it disregards other factors required for efficient use of the technology such as level of education, availability of credit, and maintenance
- some technology has not taken into account the posture of women users, the scale of women's operations, culturally dictated tasks, and product preferences (ILO/ UNDP/FDRD 1987; Akande and Awosika 1994)

Thus, new technology has not been adopted by rural women because of:

- low literacy of women
- lack of access to resources such as land, credit, farm inputs, and extension information
- cultural factors such as the seclusion of women
- lack of follow-up services after the introduction of new technologies (Akande and Awosika 1994)

Given rural women's important roles in food production and processing, it is essential that appropriate technology be available to them in order to reduce the drudgery of manual operations, raise productivity and incomes, and reduce crop wastage.

*Land.* Under traditional inheritance systems in many parts of Nigeria, women have no individual rights of access to land, since family land is inherited by males. Women depend on their husbands for small portions of land on which to farm. In focus group discussions with men in Okhuesan in Edo State, the men said that they divide their land into three parts (not necessarily equal). One part is for themselves, a second portion is for their wives to plant food crops to feed their families, while the third part is for their wives to plant crops for sale, the proceeds of which they use for the maintenance of themselves and their children (Okojie 1992). Consequently, women's plots are usually small. They cannot use such land as collateral for obtaining credit.

*Extension Services.* Agricultural extension information is required to impart knowledge about new forms of agricultural technology, especially biological and chemical technology, which can help women achieve higher output on their small farms. Rural women have limited access to extension information. In Bendel State (now Edo and Delta States), out of 531 female farmers, only 30 reported any contact with extension agents (Okojie 1989). The situation had not changed in a later study of Okhuesan women in 1991 (Okojie 1992). It is only in recent years that Agricultural Development Projects (ADPs) incorporated extension services to women within their programs. However, lack of female extension agents has limited their coverage of women farmers.

*Transportation/Marketing Services.* Access roads to many rural areas are very poor, making it difficult for women to transport their farm produce to nearby towns for sale. As a result, much of their perishable items (especially vegetables) waste away. Middlemen who brave the bad roads to the village reap all the profits by buying at giveaway prices from the farmers and selling at exorbitant prices in urban markets. There is a need to assist rural women by providing transportation and marketing outlets in order to increase their incomes and encourage them to expand their output.

### Sociocultural Constraints

Various cultural restrictions inhibit women's economic activities. Women are seen as subordinate to men both within and outside the home. A common feature of many Nigerian societies is their patriarchal structure. Patriarchy is a system of social stratification and differentiation on the basis of sex that provides material advantages to males while at the same time placing severe restrictions on the roles and activities of females (Koenig and Foo 1985). Various legal, social, and economic institutions support the institution of patriarchy. One dimension of patriarchy that limits women's economic activities is the practice of purdah, or female seclusion, whereby women are confined to the household. Furthermore, patriarchy restricts women's access to economic resources such as land, credit, extension services, and so on. It also explains men's attitudes toward women in society and the neglect of women in the planning process. Education and information campaigns are needed to break down these cultural prejudices (Okojie 1985).

### IMPACTS OF GOVERNMENT PROGRAMS ON RURAL WOMEN

In the 1980s, especially after the Structural Adjustment Programme was adopted in 1986, women's issues received greater policy attention under the Babangida administration. Various programs targeted at women were introduced. Because of the administration's emphasis on rural development, rural women received a lot of attention.

These programs were of three types: (1) programs that include components for women, for example, ADPs with women-in-agriculture components; (2) projects designed mainly or solely for women, for example the National Commission for Women and the Better Life Programme for Rural Women/Dwellers (BLP); and (3) mainstream or general programs that included women, for example, the Directorate for Food, Roads, and Rural

Infrastructure (DFRRI) and the Peoples Bank and Community Bank Programmes.

## 1. Programs that Include Women Components

In this category, we have ADPs that were introduced into Nigeria in the 1970s as a World Bank–assisted program. In the 1980s, the program was extended to all states of the country. The basic objective of ADPs is to increase food production and incomes of small farmers by introducing new technology packages based on fertilizers and inputs. For many years, the focus of ADPs was on male farmers (Okojie 1987). It was not until 1986 that a program for extending extension services to female farmers was included. Criteria for identifying women contact farmers were developed since women grow a substantial proportion of the crops being promoted, such as cassava, maize, rice, sorghum, millet, and plantain. The neglect of women has begun to be corrected, but the program is hampered by a shortage of female agricultural extension officers (Okojie 1990c).

## 2. Projects Designed Mainly or Solely for Women

*The National Commission for Women.* The National Commission for women was set up by Decree Number 30 of 1989. Among its objectives are:

- to promote the welfare of women in general
- to promote the full utilization of women in the development of human resources and to bring about their acceptance as full participants in every phase of national development, with equal rights and corresponding obligations
- to stimulate actions to improve women's civic, political, cultural, social, and economic education
- to work toward total elimination of all social and cultural practices tending to discriminate against womanhood

The functions of the commission include:

- promoting, developing, and concretizing income generation and employment through loan schemes, home and cottage industries, acquisition of skills for the improvement of arts and crafts and food processing and such other educational training of women within the context of their assessed needs and potentials
- monitoring and submitting reports on (1) women's education and counseling, and (2) the health of women and children
- ensuring the self-reliance of women

• conducting research and planning aimed at improving the status of women and
the attainment of policy objectives in relation to women

The National Commission for Women has its headquarters at Abuja,
while there is a State Commission for Women in every state. The commission is responsible for implementing government policies and programs targeted directly at women, for example, the Better Life Programme for Rural
Women, and the newly introduced Family Support Programme. If the functions of the commission are properly executed, many of the constraints on
women identified earlier can be eliminated. The commission has suffered
from lack of funds and the activities of some first ladies[1] who have inter-
fered in the execution of its functions.

*The Better Life Programme for Rural Women.* The program was
launched in September 1987 by Mrs. Babangida, the wife of the former
president. The objective of the program was to mobilize rural women to
participate effectively in efforts designed to improve their living conditions.
Among the notable achievements of the program were:

• the supply of farm inputs such as improved seeds and fertilizers to women farming
cooperatives
• the diversification and stimulation of interest in nontraditional farming activities
such as snail and periwinkle farming
• the establishment of processing and handicraft industries such as food processing,
weaving, pottery, tailoring, catering, and leather work
• the establishment of maternity centers, rural minipharmacies, mobile clinics, family planning clinics, and immunization campaigns in some rural areas
• vocational and other enlightenment campaigns such as adult literacy program
workshops, trade fairs, and so forth (Central Bank of Nigeria 1991, 1992; Akande and Awosika 1994)

Table 5.2 shows the number of projects established by the Better Life Programme in various states (as of 1992). There were, however, variations in
the implementation of projects and activities in different states. The scope
and spread of the program's efforts appear to have been limited and confined mostly to the rural elite and a few urban poor. In some areas, greater
emphasis was placed on fanfare and propaganda campaigns than on actual
results. By the decree establishing the National Commission for Women,
the Better Life Programme was supposed to be one of its three departments
but the program remained under the control of the president's wife.

The program generally had significant impact on the areas of activity of
rural women such as agriculture, cottage industries, and trade. Rural
women were able to access credit and farm inputs through their Better Life
Cooperatives. The program also helped to generate public awareness of the

Table 5.2
Number of Better Life Projects in Various States as of 1992

| State | Cooperatives | Cottage Industries | Crop Farms | Vegetable Gardens | Fish and Livestock Farm |
|---|---|---|---|---|---|
| Federal Capital Territory (Abuja) | 60 | 15 | 37 | 37 | - |
| Akwa Ibom | 118 | 36 | 50 | - | - |
| Anambra | 662 | 150 | 28 | 6 | 2 |
| Bauchi | 292 | 28 | 468 | 25 | 2 |
| Bendel | 669 | 77 | 30 | 4 | - |
| Benue | 1025 | 140 | 18 | 9 | 93 |
| Borno | 229 | 52 | 457 | 28 | - |
| Cross River | 154 | 46 | 29 | - | - |
| Gongola | 499 | 5 | 88 | 12 | 2 |
| Imo | 587 | 6 | 3 | 14 | 4 |
| Kaduna | 570 | 20 | 29 | 14 | - |
| Kano | 459 | 65 | 14 | - | 1 |
| Katsina | 242 | 55 | 46 | 10 | - |
| Kwara | 186 | 155 | 20 | 20 | 15 |
| Lagos | 374 | 48 | 42 | 28 | 13 |
| Niger | 212 | 13 | 2 | 1 | 1 |
| Ogun | 391 | 74 | - | 10 | 12 |
| Ondo | 288 | 122 | 70 | 5 | 14 |
| Oyo | 476 | 154 | 30 | 5 | 15 |
| Plateau | 290 | 150 | 27 | 15 | 5 |
| Rivers | 361 | 20 | 22 | 7 | 8 |
| Sokoto | 600 | 4 | 29 | 3 | - |
| TOTAL | 9044 | 1435 | 1531 | 253 | 187 |

Source: J. Akande and K. Awosika, Women in Trade and Industry in Nigeria. A Study Report Submitted to UNIFEM, Nigeria, 1994, Tables 6a–6c.

situation of rural women. Despite its potential, the program was suspended and replaced in 1994 by a new program called the Family Support Programme at the insistence of the wife of the present head of state.

## 3. General Programs that Include Women

Of interest here are the following programs: (1) the Directorate for Foods, Roads, and Rural Infrastructure (DFRRI), (2) the Peoples Bank, and (3) Community Banks.

The Directorate for Food, Roads, and Rural Infrastructures (DFRRI). DFRRI was established in February 1986 by the Babangida administration. The directorate was to gear its efforts toward the development of rural areas. Its objectives included: improving the quality of life and the standard of living of people in rural areas; undertaking the construction and repair of roads to facilitate communication and the distribution of agricultural products; and providing water and health facilities and electricity in the rural economy in conjunction with the appropriate federal, state, and local government authorities (Okojie 1990c).

While DFRRI's programs were targeted at rural dwellers as a group, women in particular have benefited from them through rehabilitated feeder roads that facilitate transportation of crops to markets and the provision of boreholes that reduce the burden of long trips to fetch water. Electricity supply has allowed food processing mills driven by electricity, which reduce women's drudgery, to be set up in villages.

The program contributed significantly to rural development in Nigeria. For example, in December 1992, 85,592 km of roads were completed; 30,728.34 km and 55,576.24 km were completed in 1990 and 1991, respectively. A total of 18,680 communities benefited from its rural water and sanitation schemes in 1992, while 506 communities were supplied with electricity (Central Bank of Nigeria 1992). However, the directorate's activities have been more or less at a standstill since it was merged with the Ministry of Agriculture and Rural Development.

*The Peoples Bank of Nigeria.* The Peoples Bank of Nigeria (modeled on the Grameen Bank of Bangladesh) was established in 1989 by the Babangida administration to cater to the credit needs of small-scale entrepreneurs who usually have difficulties in accessing credit from conventional financial institutions. The bank is administered on a zonal basis. By November 1992, there were about 206 branches and about 40 mobile banks nationwide.

To borrow from the Peoples Bank, prospective borrowers are encouraged to form trade groups (solidarity groups) of about seven to fourteen members and to open savings accounts with the banks. The first five members of the group benefit first and repayment commences after a two-week moratorium. Loans are granted for a period of one year at an administrative cost of 15 percent.

Many women's cooperatives under the Better Life Programme benefited from the Peoples Banks credit facility. Evidence shows that women have benefited more than men from the loan scheme of the Peoples Bank. Within the first ten months of its operation, about 60,000 women nationwide received a total disbursement of about 45 million *naira*[2]. Furthermore, over 70 percent of applications for loans were from women (Akande and Awosika 1994). The innovation of mobile banks and the rapid expansion of branches (about 2,000 by 1993) brought banking to the doorstep of the average rural woman. By 1992, cottage industries attracted about 12 percent of loan disbursement by the bank. Some female farmers have also been recipients of Peoples Bank loans (Akande and Awosika 1994).

The Peoples Bank of Nigeria has done a lot to facilitate rural women's access to credit. However, only a small proportion of women have yet been reached nationwide. There is a need for women to be informed about this source of credit.

*Community Banks.* Community Banks were introduced to Nigeria in

1990. The objectives were: to promote rural development through the provision of finance and banking services, to enhance the rapid development of productive activities in the rural and urban informal sector, and to improve the economic status of small-scale producers both in the rural and urban areas.

The initial capital of the banks was mobilized from the community's resources in the form of equity participation. This was supplemented by matching grants from the government through the National Board for Community Banks. A Community Bank's operations are limited to the community where it is established.

To qualify for loans, the customer is required to open an account. Loans are offered for periods of 6 months to one year, repayable in monthly installments with a moratorium of one to two months. The size of loans is related to the customer's current account balances. This requirement is not likely to work in favor of rural women.

By December 1992, there were 401 Community Banks in operation (Central Bank of Nigeria 1992). The activities of 250 of these banks were analyzed in the Central Bank of Nigeria's report for 1992. The total capital and reserves of these 250 banks stood at N166.5 million, while their total assets and liabilities amounted to N774.4 million and N474.6 million, respectively. Loans and advances stood at N132.2 million and were oriented toward rural activities and microenterprises. The sectoral distribution of loans and advances were as follows: agriculture (17.93 percent); petty trade (33.05 percent); petty restaurant (5.98 percent); manufacturing (9.23 percent); cottage industries (4.99 percent); transportation (7.03 percent); and others (21.78 percent) (Central Bank of Nigeria 1992).

Gender-disaggregated data is not generally available. However, a study of Community Banks in Lagos and Ondo States showed that on average, fewer females than males apply for loans. The study suggested that lack of adequate information about the banks' services was a constraint on women's access to credit from Community Banks (Fawole 1994). In terms of outreach, savings mobilization, and credit facilities to rural communities, Community Banks have the potential to meet rural women's needs for credit if they are adequately informed.

## ENHANCING RURAL WOMEN'S PRODUCTIVITY

It is noteworthy that women have now been identified as a target group for policy making in their own right. A major problem has been the partial abandonment, through changes in administration, of policies that have made a significant impact on rural women. For example, the Better Life Programme has been replaced by the Family Support Programme, and DFRRI and the Ministry of Agriculture and Rural Development have been merged.

The National Commission for Women's objectives and functions cover most of the constraints on women's activities identified in this chapter. Whatever programs or projects are put in place to eliminate these constraints, the following problems faced by ongoing programs should be borne in mind:

1. Funds. Many programs suffer from inadequate funding, especially since the Structural Adjustment Programme was adopted in 1986, a situation that makes implementation difficult.

2. Staff. Staff shortages hinder the implementation of programs benefiting women, for example, the shortage of female extension agents for the women-in-agriculture program of ADPs.

3. Female Education. Women's education programs should be vigorously pursued, as female education has high social rates of return (Herz 1989).

4. Research. There is need for further research on rural women's economic activities. Given variations in rural women's activities all over the country, priorities in different regions may differ. Research will identify problems or needs particular to different regions so that appropriate policies and programs can be designed.

5. Participation in the Planning Process. So far, women, especially rural women, play very limited roles in decision making in Nigeria. One way of involving rural women in decision making is through greater consultation with women's groups, that is, women's associations or cooperatives, in order to identify their priority needs.

6. Access to Basic Needs. This is a national planning issue as it affects both male and female productivity. Basic needs such as adequate food, shelter, clothing, and essential services such as safe drinking water, sanitation, health, and education should be brought within the reach of all households, whether urban or rural, in order to enhance productivity. Greater access to basic needs also implies that social development is occurring within the economy.

7. Sociocultural Constraints. These are very important, especially in the rural areas. There is a need to educate men to see women as partners in the development process who should be assisted to contribute their quota to national development. Currently, men who are the policymakers are very skeptical about programs targeted at women, thus affecting their implementation.

## CONCLUSION

This chapter has highlighted the important roles women play in the rural economy in such activities as food production and processing activities. They also engage in other income-generating activities such as spinning, weaving, trading, and sewing. The important contributions of rural women to food production and processing must be recognized if the objective of attaining food security in Nigeria is to be achieved. The constraints against higher productivity and incomes of rural women must be addressed, and policies to eliminate these constraints must be an important aspect of agricultural and rural development programs. Rural development policies and projects should continue to target women as beneficiaries.

## NOTES

1. First ladies refers to women who occupy powerful positions.
2. As of July 1996, we could not find the equivalent to the U.S. dollar.

# 6

# The Political Economy of Women's Work in Kenya: Chronic Constraints and Broken Barriers

*Collette Suda*

## INTRODUCTION

While there is a definite class, regional, and ethnic divide between the women in Kenya, there are also myriad common elements in their daily lives and working experiences that transcend these diversities, uniting them cross-culturally. To this extent, Kenyan rural and urban women of different ethnic, regional, and socioeconomic backgrounds share some common ground as a social group and face similar frustrations, job dissatisfaction, and work related stress both at home and in their workplaces outside the home.

In order to gain any insights into the working situation of the women in Kenya and have a better grasp of their everyday lives, one needs to understand the internal forces not only rooted in the diversity of cultural traditions but also in the ways in which class, gender, work, and power relations are socially constituted.

Inequalities do exist, of course, between men and women on the one hand and among different groups of women on the other. But in Kenya, as in other developing countries, these inequalities and the social construction of the female gender identity are often mediated and reproduced through ethnic and regional politics, contemporary economic systems, and patriarchal structures.

This chapter is about Kenyan women's work experiences and their daily life situations inside and outside the home. The analysis is anchored in gender, class, and ethnic relations as they are constituted in contemporary sociopolitical and economic systems. The theme that runs through this discussion is that women's experiences of work are inextricably linked to their class positions, geographical locations (regions), and ethnic backgrounds created and consolidated by existing political and economic structures. These structures are also reinforced by a system of male domination.

The primary goal of this chapter is to show the diversities and similarities in women's work situations between rural and urban settings and, within these settings, whether they are involved in biological reproduction, food production and processing, petty trade, commerce, services, politics, women's organizations, or formal sector employment. A further concern of the chapter is to acknowledge the strengths and the achievements of women as they work to earn a livelihood, alleviate their deteriorating working conditions, or struggle to break structural barriers. Of course, the specifics of women's work experiences do vary considerably across classes, regions, and ethnic communities, but many of the issues raised in this chapter are equally relevant to women of all classes.

## THE CONSTRAINTS EXPERIENCED BY WOMEN THROUGH THEIR TRADITIONAL REPRODUCTIVE WORK

About 80 percent of the women in Kenya live and work in rural areas. Although farming is the major economic activity and the main source of livelihood for the Kenyan rural population, women contribute over 70 percent of the agricultural labor and produce most of the food using mainly traditional technology and living largely on the edge of subsistence (Republic of Kenya 1992, 1993a). Rural women in Kenya are among the most disadvantaged groups in terms of their structural positions in the household and working conditions on the farms. In addition to their inadequate access to labor, technology, credit, and other productive inputs, women's control over land has been reduced by the postcolonial land reform programs that have left landless women from the poorest households to work as seasonal and casual laborers for very low wages.

A great majority of the rural women have only possession but not legal rights to land, which means that they don't have title deeds or the collateral needed to produce credit facilities from most formal banking institutions. However, a few highly educated and more prosperous Kenyan women have been, and still are, able to purchase and own land in their own right. Many of these propertied women also enjoy much greater autonomy than their rural counterparts whose lives and work situations are still heavily influenced by long-standing traditions. These women and their urban poor counterparts are the ones most desperate for change but also the most powerless to effect it, although this does not necessarily mean that the individual women are not conscious actors. Rather, they are faced with cultural and structural barriers that will take some time to overcome. On the other hand, the upper-class women in Kenya are still a distinct minority although property ownership among the new middle- and upper-middle-class women is becoming common and generally accepted.

Over 30 percent of the households in Kenya are headed by women who function either as the sole or primary economic providers (UN 1990; Feldman 1984; Achola 1991). Most of the female-headed households, particularly those in the urban slums, are severely impoverished. Most of these women and their families live well below the poverty line with almost no opportunity for upward social mobility. They predominate the informal sector and are, in many ways, trapped in a vicious circle of poverty shaped by systematic exploitation. Some of the reasons for the emergence of female-headed households include widowhood, male migration to urban areas, rising rates of divorce, and other forms of marital instability, as well as the emerging trend in which some urban women have chosen to have children but not to get married.

In a classic case of a double standard, most men who are divorced (or otherwise estranged from their wives) are more likely than their female counterparts to remarry or lead a fulfilling family life. This situation is primarily created out of social prejudices against women and shared expectations or assumptions about their culturally defined roles as wives and mothers. Fransella and Frost (1977: 19) have pointed out that "marriage and child-bearing are assumed to be an essential part of one's identity as a woman." Many Kenyan women still feel this way regardless of class, ethnic, regional, or other differences between them.

In the sphere of reproductive work, study after study from Kenya has shown that the burden of domestic work, including the responsibility of child care, falls mostly on women (Suda 1994; Ayiecho 1991; Silberschmidt 1991; Republic of Kenya 1991). Traditionally, women in Kenya do the majority of the work in the house. Their multiple domestic responsibilities include food production, processing, and preparation; child-bearing and rearing; nurturing husbands; the provision of fuel and water; maintaining the house; and all other activities essential to achieve food security and the reproduction and maintenance of all the human resources in the family. Many Kenyan women, particularly those without maids or houseboys to help them with housework, start their daily chores at dawn and work continually throughout the day until about 10 o'clock at night. They are usually the first ones up and the last ones to sleep in the family. Lower-class women put in considerably longer hours of either home or market work than most elite women.

Female reproductive labor, though vital to the survival and continuing reproduction of human resources in the household, is usually taken for granted and unpaid because it is not defined as "real" work for which wages are paid. This work is not reflected or accounted for in national statistics as part of a conceptual and social bias in the definition of labor that is erroneously equated with wage employment. What is implied here is that all the labor that goes into the production of family life, including the labor of giving birth to a child and taking responsibility for children, is natural and not cultural or social. The underremuneration and devaluation of women's reproductive work not only accentuates hierarchical gender-power relations but can also be viewed as part of a social process that furthers structured social inequality among women themselves. Although the demarcations of class boundaries are difficult to discern and highly subjective, many Kenyan middle-class women and their counterparts higher up the socioeconomic ladder tend to hire domestic help (mainly poor men, women, or young girls) to assist them with household chores. Most of these domestic workers are usually overworked and underpaid.

In the past few years, the living and working conditions of many poor rural and urban women in Kenya have deteriorated significantly primarily due to high inflation rates and a series of economic reforms that are all part of the ongoing structural adjustment programs. In the absence of laborsaving techniques, much of the work done by most women at home is labor intensive, difficult, repetitive, time consuming, and often unpleasant but essential. In addition, almost all the care-giving roles are not shared equally between the sexes because of deeply rooted cultural prejudices and an ingrained gender hierarchy and insensitivity at the household and village levels. These and other forms of social impediments have led to an asymmetrical gender division of labor. The imbalance in gender division of labor can be seen as a major structural constraint to women's empowerment in Kenyan society. Among other things, it leads to tremendous increases in the workload for women as they combine motherhood, domestic roles, farm production, and participation in the formal or informal economic sector (UN 1990; Ferber 1982). Consequently, many working mothers are experiencing difficulty balancing family and work obligations. In urban situations in particular, traditional female roles often constitute sufficient grounds for aggravation and occupational segregation, conflicting as they do with the demands and obligations of modern professional life (Kimani 1994).

For many working women in Kenya, the need to balance the demands of family responsibility and paid employment outside the home affects not only their participation in the workforce but also their involvement in public life, particularly in the upper niches of the power structure where they could share in decision making. Very often, these conflicting demands deny a number of women a chance to take practical advantage of education, training, and other opportunities, hence limiting their competitiveness and diminishing their prospects for promotion to better jobs. Women's work affects their status in several ways. As Mebrahtu (1991) argues, under subsistence production, the time devoted to housework, food production and processing may also determine the time available to pursue a career, seek health care, or engage in paid work outside the domestic domain. Some working women have had little time to participate in other self-fulfilling activities that could help to empower them. As much as motherhood can be a very fulfilling experience, single mothers who bear the full responsibility of parenting experience varying degrees of emotional, physical, and economic stress. Combining motherhood with full-time formal employment outside the home is undoubtedly demanding and challenging. Apart from a small group of upper- and upper-middle-class urban women who can afford to take their children to the few and very expensive day care centers, the majority of working-class women (particularly single mothers and married women in the informal sector) are severely constrained. For the average urban working woman, the problem is exacerbated by the difficulty of finding experienced, reliable, and dedicated domestic help to look after the children and to keep the house during working hours. Family support systems are also currently on the decline as the extended family system weakens. Rural women who do most of the farm work in addition to their domestic duties are also faced with chronic labor shortages as their older children are in school and cannot help on a regular basis. Other relatives who may be willing and able to help with household and farm work are increasingly beginning to expect to be paid in cash and rarely in kind.

Despite the fact that women are usually used as a cheap source of labor in factories, industries, and on commercial farms, sexist ideology and stereotyped reproductive roles still serve as important factors in the process of gender discrimination and female subordination at work. In many instances, the discrimination is quite subtle. Employers often have a negative attitude toward hiring female employees because of their responsibility for biological reproduction. A woman is not considered to be as reliable as a man because she will leave to have babies or may have to be called home to sit with a sick child or, if married, will follow her husband to another town if he is transferred (Pollert 1983). As a result of gender insensitivity and other forms of prejudice in the workplace, some women have become subordinated in the work process and experience feelings of alienation. Such forms of prejudice in women's working lives can be seen as a structural manifestation of cultural values and attitudes.

## THE WORKING LIVES OF WOMEN ENTREPRENEURS

Most Kenyan women have a great potential and tremendous capability for entrepreneurship and the determination to be self-reliant. The importance of the informal sector for job creation to augment employment opportunities in the formal sector has been underscored in a number of government policy documents such as the Sessional Paper No. 1 of 1986, the Report of the Presidential Committee on Employment of 1991, and the 1989–1993 Development Plan (Republic of Kenya 1993a). The total number of people employed in the informal sector in Kenya increased from 497,157 in 1991 to 566,029 in 1992 (Republic of Kenya 1993b). Overall, women comprise about 30 percent of those employed in the informal sector (Republic of Kenya 1993c).

The majority of women in the informal sector of the Kenyan economy are self-employed entrepreneurs who have created their own jobs in very small-scale manufacturing, transport, service, and petty trade activities. Many of them are involved in the production of handicrafts, tailoring, hawking, hairdressing, and *changaa* brewing among other miscellaneous income-generating enterprises. In practice, however, many of these informal activities do not yield enough income to reduce the growth of female poverty.

Although there are some women entrepreneurs who have developed their own businesses into sustainable private enterprises and have hired their own employees, most businesswomen are petty traders. Small-scale women entrepreneurs often experience all the disadvantages that come with informal sector employment.

Among the major constraints facing most women entrepreneurs are limited access to credit facilities from formal banking institutions because of the lack of title to property or other assets, limited education, and lack of technical and managerial skills (Berger 1989). The bureaucratic bottlenecks encountered in the licensing procedures are also a major disincentive to a number of women traders who wish to start and operate their own businesses in order to achieve some measure of self-reliance, self-actualization, and self-empowerment.

Under the Kenya Trade Licensing Act, Chapter 497, of 1972 there are certain areas in the cities, municipalities, or towns that are designated as business areas (Republic of Kenya 1972). The types of business to be conducted in such areas are also specified under the act. The licensing of businesses thus depends on the fulfillment of all the conditions spelled out in that act. Traders who carry out their businesses in unauthorized premises are usually denied a license. Most traders are small-scale women entrepreneurs who, because of their inability to pay rent in authorized premises, may set up a tailoring shop or a hairdressing salon either in their houses or in their backyards. Such petty traders are frequently harassed by the trade licensing officers who accuse them of operating their businesses illegally and in the wrong premises.

Some cultural barriers also impede women's full participation in economic activities and entrepreneurship. Because of the prevailing inequality in gender-power relations, many businesswomen still need to seek and obtain permission from their husbands before they can engage in any commercial activity or attend business meetings or management training programs. A number of them, including some professional career women, are still expected by their husbands to return home at a specified time in order to attend to their family responsibilities. There is also a general attitude that a married woman who frequently returns home from work late is neglecting her traditional roles as mother and wife. She may also be accused of hanging out with another man or being in "bad" company—a situation that could result in her being beaten or verbally abused. These social attitudes and restrictions are indicative of the social inequalities in gender relations.

Owing to its commitment to promote private enterprise and self-employment, particularly among women, the Kenyan government, in collaboration with some nongovernmental organizations (NGOs), has made some attempts to alleviate some of the problems facing women entrepreneurs. For example, the Kenya Women Finance Trust (KWFT), which is one of the affiliates of the Women's World Banking, has improved women's access to credit facilities in many parts of the country. Most of the women who have received loans from KWFT have also participated in management training. The government, through its relevant ministries and departments, has also organized some training programs for women entrepreneurs to enable them to acquire skills in trade, marketing, quality control, accounting, and management. More specifically, the Kenya Institute of Business Training (KIBT) under the Ministry of Commerce and Industry trains entrepreneurs (both women and men) in a wide range of skills at a fee. However, most women entrepreneurs have not been able to participate in such training programs primarily because of their domestic responsibilities, social restrictions, and the inability to pay the fees.

Furthermore, the training of women entrepreneurs has mainly been limited to the urban areas and a few districts with unimproved infrastructures. Most of the poor rural women from remote parts of the country and the marginal regions have been left behind and continue to miss out on this experience. Some of these economic dimensions of women's work are reflections of the colonial legacy. Although the government has district trade development officers in all fifty-one districts in the country, there is a need to further decentralize trading activities to include the divisional, locational, and sublocational levels in order to reach and help rural women in small-scale businesses.

While pointing out the ways in which the state apparatus operates to influence women's work in Kenya, it is important to assign blame and give credit where it is due. One of the steps taken by the Kenyan government to assist small-scale entrepreneurs is the establishment of the Rural Enterprise Fund, which does not require collateral. But in order to have a greater impact, this fund can be increased by giving priority to small-scale women traders, including those with very little formal education. Also, according to its national policy on gender and development, the Kenyan government has reaffirmed its commitment to provide the necessary infrastructure and support services aimed at the promotion of female entrepreneurship (Republic of Kenya 1992). Up to this point, some concrete measures have been taken to consolidate the gains made by women in private enterprise, although a lot more remains to be done through private initiative, legislation, and state intervention. Kenyan women have learned from their experiences of the past decade (since the end of the Women's Decade and the International Women's Conference held in Nairobi in July 1985, which produced the document known as the Nairobi Forward-Looking Strategies) that the political will for serious action by the state and other agencies is predicated upon women's ability to organize themselves to demand and to work for changes.

Another significant step taken by the Kenyan government is the appointment of a task force to look into the legal issues concerning women in Kenya. Part of this twenty-member committee's work is to seek, listen to, analyze, and collate diverse views from a cross-section of women (and men) with vastly different backgrounds throughout the country. A further task of the committee is to make recommendations to the government and to advocate for legal reforms as well as changes in some cultural practices, thus ensuring the protection and promotion of women's rights. The committee should also ensure that its recommendations are implemented. Participation in such a task force can be seen as an example of how Kenyan women have been working for change in their lives.

## WOMEN'S WORK IN WOMEN'S GROUPS

In order to influence further changes in their life situations and also to accelerate the self-empowerment process, increasingly significant numbers of Kenyan women have taken the initiative to mobilize and organize themselves into self-help groups at the grassroots level. Although the history of women's groups in Kenya predates the colonial period, the activities of the present-day women's groups can be seen as an attempt to repair some of the damage done by colonialism and perpetuated by postindependence political and economic systems (Karl 1984; Hay and Stitcher 1984). Despite the diversity in their activities, the primary goal of women's groups is to promote their common social, economic, and political interests by organizing themselves and pooling their resources. This initiative has been prompted not only by the fact that their individual resources are limited, but also by the recognition that both colonial and contemporary political and economic policies have undermined women's interests and weakened their positions, thereby leaving them much less powerful than men (Feldman 1984; Achola 1991).

The idea of group formation is also based upon the recognition that, as individuals, most women in Kenya have such meager resources that life with dignity is impossible. In addition, the need for women to join income-generating groups rests upon both the moral principle and the philosophical assumption that it is both necessary and desirable for women to earn their own incomes. Women's income needs and uses are as diverse as they are basic because they contribute enormously to their families' food and other basic requirements.

One of the first steps in the formation of a women's group is the identification of a common need felt by the women themselves. Although contemporary women's groups in Kenya continue to address social welfare issues, most of the activities are oriented toward income generation. Economic need seems to have motivated many women's groups to engage in nontraditional income-generating enterprises. Women also join these groups to provide psychological and physical support to one another, especially during times of crisis.

The National Women's Group Census Report, which was carried out between 1990–1991, has shown that groups are involved in a wide range of activities for various purposes. A number of them are engaged in more than one activity at a time in order to diversify their sources of income (Republic of Kenya 1993d). Due to considerable overlap in some of the group activities, it is somewhat difficult to classify all activities into specific categories. However, women's group activities do fall under two broad categories, namely: income-generating and social welfare types of projects. In general, women's groups in Kenya are involved in a variety of activities ranging from farming and transport business to real estate, merry-go-round light manufacturing, sales, service, and handicraft production. The Maasai women, who have limited opportunities to generate income within the livestock sector because the marketing of livestock is a male-dominated field, have turned their attention to handicraft production for the market. Among other things, the Maasai women produce large quantities of beads, mats, and other products for the local and the tourist markets in Nairobi, although some husbands object to their wives' participation in the bead-work project (Talle 1988). This experience is similar to that of the Kikuyu women in the production of *kyondo* bags, not only exemplifying the way in which the pastoral and subsistence agricultural economies are integrated with the market economy but also, more importantly, the possibilities of increased female access to income and the decision-making process. It is important to point out, however, that many women in agricultural communities contribute significantly to the production of cash crops but often have little or no control over the product of their labor, as the men appropriate the profits derived from the sale of such crops. In fact, many women's groups are now moving away from activities that had confined women to the traditional sector (because they were mere extensions of their traditional roles) and toward projects and enterprises involving modern technology that were previously male dominated.

The specific types of projects undertaken by the groups vary according to the local situation under which the women live and work. Broadly conceived, we are talking about the social, cultural, economic, physical, and political environment—all of which bear upon women's working lives. The choice of project is also influenced by whether the community is rural or urban, the types of knowledge or skills the women have, the availability of raw materials, and whether or not there is a ready market for their products, among other factors (Karl 1984; Achola 1991).

Although the institution of women's groups is uniquely a Kenyan phenomenon, their distribution pattern and the range of their activities vary widely from one region to another. According to the National Women's Group Census Report, there is considerable variation in the number of women's groups between different regions. The census results show, for example, that Rift Valley, one of the largest provinces in Kenya, has the highest number (4,568) of women's groups. In contrast, Northeastern Province, one of the most economically marginal regions, has the least (225) number of groups. The distribution pattern of women's groups in Kenya can generally be explained in terms of the nature of economic activities the people of these regions engage in and, to some extent, the caliber of political leadership in the area. Most of the drier districts of the Rift Valley, Eastern, Northeastern, and Coast Provinces tend to have fewer women's groups as compared to the higher potential, agroecological zones that form much of the Western and Central Provinces.

The census report further indicates that nomadic pastoralism, which is the dominant mode of production and way of life in the Northeastern Province and parts of the Eastern and Rift Valley Provinces does not favor women's group formation primarily because of the seasonal mobility of these pastoral communities. For example, because of their harsh and hazardous environments, places like Isiolo, Mandera, Garissa, Tana River, West Pokot, Kajiado, Wajir, Narok, Marsabit, and Turkana are also very sparsely populated, with security a major problem because of banditry. These factors influence the range of activities open to women.

Within the coastal region, the Islamic religion has had a profound influence on the lives and activities of most women. According to their religious tradition, Muslim women are encouraged to stay at home and look after their families. Thus their minimal involvement in women's groups and other economic activities outside the home is explained, in part, by their confinement to the domestic sphere, although they are beginning to experience some limited physical and social mobility and a greater possibility for earning independent incomes.

Kenya is a pluralistic and highly stratified society and the women's groups, like the individual women themselves, are vastly different in their activities, class positions, cultural traditions, and experiences. But there are also some similarities in the types of constraints the women and their groups face. Some of the most common problems faced by women's groups as a whole are leadership wrangles, lack of or inadequate access to resources such as land, credit, modern production technology, markets for their products, premises for their activities and meetings, and poor infrastructure. The level of underdevelopment experienced in some parts of Kenya is a carryover from past policies and a reflection of the colonial legacy. Lingering cultural practices and limited training opportunities also contribute to a lack of knowledge and skills necessary in design, production, and quality control measures (Njonjo et al. 1984). Another dimension of women's experiences in their group activities is the violence against them from some husbands who object to women's appropriation of the products of their own labor. Under the existing structure of gender-power relations, most Kenyan men fear that their power and control in the household will be undermined by the women's collective voices and improved economic status.

Structures interact with ethnic politics to determine which Kenyan woman does what, when, and where. However, this does not necessarily indicate that women's groups and other women's organizations have not brought some measure of economic independence to some women and self-empowerment to others.

## WOMEN'S WORKING EXPERIENCES IN THE FORMAL SECTOR

Although Kenyan women have joined the labor force in large and increasing numbers over the past two to three decades due to increased access to education, the vast majority of them are still concentrated in traditional "female occupations" and "pink-collar" jobs. Most of these so-called traditional female jobs lack prestige, are low paying with poor fringe benefits and working conditions, and hold little prospect for upward mobility.

The urban labor force participation rate for women in Kenya increased from 39 to 56 percent (Ongile 1992; ILO 1991). Despite their growing participation in the workforce, there are still very few women in the top echelons of public decision- and policy-making positions in Kenya.[1] The gross underrepresentation of women in high profile careers and positions and the concentration of women in certain occupations is mainly due to labor market segregation, social attitudes, lack of training, ethnicity, and the quest for balance. Owing to the multiple constraints experienced by the groups, many of them, particularly those working in the rural areas, lack the capacity to deal with the complexity of export, marketing promotion, advertising, foreign exchange, and licensing procedures. Part of the reason is that most of these women have never done any of these things before, although their work represents an effort to resist exploitation based on gender and class. Under the circumstances, the achievement of their goals may be difficult without some form of economic and political support.

Consequently, some women's groups have received various types of assistance from local and international organizations in the form of loans, training, cash, equipment, technical advice, seminars, and supplies.

Much of the growing interest in women's group activities stems from the recognition that they constitute the easiest and most direct way of reaching the local communities. Because of their local representation and the diversity of their activities, women's groups often serve as entry points for donor agencies and other organizations working with the local communities to bring about some changes in women's lives. In effect, the groups represent grassroots efforts that preempt development interventions from the state and other national and international organizations.[2]

Apart from the women's groups operating at the grassroots level, there are also a number of national women's organizations in Kenya through which women can work to bring about changes in their situations. Two such national organizations are Maendeleo ya Wanawake (Progress for Women) and the National Council of Women of Kenya (NCWK). However, a closer look at these umbrella organizations indicates that they tend to be used by a few elite women as springboards to further their own political interests (Stamp 1991).

A fundamental point to be made about the working experiences of Kenyan women in group activities is that they share the common goal of bringing about qualitative change in their lives mainly through their own initiatives and pooled resources. But, at the same time, they also tend to face similar types of constraints. The problems of regional inequality and the structures of gender hierarchy within families have proved formidable. As a result, to say that women's participation in group activities alone will lead to dramatic changes in their status is to overlook the complexity of the whole situation. This is because such an assumption ignores the subtle ways in which gender relations and class appointments to senior public offices, and the promotion system in general, tend to be influenced by other considerations. These include the quest for gender, ethnic, and regional balance, party affiliation, class position, the "godfather syndrome," and the ideological inclination of the individual. With regard to social attitudes, for example, there are some men who strongly believe that they cannot accept supervision by women because of real or perceived interpersonal difficulties. Similarly, some male employers or bosses still believe that women cannot make good supervisors or managers because some of them are thought to be bossy, quarrelsome, or firm. In Kenya, this attitude seems to influence the working environments of all women regardless of their class and ethnic differences. Even highly educated, experienced, and capable women who are working in those fields previously reserved for men have to work nearly twice as hard to be considered half as good by their male colleagues.

Despite the complexity of the factors influencing a woman's working life, the relationship between education, training, and formal sector employment remains important. When women have more opportunity to receive high-quality education and training, they increase their chances for better-paying jobs even though unemployment is rampant in this developing and dependent economy. But the situation of women's work is much more complex than that. As was the case during the Kikuyu political and economic domination, under the present Kalenjin political hegemony, ethnic chauvinism, and rivalry have reemerged as potent factors in the distribution of resources and the creation of job opportunities. Under the current dynamics of ethnic politics and patriarchal ideology, most women and men from parts of Nyanza and the Central Provinces and their colleagues from other ethnic communities designated as "opposition zones" are increasingly marginalized from the political mainstream and are becoming concerned about job security in every sector of the economy.

Compared to their urban counterparts, most rural women have less formal education. They are subsequently more economically dependent on their husbands and are disempowered. In addition, many poor women are too busy struggling to feed and clothe their families to think about how to change their situations as women (Azevedo 1993).

One of the ways in which the contemporary political system is attempting to change educational opportunities for women is through the 8-4-4 system of education. Under this system, boys and girls receive the same type of education and, one can assume, are prepared for the same type of careers. Ideologically, the 8-4-4 system is primarily intended to expand the range of occupations women can pursue in the workforce and to bridge the existing gender gap in education and employment.

## WOMEN'S WORK IN POLITICS

In terms of participation in the political process, there are definite signs of women's empowerment as they gradually break the long-standing traditions and male-dominated structures. Kenya made a modest improvement in the representation of women in parliament after the 1992 second multiparty general elections. Six women were elected to parliament out of 188 possible seats. All women members of parliament except one are in the opposition. During the same period, fifty women were elected civic leaders in various local authorities. But given the fact that Kenyan women constitute slightly over half (52%) of the total national population, thus constituting the majority of voters, their votes are obviously critical but their representation is still minimal. The range of political participation by women, apart from voting, is being expanded as part of the democratization process. Voting alone, though crucial, is not enough because the road to high-level legislative, executive, and judicial offices is usually via appointments, nominations, and promotions rather than through elections per se.

With the reintroduction of political pluralism in Kenya, many women have played a more active part in attempting to redefine their historically marginal political positions. Through many generations, Kenyan politics has been a man's world shared by a handful of women with similar socio-economic backgrounds. Almost all the women in senior government positions owe their positions to the existing political establishment and are generally ambivalent about, and ineffective with regard to, the women's movement in Kenya. Although it is starting to gain momentum, a Kenyan women's movement still faces a great deal of hostility. Not surprisingly, the movement is resisted mostly by men. However, many senior women public officials sometimes consider it politically suicidal to overtly champion women's causes or to publicly identify with them.

Viewed in relative terms, Kenyan women are still extremely underrepresented in politics. The six female members of parliament constitute only 3.2 percent of the total seats in the national legislature while the fifty civic leaders represent only 2.7 percent of the total number of councillors in all the local authorities (Republic of Kenya 1993e). More significantly, a woman has never held a full ministerial position in Kenya. Right now, there is only one female assistant minister and no female nominated member of parliament. Perhaps these realities are the best expression of the depth of gender inequality in Kenyan polity.

Although Kenyan women are slowly making strides and moving into the male-dominated workforce and political structures, their underrepresentation in the current political system can be attributed to many factors. One factor is that many rural women, who also constitute the majority of the voters, are uneducated and so it is more difficult for them to be organized, sensitized, and educated into well-informed voters. This is partly attributed to inadequate networking and poor linkages between the rural and urban women whose lives, experiences, and status are sometimes quite different. The other factor keeping many women out of politics is that when a woman runs for a political office, her private life is usually put under scrutiny, something that does not seem to be the case with male politicians. Following from this example of a double standard is the idea that men can be appointed but women have to be elected to political positions. Other factors and reasons include women's lack of political education and confidence in themselves, the public's perception of women's political abilities, women's attitudes toward female leaders, and women's overall economic situation. As in many other poor, economically dependent African nations undergoing economic and political transformation, a great majority of Kenyan women still lack the political will and economic means with which to run for public office and/or improve their working conditions.

## CONCLUSION

As in other African countries, Kenyan women live and work under different environments in a gender and class-structured society in which the entire equation is a factor in the distribution of resources. Although their living conditions and working experiences vary a great deal between classes, regions, and ethnic communities, their overall contribution to the household, local, and national economy is both vital and visible. Women's contributions and experiences in the household, workforce, informal sector, entrepreneurship, women's groups, and politics are at once similar and diverse, as are their backgrounds and abilities.

This chapter's intention has been to contribute to a structural understanding of women's working lives in Kenya by focusing on some of the obstacles they face and the achievements they have made. The discussion has been devoted to examining the ways in which different groups of Kenyan women are working either autonomously or through existing economic and political organizations to overcome barriers and bring about change in their situations and in their futures.

Although there have been some concrete improvements in the working lives of some Kenyan women, they have been slow and fragmented and a great deal still remains to be done. Within the context of a highly stratified and ethnically conscious patriarchal society that is also in the process of rapid economic and political reforms, meaningful change in the lives of most women will have to be preceded by and achieved through conscious changes in the social, economic, and political systems.

In order to improve the working situation of women in Kenya, social attitudes toward them must change, particularly those attitudes defining "male" and "female" domains. Another key to breaking gender and class barriers is increased access to education and economic opportunities that make individuals feel empowered to take control over their own lives. Persistence in the fight for equal benefits in the work place could also help women overcome segregation in the formal labor market.

Given the class and regional differences between women, the well-educated and more prosperous urban women have been leading the way for women's empowerment in Kenya. But the key to dealing with women's work-related issues and bringing about change in their daily lives and work experiences is through unity in diversity. More recently, a growing number of women from diverse backgrounds are beginning to challenge Kenya's male-nominated political and economic structures and to advocate for change. After all, this is one of the ways to remind Kenyan society that its women hold up half the sky.

## NOTES

1. Although the Kenyan government ratified the recommendations of the Nairobi Forward-Looking Strategies (NFLS), the implementation of many of these recommendations has been slow and the overall situation of the average Kenyan woman has changed little (UN 1985). This systematic problem arises from institutional and structural deficiencies. One of the recommendations of the NFLS was to increase the participation of women in high-level legislative, judicial, administrative, and management positions. For example, paragraph 8 of the Nairobi Forward-Looking Strategies stresses the need for governments to use administrative and other measures to increase the number of women in senior management positions at the national and local levels through recruitments, nominations, and promotions. In accordance with this recommendation, the Kenyan government has appointed a few women to hold high-profile positions in the diplomatic service, in the state-owned parastatals (including the public universities), in the judiciary, and in the civil service. In fact, the judiciary is one of the sectors where significant improvements have been made with respect to appointments and promotion of women to senior positions such as high court judges and chief magistrates. The posts of attorney general and chief justice have never been held by a woman in Kenya.

2. And as Stamp (n.d.: 41) has acknowledged, the Kenyan government has encouraged self-help activities through the ideology of *harambee*, which has been widely used to augment state development efforts in the provision of social services, particularly in the rural areas.

# 7
# Women and Garden Produce of Kinshasa: The Difficult Quest for Autonomy

*Gertrude Mianda*

This chapter focuses on women and the organization of garden production in Kinshasa, Zaire. It analyzes how women organize their work in order to have access to resources and to attain a certain degree of autonomy. Many studies on women in the Third World see women's lack of control and limited access to resources as factors limiting their contribution to the economic development of their countries. This marginalization of women in development is explained on the basis of unequal gender relations. These studies put the emphasis on the sexual division of labor constraining women to spend a greater part of their time on domestic activities (Beneria and Sen 1981: 282–93). The sexual division of labor is, in effect, the basis for the social construction of sexual differentiation (Rubin 1975: 159–210) and thus of the gender relations.

When speaking of women of Zaire, MacGaffey highlights the impact of gender on women's access to resources and the limited control they exercise over them (MacGaffey 1987, 1991). On one hand, women merchants of Kinshasa struggle to insure the survival of the family while their husbands try to control the revenues generated from their activities (MacGaffey 1991: 145–51). On the other hand, the women entrepreneurs of Kinshasa have succeeded in avoiding both control by males and by institutional constraints. They have independently undertaken their commercial activities (MacGaffey 1987: 165–83). Within this perspective, we analyze the organization of garden produce in Kinshasa and its impact on gender relations and on the women gardeners.

Gender relations are primarily power relations (Scott 1988: 141). In this sense, our analysis focuses on power relations in the organization of production between women gardeners, their husbands, and all males involved in production. In order to do so, we must define the concept of power. Following Foucault, we define power as a relationship and not solely as an attribute of the actors (Foucault 1975: 31–32). Power is related to a situation. It is always changing and unstable. According to Foucault, one must decode within the sphere of power a network of relationships that remains always tense, always active, and must be perceived as an ongoing struggle (ibid: 32–33). This concept of power suggests considering power in technical terms, that is, the manner in which it manifests itself (Foucault 1976: 112–13; Finas 1977: 4–5). Thus, the exercise of power is defined as a mode of action of one group over another (Dreyfus and Rabinow 1984: 308–13, 318–19). This mode of action is a strategy and/or tactic. The latter is made up of all the means used to mobilize the available resources in the society in order to gain advantage over the other group (Foucault 1980: 256). In our case, we define strategy and tactic as all the elements that women gardeners use, in the sociocultural, economic, and political context of Zaire, to gain advantage over their husbands and the males involved in the garden produce. We should point out that while a strategy can succeed in overthrowing the relations of power, a tactic, on the other hand, is never successful in doing so. Furthermore, a tactic, as opposed to a strategy, grasps a fleeting opportunity. It is the recourse of the weak, a ruse (de Certeau 1990: 59–63). Therefore, we can say that a tactic, in power relations, hinders the constraints of the strategy.

The conception of power that we adopt in this chapter is not supported unanimously. Hartsock, for example, refutes it because it implies passivity and resistance, not transformation (Hartsock 1990: 167–70). However, we hold that the analysis of the mechanisms of power in a concrete situation, such as the case of garden production, will allow us both to grasp the nuances with which the different social groups exercise power and to account for the dynamics of the social construction of gender. It is important to understand how "gender hierarchies are constructed, legitimated, challenged, and maintained" (Scott 1988a: 11) in specific contexts. This objective underscores our analysis of women and garden produce of Kinshasa. First, we provide a brief historical overview of the garden production. Second, we discuss the situation of women in Zaire that enables us to understand how the strategies and tactics of female gardeners shape production.

## A HISTORICAL OVERVIEW

Officially, following land distribution by the colonial administration, garden production was set up in Kinshasa in 1954. In the marshy area of the Ndjili River, land was distributed among women and the unemployed as a policy to create a horticultural peasantry. Years before that, E. Capelle, the colonial administrator, had suggested the creation of a greenbelt around the city of Kinshasa to keep women busy, thus putting an end to the leisure they experienced when they migrated to the city (Capelle 1947: 51–52). The colonial administration gave land, divided into three categories of domains, registered, and native lands, to women in accordance with the land ownership law established at the time (Paulus 1959: 15–19). The first category of land was directly under the colonial authority; the other two were administered according to the common law. Access to land was determined by custom. Therefore, land is owned collectively by lineage and ownership is inalienable.

After independence, the colonial project of settling a horticultural peasantry in the marshlands of the Ndjili River was resuscitated in the hope of promoting garden production. This production plays an important role in the provision of fruits and vegetables to the capital, especially in view of the population explosion facing the city of Kinshasa. In fact, population increased from 400,000 inhabitants in 1969 to two million in 1980 and was estimated at 3.2 million in 1990 (de Maximy 1984: 123; Braeckman 1990: 6). In spite of its economic importance and the presence of diversified industries, the city of Kinshasa cannot meet the employment needs of its ever growing population. The economic crisis has been felt in a dramatic fashion since the end of the 1970s. In order to survive, the population has increasingly turned to the informal economy (Houyoux 1986: 174–75). This sector covers even the smallest commercial enterprises. In these circumstances, one can understand the importance of garden production, which is promoted by the Department of Agriculture and Rural Development along with the help of French cooperation. Thus, the scope of the initial project of the colonial era is widened to encompass new territories and help vegetable producers to set up cooperatives. In the meantime, land ownership is undergoing major changes. In 1966, the bakajika law suppressed colonial land ownership. The law, adopted in 1973 and revised in 1980, makes all land and the substratum of Zaire the property of the state. Henceforth, individuals can only have the right to use land through the acquisition of the land title (Lupungu 1982: 103–5). Normally, in light of this law, all the kinship rules that determine access to land become invalid. However, in reality, these rules coexist with the law of 1973 that was modified in 1980. As a result, those who wish to undertake garden production in Kinshasa must first negotiate with the chiefs and then acquire the title to the land from the civil authorities. In the course of the last twenty years, garden production has enjoyed considerable growth, utilizing an increasingly available male labor force, even as it remains, fundamentally, an area of employment supervised by the female sector. In order to maintain this production, women must overcome sociocultural, economic, political, and legal constraints that are found and justified, in part, in women's representation grounded in the society of Zaire. These constraints are more acute in an urban area such as Kinshasa that is governed by a patrilineal urban culture dominated by male ideology (Mianda 1996).

## WOMEN IN ZAIRE

We attempt to limit our examination of the image of women in the society of Zaire, especially in the city Kinshasa, by focusing on women's access to resources. In order to accomplish this task, it is important to refer to the two kinship systems found in Zaire, as well as to the colonial influence on gender relations.

Women's access to resources does not generally differ in the two kinship systems. During the pre–colonial period, land, the principal means of production, was considered a collective property. Access to land was determined by customary rules. The same held true, under colonial rule, for native lands. Through marriage, women became members of their husband's lineage. They were placed under the authority of their elders and husbands. Women performed their agricultural work within the framework of the lineage and its sexual division of labor that allocated this work exclusively to women. Women produced within the boundaries of lineage, but had the right to use land regardless of the type of kinship system. They could also use the fruits of their agricultural production. From this point of view, they had relative economic autonomy. In respect to personal belongings, the matrilineal system, as opposed to a more restrictive patrilineal system, allowed women to decide how they would dispose of their personal possessions. However, under both systems, women were generally not allowed to inherit and were subordinated to their husband's authority. Colonization fundamentally changed this structure. It manipulated the inequality between men and women at the expense of the latter. It also imposed a patrilineal system where none had previously existed (Boserup 1983: 65–66; Comhaire-Sylvain 1950: 123).

We must note that under colonial rule, civilization was understood as the place of writing and French as the official language opposing oral and various local languages which were perceived as the place of noncivilization. Colonization established cities such as Kinshasa as privileged spaces where modernization, and therefore civilization, took place creating a new scale of social differentiation. Migration to the city meant upward social mobility for all. However, for women under colonial rule, it meant the beginning of economic dependence and institutionalized subordination.

Women were not, for the most part, allowed to migrate to the city except as dependents of males. In general, they arrived in the cities to join their husbands who had moved there to work. Women were even deprived of an identity card. The information related to women was written in the identity booklet of the household head, a man (Comhaire-Sylvain 1968: 28–29). Thus, the colonial administration instituted a radical distinction between the sexes. It did not legally recognize women's, and especially wives', existence except through the intermediary of males or husbands. The identity card, written document, and French language were instruments that legalized and consolidated male power in the colonial society. In effect, colonialism, employing these means, gave a new face to gender relations.

Colonial administration required by law that women obtain written permission from their husbands to work in the public service. In the meantime, the educational system, largely dispensed by missionaries, trained girls in local languages and in domestic chores, with a shorter curriculum than the boys. The latter pursued more advanced secondary training in the French language (Yates 1982: 127–28). From the start, women's chances of getting jobs in the modern sector of the economy were compromised. The educational system aimed to produce good housewives corresponding to the colonial vision of women. "Our policy in Africa intends to liberate native women from their hard labor to enable her, like women in the civilized countries, to dedicate her time and strength to the traditional role of wife and mother" (Bulletin agricole du Congo Belge 1954: 1129). The exclusion of women from wage labor, especially in the field of agriculture, seems to be justified by this policy. As a result, men were paid to produce the mandatory crops that were required of all healthy males, when in reality, the traditional sexual division of labor dictated that such work fall on the women (Coquery-Vidrovitch 1985: 150).

Thus, in the name of civilization, colonization instituted a socioeconomic, legal, and political framework that granted more privileges to men than to women. It promoted, in colonial society, the image of housewives and women over whom men must take charge. In the eyes of the colonial administration, women could legally have access to economic resources and the right to administer them only through the intermediary of men and husbands. The latter were portrayed as providers of the family, subjects with rights to whom the wives must legally submit. In a city such as Kinshasa, these institutional constraints, combined with those of the kinship systems, created, in reality, a confining space for women. The very fact that the husband is seen as the provider of the family obliges him, in an urban environment, to take care of his wife and family. Therefore, the brunt of the household work falls on the wives. Thus, in Kinshasa, a working wife underscores the failure of the husband as a provider. This is why men refuse to allow their wives to work outside the household (Mianda 1996). In this context, the ever growing number of women in the marketplace is an indication of the extent to which the economic crisis undermines the financial credibility of men.

In Kinshasa, men tend to control and to manage the affairs of their spouses. Furthermore, the present legal framework in Zaire not only replicates the same representation of women stemming from the colonial period but serves to consolidate the domination of men over women. As well, the Family Code of 1988 limits, as under colonialism, women's access to resources (Code de la famille en République du Zaire 1988). As outlined in article 488, it further subordinates women to their husbands when it comes to all legal requirements that they must fulfill personally. Wives, according to article 450, can neither testify in civil matters nor acquire or sell property without the permission of their husbands. As well, the right to oversee their personal possessions is limited in accordance to article 497, paragraph 2 of the code. Furthermore, article 444 of the code stipulates that the husband is the head of the household and that it is his duty to protect his wife, who must obey him. The sociocultural, economic, and political ambience of Zaire, just as that of Kinshasa, also appears to be constraining for women. However, in the example of garden produce, women employ various ways to achieve relative autonomy, as illustrated in our analysis of the organization of garden production.

## WOMEN AND THE QUEST FOR AUTONOMY

Women undertake garden production to acquire economic independence vis-à-vis their husbands, as well as, to meet the ever growing financial needs of their families. Since society still associates women with the household and subordinates them to male authority, women cannot take part in garden production without the prior consent of their husbands. Furthermore, agricultural activity in an urban environment is considered to have low status. In reality, garden production becomes a game of power relations between wives and husbands. Similarly, the management of this production is a play of power relations between women producers and their husbands. The actual production process involves moments where women gardeners develop strategies or tactics in order to gain advantage over their husbands for initiating the production and exercising control over it. First, we examine strategies or tactics that pertain to production. Later, we discuss those used in the management of the production.

In order to reverse the power relationship vis-à-vis their husbands and undertake garden production, women have used a strategy that rests on the sexual division of labor. This strategy sets in motion the social duties that the society of Zaire gives to women related to child care and agricultural production. It also makes use of the moral obligation of solidarity towards the family of origin (Mianda 1996). In a precarious financial situation, men are no longer capable of fulfilling, by themselves, their role as providers. Women take advantage of this situation, using the notion of a shared obligation toward their children, to get the approval of their husbands to start garden production. Women reclaim this production by stressing the agricultural nature of the work. In reality, according to the traditional sexual division of labor, agricultural work is a feminine activity. Women therefore manipulate the sexual division of labor, despite its constraints, for their own benefit. Women also use the moral obligation of solidarity that they feel toward their family of origin. Indeed, due to the socialization of girls that leads them to be closer to their families, women, more than men, have solidarity toward their family of origin.

Having succeeded in initiating production, women gardeners cannot claim total autonomy without establishing control over it. However, before dealing with the strategies or tactics employed by women gardeners to manage production, it is essential to specify what it entails: the management of the work in the garden; control over marketing; and control over revenue derived from production.

The management of activities relates to the work of male and female workers. Here, the technical sexual division of labor plays a major role. This division of labor was introduced by national policymakers and those who cooperated in its formation. They trained men to use phytosanitary products, thereby enabling men to manipulate technology better than women. Women gardeners, however, despite their lack of technological expertise, still succeed in supervising certain activities involved in garden production by relying on their wide experience in and knowledge of agriculture production. In reality, management of the work in garden production does not necessarily give rise to power relationships between women gardeners and their husbands because it emphasizes the relationship between the landowners and the workers. However, it offers us an opportunity to understand the process of the social construction of gender. Whenever women gardeners have a more active role than their husbands in the management of production, even though men are still involved in the production process, women are then symbolically perceived as men. Correspondingly, their husbands, because they are not as active or do not sufficiently take charge over the agricultural activities, lose, in the eyes of workers, their social credibility as men (Mianda 1996). From the perspective of their social surroundings, women gardeners who supervise agricultural activities inherit a masculine nature. Thus, women who undertake an activity that is culturally reserved for men are symbolically represented as men.

Similarly, when laborers assume tasks that are culturally assigned to women in garden production, they appear as women. In reality, male workers in garden production undertake all activities related to production, even the tasks that the traditional sexual division of labor defines as female. For example, male workers carry loads on their heads in basins or even bags filled with household trash that serves as fertilizer for production. However, men who work independently delivering household trash refuse to carry such loads on their heads, using wheelbarrows instead. In the culture of Zaire, men do not generally carry loads on their heads, although this is seen more so in urban environments, particularly in a city such as Kinshasa. We can state, through these examples, that economic position intervenes in gender differentiation and that the attributes associated with one sex constitute, in themselves, a social construction. Women, like men, can come to symbolically bear the attributes of one sex or the other depending on the type of work they undertake in their economic position. Women gardeners, for example, in their position as landowners, manage the work of production, control the labor of men who are employed by them, and subsequently are perceived as men. Male laborers who undertake tasks that are culturally defined as feminine are symbolically perceived as women. Because of this, independent male workers refuse to execute such tasks. The management of garden production activities, thus does not give rise to the development of specific strategies or tactics on the part of women. The opposite is true in the area of marketing.

Before presenting the strategies, we must stress that the management of marketing is related to decisions made around establishing market prices. It equally involves the sale of vegetables as well as the products of husbandry. Women gardeners' strategies to control marketing in an autonomous manner are grounded principally in the sexual division of labor. On the basis of the sexual division of labor, men do not sell green vegetables such as lettuce, carrots, cucumbers, leafy vegetables, and so forth, in the marketplace. Rather, men are directly involved in their production, claiming that women cannot take care of such vegetables because their preservation is a fairly delicate process. In reality, the production of this type of vegetable is related to higher revenue than to the equivalent quantity of local vegetables. However, women gardeners rely on the sexual division of labor, which establishes the marketing of vegetables as an entirely female activity, in order to control the whole process of production from price setting, to price negotiation, to the selling of the products in the marketplace. Women, in turn, claim that men do not know how to negotiate the price of vegetables. Therefore, in this way, they use the sexual division of labor to gain the upper hand over their husbands.

On the other hand, some female gardeners prefer to sell their vegetables directly from their garden. When their husbands try to grasp this opportunity in order to sell the vegetables, women gardeners then choose the option of selling in the marketplace. By adopting this course of action, women keep their husbands at a distance from the sale of vegetables without necessarily changing the power relationship. In this sense, women enact their tactics. We must emphasize that a tactic takes advantage of a fleeting opportunity, as opposed to a strategy, which induces and constrains. Taking the definition given by de Certeau into account, tactic simply limits and prevents (de Certeau 1990: 60–63). Nevertheless, women gardeners, in this way, manage to control the marketing of their produce by directly negotiating the sale price in the marketplace. Women gardeners' tactics thus amount, in the long term, to a strategy of regaining control over marketing.

Women adopt strategies to manage the revenue gained from garden production because in the urban environment of Kinshasa the male is responsible for managing the goods of the couple. Article 490 of the Family Code of 1988 clearly underscores this responsibility. Strategies are subsequently put in motion, particularly by women gardeners who are co-owners or do not own land. In the case of women gardeners who are landowners, such women should theoretically manage their revenue in an autonomous fashion as prescribed by established practices of their matrilineal kinship system. However, since these women live in Kinshasa, they associate their husbands with their commercial undertakings as a means of avoiding social pressure. One must also take into account that their husbands find advantages in adopting the Kinoise culture, which follows the rules of patrilineal descent. Under these circumstances, the management of revenue, for women gardeners who are also landowners, becomes a game of power relationships and necessitates using strategies.

As in the case of production, women gardeners' strategies for controlling revenue rely on their obligations as mothers toward their children (Mianda 1996). Women gardeners who are not landowners demand their share of the revenue derived from production because they are the ones who are primarily responsible for the care of the children. However, when they do not succeed in gaining the upper hand over their husbands, they resort to a womanly ruse. Women often retain part of the money from their sales without the knowledge or consent of their husbands. While still in the marketplace, they entrust this money to a person who manages a kind of floating banking system called *the card system* in Kinshasa. Other women prefer to trust women friends or their children with this money. Still others quite simply deposit the cash in a secret place, alluding to the metaphor of the kitchen pot. The general belief is that men do not touch their wives' pots and pans to avoid being the victims of sorcery.

This metaphor of the kitchen pot symbolically illustrates the differences between the two sexes. It refers to something that belongs to the women's realm and is inaccessible to men. The reference to sorcery, which can curse males, links this metaphor to the menstruation cycle. In some ethnic groups of Zaire, custom has it that the menstruating wife keeps her distance from her husband, unless she is preparing meals for him, in order to avoid subjecting him to sorcery (Mbuyi and Smal 1973: 43–44; Doutreloux 1967: 62). Alluding to the metaphor of the kitchen pot in order to withhold part of their revenue from their husbands, women gardeners turn to their advantage a taboo that originally served to marginalize them. The menstruation cycle is seen to be a time of impurity, when women are required to be kept apart from society and when the perceived negative powers of sorcery are attributed to women. Therefore, the metaphor of the kitchen, in our view, is an expression of the social construction of inequality between the sexes. The manner in which women gardeners co-op this metaphor to their benefit provides evidence that they have knowledge of their sociocultural environment and are aware of sexual inequalities.

On the other hand, by putting aside a part of the revenues derived from production in order to circumvent the control exercised by their husbands, women gardeners are motivated by a tactic. They do not invert power relations vis-à-vis their husbands. Nevertheless, they widen their sphere of influence and achieve a certain degree of autonomy. Tactics, according to de Certeau, are the recourse of the weak. They are a ruse (de Certeau 1990: 60–63). Women gardeners define withholding part of the revenue from the greed of their husbands as a womanly ruse. This ruse is a practice that is learned, since facing multiple obstacles leads women, on the basis of their experience, to acquire a practical sense and to subsequently put aside some money. In these circumstances, womanly ruse can be understood as a strategy, as defined by Bourdieu, which results from a practical sense acquired from childhood by participating in social activities (Bourdieu 1987: 79–90). Behind the womanly ruse then, derived from the practical sense, is a conscious and rational calculation.

For the majority of women gardeners, the revenue derived from production constitutes the principal source of family income. By succeeding to manage this revenue independently, women gardeners become the providers of the family, a role that the society of Zaire, particularly in urban Kinshasa, does not recognize for women. In reality, women gardeners are in charge of their families. They even see to it that the needs of their husbands are met by giving them pocket money. When women must use the services of a third party to purchase food or other necessities for the family, they pass on their husbands as the ones who provide the money. In this way, women gardeners deflect the social pressure of their environment and appear to keep intact their husbands' status as providers. We interpret this gesture as women gardeners' tactic vis-à-vis a society that attributes the role of provider solely to men. In some ways, women gardeners thus participate in the consolidation of the traditional rules that govern the exercise of power and that favor men in this society. However, in the domestic sphere, women manage to change these rules. They also modify the traditional image of women as nonproviders through the exercise of power, even if it is not acknowledged within the hegemonic framework that finds its expression in law, the kinship system, and the social structure in general (Mianda 1996). Ferchiou defines the power exercised by women as a counterpower precisely because it does not derive from the established social order (Ferchiou 1989: 90). However, as Crozier and Friedberg have pointed out, power is inseparable from negotiation (Crozier and Friedberg 1981: 62).

## CONCLUSION

It appears that women gardeners manipulate the sexual division of labor in order to have a hold over their husbands and to overcome the socio-cultural, economic, political, and legal barriers in society. The manner in which women manipulate the obligations linked to the sexual division of labor illustrates their ability to decode the constraints deriving from gender. It also tells us how women gardeners have mastered the knowledge of their sociocultural environment. This knowledge allows them to subtly use available means in order to invert the power relationships vis-à-vis their husbands, and to change, at the level of production and of the household, the traditional rules that govern the exercise of power in the society of Zaire at large as well as in the urban environment of Kinshasa. As a result, women gardeners gain autonomy in the organization of their work by transgressing barriers that repeatedly arise in Kinshasa and in the society of Zaire. They thus modify, both at the level of garden production and at all levels of power related to this production, the traditional image of women.

## NOTE

Translated from French into English by the editors.

# 8
# Negotiating Ideal Womanhood in Rural Philippine Households: Work and Survival
## *Tuula Heinonen*

## INTRODUCTION

This chapter focuses on gender relations and women's work in rural Philippines. In the first section I provide a general background for understanding the factors that contribute to the invisibility of women's work. The second section aims to question the narrowly defined ideological basis of women's position in the division of labor. It is shown that women's work is multidimensional and is indispensable to the survival of the household. The final portion of the chapter draws from my field work and provides concrete examples that challenge the established ideal of womanhood in the Philippines.

## THE PHILIPPINE CONTEXT

Precolonial Philippines was characterized by independent settlements organized mainly on the basis of kinship and stratified according to traditional laws (Mananzan 1987: 7) and a gender division of labor (Infante 1975). Hispanic colonization, beginning in 1565, was characterized by aggression, domination, and subjugation of tribal groups (Zaide 1957: 142). Spanning three centuries, the introduction of Hispanic cultural and religious ideology deeply affected class relations and the structure of landholding. It was successful in delineating female and male expectations of behavior in many areas of personal and public life. The introduction of religious ideology and legislation pertaining to the responsibilities of men and women served to transform the social position of women in relation to men, thereby curbing women's individual freedom (Mananzan 1987: 27) and leading to a concept of ideal womanhood (Rojas-Aleta, Silva, and Eleazar 1977). When the United States won the war of conquest over the Philippines from Spain in 1898, Filipinos found themselves a colony again, this time of the United States. Although the American colonial period lasted only until 1942 (Goodno 1991: 34), its economic policies shaped the export agricultural market and private interests. The Americans institutionalized the status of the Philippines as a producer of raw materials: sugar, tobacco, abaca (Manila hemp), and coconut products (*Solidaridad* 1988: 15). After independence, U.S. relations with the Philippines were decided upon largely favoring American terms of trade in exchange for a set amount of U.S. financial aid (Goodno 1991: 41–42). Generally, the structures and systems of the government administration changed little. Trickle-down economic theory guided social policy. During the American period, existing structures of class and gender were left intact.

Rural people were affected by serious problems in terms of access to land, while many urban dwellers faced the hazards of life in slum conditions. Despite the restrictions on women's freedom of movement and limited educational and employment opportunities, some Filipinas in rural areas engaged in private business that enabled them to work from home, such as in the operation of farms and in small-scale commercial enterprises (Alzona cited in Torres 1989: 9). In fact, rural women who lived in areas less influenced by Spanish standards of behavior enjoyed more personal independence than their urban counterparts (Szanton 1982: 132). But their relative independence in comparison with wealthier, urban women did not bring an easier life, since poor, rural Filipinas could not afford to remain economically inactive (Eviota 1992: 38).

The gap between poor and wealthy women widened. Well-to-do and middle-class women began to enter public life and the professions. Upper-class women, discouraged from economic activities and valued for effectively managing their households and caring for their families, were able to hire help to relieve them of household drudgery.

Today, Filipino women in urban and rural areas are generally employed in different types of work. In the cities, their work is in industries, retail sales and services, and the professions. In rural areas, where employment opportunities for women are scarce, they are engaged mainly in agricultural work and small-scale, informal sector activities such as vending, hawking, hairdressing, laundering, and as domestic helpers (Alonzo 1991: 42).

The male's role as breadwinner and the female's role as homemaker were considered traditional and customary. If a healthy, married man failed to perform what was considered his family obligation, he faced criticism from relatives (especially in-laws) and peers. Such failure was found to be a source of shame for men because it was felt that women should not need to work outside the home. A married woman who worked outside the home might become proud and dominant over her spouse, an undesirable outcome (Heinonen 1994). It was inappropriate and unusual for a woman to take on the role of primary income earner unless she had no male partner.

Although cultural ideals define men's work as outside the home (i.e., in wage work and farming) and women's work as within the home (taking care of others and performing domestic chores), the survival needs of family members necessitate some shifts in actual practice (Illo and Polo 1990: 108–10; King and Evenson 1983: 54).

As in many parts of the world, an attitude persists that the male should be dominant and the female subordinate, particularly in rural areas of the Philippines (Women Studies and Resource Center 1988: 40). Men are considered household heads and breadwinners. A man's identity is integral to his capacity to support his family adequately. If his wife takes on a job, the potential for marital conflict rises (*Solidaridad* 1988: 33).

Linked to women's status are the kinds of tasks they are expected to perform in, for example, subsistence agricultural work, child care, and wage labor.[1] Research from the Bicol region showed that women were proud to help in supporting their families and the sacrifices they made in doing so added to their feelings of self-worth (Illo and Polo 1990: 111). Further, in rural households, where children are especially regarded as an investment (Evenson, Popkin, and King 1980), the work of women as child bearers and nurturers adds value to being a housewife.

Women's child care responsibilities focus their attention in the home for a large part of their adult lives. When women frequently have four or five children, child care involves a great investment of time and energy on their part. Unless they have access to child care help, they are not able to take on employment that conflicts with children's needs (Israel-Sobritchea 1990: 38).

Labor statistics tend to underestimate the income-generating work done by women (e.g., informal sector activity) and do not assign value to the work done in the household. The important economic contribution of homemakers in labor and earnings tends to be underestimated in government statistics.

In the following sections I will discuss the reality of women's work in rural Philippines.

## IDEOLOGY AND REALITY OF WOMEN'S WORK

A study of women's work concluded that the range of activities accomplished by women appeared to be more varied and more complex in comparison to men's, entailing longer work periods for women as well (Illo and Veneracion 1988). A study of the daily time allocation of mothers and fathers in rural Laguna households with an average of four children showed that although mothers spent less time than fathers in farming and other labor market activities, mothers spent more time than fathers in household work, resulting in longer work days for mothers (King and Evenson 1983: 39). In addition, mothers spent less time in recreational activities than fathers.[2] The term "housewife" used as an occupational category is misleading in that it gives little information about the extent and variety of women's work, paid or unpaid. Philippine research indicates that the activities of a housewife include all of the work done "as part of a wife's duty to help the spouse support the family" (Illo and Polo 1990: vii). In the case of poor women, paid work is seen as an extension of their traditional housewife roles.

In the Philippines, agriculture is generally dominated by males (70 percent of agricultural workers are males); however, it is a major employer of rural women, involving 40 percent of employed females in rural areas (National Commission on the Role of Filipino Women 1985: 56). There were more than 1.8 million unpaid female family workers engaged in agriculture in 1982, representing the largest category of employment performed by unpaid female labor. The women were defined as "members of the family who assist another member in the operation of the family farm or business enterprise and do not receive any wage or salary for their work" (National Commission on the Role of Filipino Women 1985: 34). Most of these women were employed in rice and corn farming. Other types of agricultural activities in which women were engaged in paid or unpaid work included coconut and sugar production and livestock and poultry raising. Castillo found that women contributed about 21 percent of labor in various farm operations (National Commission on the Role of Filipino Women 1985: 56). However, due to increasing landlessness and diminishing employment opportunities, particularly in rural areas where seasonal underemployment is common, women commonly take on many different types of work (Rutten 1990: 247).

A category of work performed mainly by women is the home-based production of handicrafts or garments (Rutten 1990; Pineda-Ofreneo 1990: 42). Despite the poor working conditions, home work may contribute substantially to household incomes. In an ILO-sponsored study, it was found in Sorsogon province that homeworker respondents earned more than their spouses and other income earners in the household (Vasquez 1989: 12–13). Women have also found work in entrepreneurial endeavors; a recent study shows that 62 percent of informal sector enterprises were headed by females (Alonzo 1991: 46). These women earn income from the work they do without having to significantly reduce family and household responsibilities or incur transportation and other expenses outside of the home (e.g., sari-sari store operators who buy goods in town and sell them for a profit from their homes) (National Commission on the Role of Filipino Women 1985: 41).

Women's participation in rural communities has been shown to be mainly limited to attending local barrio meetings, participating in agricultural extension programs, including those concerning health and nutrition issues (e.g., Rural Improvement Clubs), neighborhood improvement programs, fiesta committees, and religious activities (Arca-Alejar 1988: 26). In local politics, women seldom participate in leadership roles (Aleta, Silva, and Eleazar 1989: 114). Rural organizations often only represent male farmers, making it difficult for women to bring forward issues of interest to them. Women leaders in these organizations are rare (Tidalgo 1985: 402), although some may participate on behalf of their absent husbands (Ancheta 1982: 5). Women's involvement in organizations tends to be more informal and as auxiliaries of the larger, male organizations. Most women's groups focus on traditionally female areas of concern: health, nutrition, small-scale income generation, and the kinds of issues rural women identified as being important to their well-being and to that of their families (e.g., "Organizing Women Through Integrated Health") (Bulletin of the Philippine Development Assistance Program 1991: 19). Currently, rural women are being targeted by the Department of Health for training in health delivery as volunteer health workers for their communities (Osteria and Ramos-Jiminez 1988: 223).

Due to increasing impoverishment, people are forced to make use of kin and community support more than ever before. Women, as household managers, play an important role in sustaining their households by drawing upon various strategies and resources (Illo and Polo 1990).

With the money given to them by their husbands and other family members,[3] women are required to purchase food and other goods on behalf of family members. This responsibility is one that contributes to anxiety about making up shortfalls (Makil 1989: 145; Illo and Veneracion 1988: 123). If there is not enough money to sustain the family, it is women who shoulder the burden of borrowing the needed cash or food (Bautista 1987). Thus, women's work is indispensable for the survival of the household.

## CASE STUDY: THE RESEARCH SITE

The research was conducted in a municipality of Sorsogon province in Southern Luzon. Sorsogon is characterized by a mountainous terrain, a tropical climate with frequent rainfall, rich, volcanic soil, and a long coastline. The three barrios that make up the research area each consist of 100 to 200 households and contain their own small chapel, primary school, day care center, sari-sari stores, and transportation access points. The communities vary in some ways, such as location in relation to transport, water, and other amenities, as well as in local production activities. The municipality's economy is based on agriculture; mainly rice, coconut, abaca (hemp), and fruits ("Bicol Express" 1988: 4). In the research site, rice farming is the most common agricultural activity; however, declining prices for farm products, small farm size, inadequate land tenure arrangements, costly agricultural inputs (Angeles-Reyes 1987), periodic typhoons, and inadequate infrastructure facilities hamper agriculture, reducing production and employment opportunities.

Existing data suggests that Sorsogon residents enjoy less ownership of land and have more tenancy arrangements than do residents in other parts of the region (Republic of the Philippines, Regional Development Council, Region V 1986: 118). This pattern is evident from my research area survey data (Heinonen 1994), which showed that owning land was not as common as working others' land or tenanting. Those households having no land of their own to till (either leased or owned) and in which members had no nonagricultural jobs, suffered the greatest financial hardship. They relied on farm laboring (earning about 40 to 50 pesos per day)[4] or whatever work could be found to support themselves. National research concluded that the relatively low level of wages and postharvest payment of earnings to laborers made them and their families very vulnerable to slight changes in job prospects and prices of basic goods (Republic of the Philippines and UNICEF 1990: 27). The distribution of land tenure arrangements among the households included in my research shows that in 75 percent of households, the members owned no land.

In rural areas of the province, 81 percent of households fell under the poverty line[5] (Republic of the Philippines, Regional Development Council, Region V 1986: 118). The 1988 Family Income and Expenditure Survey data showed that although most of Sorsogon's families had annual incomes between 15,000 pesos to 19,999 pesos, 11 percent earned less than 10,000 pesos per year. Incomes in the region were among the lowest in the country even in 1983 (Angeles-Reyes 1987), showing that poverty is a chronic problem in the area. In the research site, the average incomes reflected this pattern.[6]

In this research, a survey involving 101 households, including 92 men and 98 women, was conducted to gather information mainly on illness incidence, but also on living conditions, household membership, work activities, income, land tenure, and assets. Households in which the female partner was below the age of 45 were chosen primarily because of my interest in researching the situations of women who were of reproductive age. Based on the data generated, fifteen men and twenty-one women were chosen for in-depth interviews about work and illness. The average age of the male participants was 37; whereas the average age of males in general was 35. In addition, key informants (community leaders, traditional healers, teachers, and health care workers) were interviewed for further information on local practices. Three focus group meetings (one in each barrio participating in the research) were held in order to present initial findings for discussion and verification. It was during these events that the ideology of womanhood and women's work in contrast to the local reality came into sharp relief.

## Research Findings

In my research findings, I noted some underlying contradictions between the ideal and actual behavior of men and women. These are discussed in relation to qualitative information gathered from the research site. The idealized roles of men as breadwinners and women as homemakers did not reflect actual behavior.

Women stated that it was alright to earn an income if work was done from inside the house. However, because few modern-sector work opportunities were available in the research site, the ideal gender division of labor was often left unchallenged. Furthermore, working from inside the home served to make the work of women invisible, hiding the true level of their economic contribution.

Research respondents claimed that women were physically weak and therefore could not do certain agricultural tasks requiring the muscle strength of men. It was felt that work in the home environment required less physical strength and thus was more suitable for women. This, they said, was why most men were found in jobs calling for heavy lifting, pushing, pulling, climbing, and cutting. However, I observed that it also went against the local expectations for women within marriage to work outside the home. As one respondent explained, "It is shameful for an employed man to have a wife who works outside of the home. It is better if she works at home. Wives must obey husbands and stay in the house."

Most farming work was in lowland rice fields, while some was in upland areas where coconut and abaca trees were plentiful. Three-quarters of all the men stated that they also worked at sideline activities (mainly other types of agricultural labor) because the agricultural cycles did not keep them employed year-round. Men performed only one main kind of work during the day (i.e., farming), which made their work days less varied than women's. It was concluded by respondents that women's work was more difficult than men's because it entailed more hours of work with many kinds of tasks to perform and think about. "With only one job you keep more of your energy. Women are overworked because they have too many tasks to do. They need to think about them all."

The types of work women performed were generally home-based, allowing them to care for their children and carry out domestic chores. From their houses, women produced and sold food, clothing, handicrafts, and other goods. They also performed services for pay such as laundering and childminding. They said that it was easy for women to obtain this type of work because men would not do it; it paid poorly and did not provide a secure source of income.

Women tended to work longer hours than men. They generally rose earlier to begin preparations for the morning meal and continued to work in the home after their partners rested following their work day. Women combined household chores, child care, tending crops, and income-earning activities into a single day. For example, cooking, child care, and handicraft-making were often carried out at the same time. The abrupt switch from one kind of work to another and the lack of time to complete all jobs properly was mentioned as being especially difficult and challenging for the women. Respondents explained that men's work, although physically demanding (and sometimes risky), was easier than women's in the sense that it entailed thinking about and doing only one main type of work each day. Women complained of stress and fatigue due to the need to manage many tasks at one time.

Washing laundry was their most arduous task, involving manual scrubbing, beating, wringing, hanging, and carrying of wet clothing. In most cases, community faucets and rivers were the places where children were bathed and laundry was washed. Women invariably carried out this work (except directly after giving birth) by taking the children and clothing to the water. Women did not usually handle ploughs or work animals, but instead raised pigs, chickens, ducks, or goats. They could do this work while tending to children or performing other tasks at home. Having animals gave people a hedge against lean times because they could be sold quickly to acquire cash for emergencies. Raising poultry was relatively common, whereas having one or more pigs indicated a measure of economic security. Other prized assets were those enabling the owner to earn some income. For example, a Betamax set, although requiring a large initial investment, was used to show video films for which admission was charged. Sewing machines enabled their owners to sew clothing for sale, whereas having a refrigerator provided opportunities to produce and sell ice candy. These activities were generally the domain of entrepreneurial women.

Despite the view that agriculture was a male occupation, I noted that women often transplanted, weeded, and harvested in the fields alongside men. They were also engaged in subsistence agriculture, laundering, and other work requiring considerable physical strength and endurance. Further, men, not women, were employed in work not necessarily requiring physical strength, but requiring skills in the operation of machinery and tools. Several women said that men had the ability to do such work (i.e., driving, equipment maintenance and repair, cutting wood, building houses) but that women did not.

In my research, all respondent women were in their reproductive years, which did not enable a study of how life cycle affected the women's employment. However, the case study data suggests that younger women with small children were least able to take on additional employment because they were fully occupied with household chores and child care, while women with older children (particularly girls) were able to assign household chores to them and take on other activities. I was told, "It is easier if there are older girls in the household."

In most areas of the Philippines, kin play an enormous role in the lives of individuals and families. Married Filipinas nurture and maintain these relationships, especially with their own relatives (Sevilla 1989: 39). Not only are the typically bilateral relationships important, but so too are networks of godparents and foster families (Yu and Liu 1980: 240). All of these relationships may be considered potential sources of economic or emotional support. Women revealed that they relied on neighbors, kin, or a local shop to help out when they ran short of food or when they required emergency funds. Their partners did not usually borrow or ask for credit unless the amount was large and then often at the request of their wives. "Men are ashamed to ask for credit or help," said several women.

My research found that making ends meet was a difficulty that women faced firsthand because they purchased what family members needed from the money given to them. "It is harder for women than men because women feel the effects of poverty and hardship in the house more directly. They suffer if there is no food. Men can still carry on." Although it was the obligation of men to earn the primary income for the family, this income was often inadequate to provide for all the members' food, clothing, education, and health care needs. Even when men had secondary employment, the women found that it was not enough to sustain the household; prices of many needed items had risen while wages had not kept pace. "Before women only stayed home. Now it's different. We must help each other," stated a male respondent. Household managing and budgeting often forced women to seek ways to make ends meet.

Most women respondents raised garden vegetables, poultry, and pigs that were sold or consumed in the household. A large majority (ninety-five out of ninety-eight women) stated that they worked "at home" (sa balay). Sixty percent (59) of the women survey respondents claimed that they were engaged in income-generating activities as sidelines. Of the fifty-nine women earning some income, thirty-three were involved in farm work, sometimes in combination with other types of work. The remainder were engaged in sales, service, handicraft, and the raising of livestock. Thirty-nine women stated that they were fully engaged in domestic work in the home for which they were not paid. The income they earned was necessary to supplement otherwise inadequate household incomes.

In barangay group discussions, it was concluded that it was acceptable for women to help their husbands provide for the family by earning income if it was necessary. "Because of poverty, men let their wives work outside of the home. Men are ashamed and pity their wives, though." Another male respondent added, "It's good that our wives have some income because they can help us provide for the family." Gender-based roles were thus diffused by the poverty of respondents. However, men were still seen as the principal earners while women assisted them in fulfilling male household obligations. Without the women's help, the survival of household members was threatened.

The traditional boundaries of the gender division of labor were blurred due to household survival needs. However, strategies aimed at increasing household incomes were affected by problems in the local economy, which were in turn affected by broader economic factors. For example, the rising prices of food and medicine were sources of concern.

## CONCLUSION

The ideal of womanhood defines gender and makes women's work invisible. This study shows the multidimensional nature of rural women's work and its importance for the survival of the household.

Women who were effectively supplemental wage earners engaged in activities added to their household chores. Traditional expectations and attitudes about women's role (homemakers dependent on breadwinner-partners) had been expanded and transformed by the exigencies of family survival. Women referred to the fact that, by earning money informally, "we help our husbands provide for our families." Women and men referred to the importance for men in maintaining a dominant position in marital relationships and the need to acknowledge men's role as primary breadwinners for maintaining harmony in the household.

## NOTES

1. Married women who earn their own income may have more decision-making authority in the allocation of funds and other resources in the family. They may be better off in terms of health and nutrition, as are their children (Popkin 1983). The survival of household members is thus enhanced when women acquire and use their own money.

2. It has also been suggested that women's work is valued less than men's which results in women carrying heavier workloads (Illo and Veneracion 1988: 124). At the same time, women's work is classified as easy; men's work as difficult (ibid.).

3. The contribution of children's labor and earned income to rural Philippine households has been shown to be important (King and Evenson 1983: 38). Research findings, conducted in households with an average of four children, concluded that children were involved in a variety of tasks, including crop cultivation, livestock raising, and fishing. Girls take on a heavier share of work than boys, particularly in household chores and child care (Folbre 1984: 312–16).

Migration patterns in the Philippines, reflecting a female-dominated form, show that single women (mainly aged 15 to 24 years) leave their parental homes in rural areas for factory or service work in urban areas. Daughters rather than sons are relied upon to help support their parents, brothers, and sisters because they "are likely to be trusty remitters" (Stark 1991: 41). Although the money earned and remitted by migrants to their families averaged a low 231 pesos, it made an important contribution to the overall incomes of poor households (Lauby and Stark 1987: 23).

4. In 1991, $1 U.S. = 24 pesos.

5. The incidence of poverty is based on a poverty line used by the National Statistics Office in the 1988 Family Income and Expenditures Survey. It is a calculation estimating the cost of meeting 100 percent of the minimum annual nutritional requirements and other basic needs of a family of six (Nuqui 1991: 12).

6. In January 1991, the average household income was 664 pesos (range 0–2,300). Women's average income was 143 pesos (range 0–1,300). The men's average income was 521 pesos (range 0–2,200). In thirty-three households, the members were receiving financial or in-kind contributions from kin to enhance household income (Heinonen 1994).

# 9

# Moral Regulation and Microlevel Politics: Implications for Women's Work and Struggles

## Suzan M. Ilcan

This chapter attempts to redirect our understanding of moral relations from the boundaries of religious or legal doctrine to the field of discourse and microlevel politics. Too often external criteria, such as religious codes or state laws, are used to determine and evaluate what is appropriate or inappropriate social behavior. Placing such a heavy emphasis on these centralized positions of power, however, ignores the more subtle and multiple forms of power relations that are involved in guiding and changing people's conduct and activity.[1] In this chapter, I emphasize the role of moral discourse as a technique of power in shaping social and economic relations and in directing the action of people by circumscribing arenas of obedience and duty. Specifically, my research in rural Turkey highlights how everyday moral discourses and practices incite, undermine, and authorize women's and men's relations, as well as mediate economic transformation. In the spheres of social class, work, and gender relations, moral discourses are shown as both instruments and effects of power, as well as points of resistance.[2] In this way, the first section of this chapter conceptualizes morality within a genealogical frame of reference, emphasizing the connections and relations between people by locating the power struggles of these relations. The second section highlights how moral discourses at both the national and local level negotiate economic development and influence gender and work dynamics. In the context of the northwestern region of Turkey, I analyze how the availability and moral value of migrant (male) wage labor altered landlord-peasant relations and introduced a series of new developments and challenges in women's work responsibilities. This section also elaborates on contemporary relations in the community, including the process of the feminization of subsistence agriculture, the regulation of women's work and activities through a masculinist moral discourse, and the everyday forms of resistance by women.

In the Middle East, conceptions of morality customarily hold that Qur'anic moral/legal codes are directly correlated with everyday "reality" (Bauer 1985; Rassam 1980; Youssef 1976; Sedghi 1976). Likewise, and within the Turkish context, some scholars deduce certain forms of social behavior, such as polygamy and inheritance, gender, family, or property relations, from the Qur'an (e.g., Petek-Salom and Hukum 1986: 93–94; Vergin 1985: 572–73; Coşar 1978: 129). However, while Qur'anic law and rhetoric are powerful tools for understanding certain social and political environments, as a master narrative they cannot always provide a sufficient account of patterns of social behavior, especially variable patterns of gender relations. As Najmabadi (1991: 63–64) states, "There is a tendency toward an essentialist conception of Islam, reducing Islam to a given set of doctrines, with a given set of edicts on women, and attributing the current practices and ideology of Islamic movements to the implementation of these doctrines." In other words, religious or legal perspectives defer to the authority of the text or adopt authoritarian dogma as explanations of social relations. Such totalizing strategies are unable to fully explain or recognize the complexity, contradictions, and transformations of gender relations. It is therefore important to document other less formal techniques that influence and shape gender and work dynamics.

In moving away from positing official Islam as the basis for understanding moral action and belief (cf. Marcus 1992: 64), it is essential to highlight a more genealogical approach to morality. Differing from legalistic approaches, a genealogical[3] approach to morality involves researching or tracing the connections and relations between people *by locating the power struggles of these relations* (see also Abu-Lughod 1990; Foucault 1983; Fraser 1989). This methodological approach acknowledges that there is a difference between people's accounts of their connections to others and the social struggles within which these discourses emerge in the first place. In other words, the moral discourses people use to connect themselves to (or disconnect themselves from) others, do not fully disclose the nature of the underlying relationship between discourses and power contests. Everyday moral rhetoric (i.e., that one should do this or that; that one ought to act in such and such a way; that things ought to be like this, etc.) only marks the site of contested relations; it does not specify the character of the power struggles (or the forms of resistance) that underscore them. Therefore, it is the role of the analyst to discover the nature of the power struggles and to recognize that there are diverse techniques through which the actions and judgments of individuals and groups can be linked to political processes.

Simply to translate how people understand their relations with others, what they judge as appropriate and inappropriate, good or bad, right or wrong, would be to understand these claims only as rationalizations and defenses of their way of life. In so doing, however, there is always the potential problem of being caught up in the reasoning certain groups give for why they think and act the way they do. It is often the case, for example, that scholars take people's purposes, interests, or intentions as the origin of the discourse, without examining the discourse's internal relations and the generative aspects of the relationships to which it speaks. In an effort to avoid functional or teleological explanations for "the ways things are or should be," it is essential to separate the alleged purpose of morality (what moral discourse says it does) from its origin (power relation). In this regard, I show how moral claims, rather than preserving, defending, or protecting something, emerge from a form of power that attempts to guide people's possibility of conduct in the present or in the future. In this way, I present morality as a form of regulation. Instead of simply analyzing moral relations[4] as devoid of social conflict, this methodological technique conceptually distinguishes the discursive from the non-discursive or moral discourse from everyday power struggles. Such an approach permits a sociological analysis of the northwestern community of Sakli's moral economy and an excavation of patterns and exercises of power. In what follows, I illustrate how moral discourses at both the national and local levels are critical for understanding social regulation and power relations, especially in the way in which they mediate development regimes and shape gender and work dynamics.

## DEVELOPMENT REGIMES AND SOCIAL CHANGE

Many rural development regimes, including policies and state subsidies geared to bring about market expansion, industrial employment, or production for profit, are often based upon the explicit or implicit moral assumption that the standard for evaluating "the good life" is Western society. The question of how rural peoples attain "the good life," is usually answered in terms of their incorporation in market or commercialized production or, more generally, as state citizens or subjects embodying this moral character (see Valverde and Weir 1988: 31). Ultimately, for rural transformation to occur, changes are expected to take place at various social, cultural, and political levels, and in development discourses it is often assumed that these changes bring about benefits to local regions, nation states, and the international market system (see Mies and Shiva 1993). A common and overly economistic argument is that development regimes are primarily responsible for transforming rural societies and village traditions (i.e., large kin networks as sources of insurance and labor pools based on family, kin, class, or neighborhood). However, such views envision and promote "rural communities" as static, rule-bound entities, ignoring the exercise of moral beliefs by rural peoples in the context of social change and power struggles.

Local political and cultural settings play a vital role in mediating development regimes. I say this because rural peoples who begin to leave subsistence agriculture, to start cash cropping or selling their farm products for world markets, or to engage in wage labor relations, do so in ways that are shaped and influenced by moral discourses. This is not meant to suggest that moral relations resist economic development or preserve and protect anything (i.e., tradition, family unity, community, etc.). Far from adhering to such functional matters, it is precisely moral subjects that respond to material and economic conditions in ways that cannot be considered permanent or traditional but rather are considered to be transformative. Moral judgments, that "one ought to do this or that," are beliefs interpreted as choice or duty, and direct the action of people by restricting them to spheres of conformity and responsibility—with such regulation inevitably permeating various development processes and social relations. For these reasons, I wish to present a view of power relations that moves away from a centralized position of force (i.e., state, Islam, etc.) that controls and structures the field of possible actions, to one which focuses on a multiplicity of force relations that brings about change and guides people's activities (see also Abu-Lughod 1990: 42; Foucault 1983). In addressing such issues, the following discussion provides a brief background into the historical character and processes of development regimes in rural Turkey generally, and in the northwestern community of Sakli specifically.

Since the formation of the Turkish Republic in 1923, various attempts have been made to change political, economic, and cultural landscapes in the countryside. These changes have contributed, in part, to the formation of moral subjects and to the development of new gender divisions of labor. In particular, the role of the Turkish state in initiating rural transformation has broadly defined how people "should" behave and what they "should" deem good or bad. Central to Ataturk's political regime of modernization beginning in the early 1920s, state policies and plans played a primary role in improving the country's position in exports, increasing production to generate a large agricultural surplus, nationalizing coal mining operations, and taking over main railways, utilities, transportation, and port facilities (see Finkel and Sirman 1990; Morvaridi 1992, 1990; Keyder 1989; Berberoğlu 1982). This modernization regime was geared to foster a demand for industrial work, wage laborers, and export and internal markets. It also imposed the standards of fashion (e.g., outlawing the fez and replacing it with the Western hat), the use of language (e.g., displacing the Arabic alphabet with the Latin alphabet), the organization of work schedules (e.g., replacing the Islamic lunar calendar with the Gregorian calendar) (Finkel and Sirman 1990: 4; Kocturk 1992: 30–32), and introduced several new civil laws abolishing polygamy, equalizing property inheritance for men and women, and regulating divorce, marriage, and child custody procedures (Toprak 1994: 298; Kandiyoti 1991: 38; Abadan-Unat 1991: 178–79; Tekeli 1990: 270–71). All of these social and cultural changes were done in the name of "modernity": a process that attempted not only to mobilize and discipline populations but also to morally regulate and create subjects that would comply to certain ways of modern thinking, acting, and behaving.

State-initiated development during this early modern period sought to transform rural agrarian relations through the abolition of *aşar* (crop tax) in 1925, the introduction of state subsidies for agricultural production in 1926, and the acceleration of state-supported capitalist development, especially after World War II (Akgündüz 1993: 170). However, it is difficult to claim that state-initiated regimes alone are responsible for governing and transforming rural life. To do so would be to ignore the multiplicity of social forces involved in the regulation of groups, communities, and populations. In contrast to such a totalizing view of power, a microlevel analysis permits us to better understand local economies of power and the manner in which these intercede economic processes. It also enables us at the same time, to identify how certain groups become linked to regional or national economic development while others remain peripheral to it. In what follows, I will show how capitalist expansion and the demand for rural migrant labor in Turkey articulates with landlord-peasant moral relations and gender divisions of labor in the northwestern community of Sakli.

## MICROLEVEL POLITICS AND COMMUNITY RELATIONS

### Landlord-Peasant Relations during Modernization

Sakli is a mountainous rural community in the province of Zonguldak. Under Ottoman rule and long before the formation of the Turkish republic in 1923, the village was inhabited by a few subsistence farming families. Over two centuries ago, three families from the Bolu region of Turkey established an *ağalik* or landlord system in Sakli—a system of social and economic relations common to various parts of Turkey up until World War II. Under this system, local villagers, including women, men, and children, were compelled to work as sharecroppers for these village landlords who controlled all of the land in the area, owned over 250 sheep, and employed village shepherds, servants, barbers, and garden keepers. Until the 1920s (and to a lesser extent until the late 1950s), agricultural production was largely under *ağalik* control. The vast inequality in the ownership and regulation of land enabled Sakli landlords, and landlords from other regions, to dominate social, economic, and moral relations. In fact, during the Kemalist regime, some 2.5 million small and impoverished peasant families in Turkey were under the rule of wealthy landowning families (Berberoğlu 1982: 58).

Gender and class divisions of labor in subsistence production characterized this early modern period. Peasant women, men, and children worked the land for their own consumption needs as well as for village landlords. During field preparation and planting, both men and women participated but each performed separate tasks. Men generally led the oxen in the ploughing of fields and women and young children followed behind, removing rocks and planting seeds. Other tasks associated with field work, such as the cooking for kin in the field, was the domain of women, while the delivering of food and produce to landlords was the domain of men. Furthermore, the division of labor in agriculture was highly class specific in that peasant women and men were the ones responsible for farm production, whereas village landlords were responsible for distributing the produce back to the peasants, minus their share. During this time period, social class conflicts characterized community relations and local politics.

The *ağalik* system was responsible for maintaining a well-trained and compliant farming population. Since peasants did not own any land, landlords forced them to clear the forest for land, to seed, to harvest, and to transport the produce back to the landlords' manors. In addition to this economic domination, landlords also attempted to regulate the peasantry through moral means. Villagers were expected to ask the landlord's approval of their daughter's or son's marriage partner. Even the appropriate bride-price payment was negotiated between the groom's father and the landlord (see Ilcan 1994b). Often, villagers could not afford to pay the bride-price and relied on the landlord to help them financially. In addition, villagers were compelled to pay part of the bride-price money (usually half) to the landlord upon the marriage of their children. In their attempt to preserve the *ağalik* system, landlords approved only marriages between those families that were compliant and forbade marriages with households with whom they had conflicts. Due to their domination, landlords were in a position to create a sense of moral obligation among the peasantry by defining the parameters of appropriate interaction between landlords and peasants and between males and females. Noncompliance with landlord expectations could result in villagers being beaten, sexually assaulted, killed, and/or having their homesteads razed. As one elderly woman said, "*yediler bizi*" (literally, "they ate us"), "they took everything from us." As a notable moral expression in Sakli, the verb "to eat" (*yemek*) means to spend or to consume and villagers commonly use it to describe their state of exploitation and other forms of injustice (for a similar view see Scott 1985: 187).

Peasants rebelled against this oppressive system in numerous ways, especially during the late 1920s and early 1930s. In some situations, couples formed marriages without the consent of the landlords. A type of marriage known as *kiz kaçirma*[5] (literally, "girl kidnapping" or elopement) emerged to curb landlord control and to avoid the landlord's marriage tax. A villager could accomplish this by "carrying away" a woman to a cleric (*imam*). In other cases, some peasants reacted to the demands of the *ağalik* system by clearing small plots of land from the forest without the landlord's consent. This enabled them, if they did not get caught, to increase their harvest without increasing the share owed to landlords. Others simply stole from the landlord's granary what they thought was rightfully theirs, while some resorted to magical spells (*muska*) in an effort to gain control over the landlords. The landlords, for their part, developed countermeasures of their own. By controlling the distribution of goods, the landlords made it difficult for peasant families to steal or hide produce. They closely surveilled the peasantry during the harvesting season and often employed other villagers as spies to report on those who did not comply.

By the late 1930s (through to the 1970s), the state's role in expanding industrial development, in economic investment, and in the intensifying of economic relations with the West provided employment for many male peasants. Farmers from Sakli and surrounding areas seasonally migrated to the nearby city of Zonguldak for work in the coal mining industry. Facilitated by the state's Second Five Year Plan to implement industrial development, Zonguldak witnessed the establishment of heavy industry based on raw materials, the improvement of transportation facilities, and the construction of a modern port for the export of steel and coal (Berberoğlu 1982: 40). With the growing demand for wage labor in the Zonguldak area, the stronghold of the *ağalik* system in Sakli was clearly reduced. Specifically, this period witnessed the first decline in sharecropping practices, the emergence of land rental arrangements between landlords and peasants, and the ability of peasants to purchase small pieces of land for subsistence purposes.

The decline in landlord domination, however, stems from factors other than the male peasantry simply being pulled externally from sharecropping into migrant work. Sakli peasants came to consider the value of migrant labor in moral terms, enabling many of them to mitigate landlord domination. Peasants did not regard the "value" of work in the context of what it earns in the market. Rather, the meaning of migrant work came to be viewed in terms of its value in changing previous relations of domination and subordination, that is, overcoming landlord domination, surveillance, and brutality. The introduction of wage or migrant labor therefore served the political purpose of reducing landlord control over the peasantry.[6] This bears similarity to how the advent of tractors, the availability of increased credit, and the emigration of peasants to urban areas after World War II contributed to a decline in sharecropping arrangements in other parts of Turkey (Keyder 1989: 731–32).

Processes of capitalist expansion also brought about new changes to other areas of rural Turkey. Especially after World War II, many of Turkey's rural economies underwent enormous shifts, partly due to the introduction of local industry and wage labor, state-facilitated cash crop production, irrigation systems, fertilizers, or farm technology (e.g., Morvaridi 1990, 1992; Finkel and Sirman 1990; Aydin 1990; Keyder 1989, 1987).[7] However, and more specific to the theme at hand, is the manner in which local economies and populations mediate development efforts and the effects of this mediation on understanding microlevels of power and gender relations.

The following section discusses the contemporary situation of women's lives and work processes in the community of Sakli. Based on this research, I will show how complex interrelationships exist between social transformation and the moral discourses deployed to circumscribe arenas of obedience and duty[8] for those regulated by it (especially women) and the sites of resistance it engenders. The empirical basis of this discussion stems from several research methods employed during my one year of field work conducted in Turkey. Data is drawn, in part, from a villagewide household survey, in-depth interviews and oral histories with women and men, informal group discussions, and participant observation. My personal involvement with women's activities in the farm fields and in the homes has enabled me to draw upon the women's experiences and struggles, giving greater depth to the intricacies of power operating in their lives.

### Contemporary Struggles: Women's Work and Forms of Resistance in Sakli

In Sakli (population 567), and in the region generally, local residents identify themselves as Sunni Islamic, reckon descent in patrilineal terms, support arranged marriages and virilocal residence, and live mainly in three- to four-generational households. Their major economic activities include labor-intensive subsistence agriculture, together with household reproductive labor and seasonal male migrant work. Land distribution[9] among farming households[10] is fairly even, but great variations do still exist between landlords and villagers in terms of land ownership.

With the historical development and value of migrant work and subsequent changes in landlord-peasant relations, a "feminization" of subsistence agriculture and a "masculinization" of cash relations (see also Kandiyoti 1990) can be identified in Sakli today. In a situation quite different from that seen in the earlier period, most men have virtually withdrawn from labor-intensive agriculture. Usually one or two male household members (a husband or a young married or unmarried son) now work as seasonal migrants, while other household members take responsibility for the bulk of agricultural work. Women and young girls, in fact, do most of the agricultural work, including the labor-intensive operations of ploughing, hoeing, planting, weeding, and the caring and feeding of animals. Even the labor-intensive harvesting of wheat and corn is mainly undertaken by women. When men do participate in agriculture, their involvement is generally restricted to performing tasks during the peak ploughing and harvesting seasons, working in mechanized activities (in some clearing, ploughing, and threshing operations), and supervising the labor process. Likewise, young boys (especially those under 12) also participate in agricultural work, as well as help their male kin rebuild houses or barns, and paint and upgrade fences. Overall, men predominate in mechanized agriculture, restoration work, commercial transactions, and migrant labor. It is considered unmanly, however, for a male to do what is now considered traditional female work—the mundane and time-consuming work of labor-intensive farming and gardening.

Within village households, there is also a marked gender division of labor. Women and young girls perform all of the major cooking, most of the child care, and virtually all of the work associated with other household demands.[11] When not working in the fields or tending to gardens, women and girls spend their time making goods for trousseaus and preparing for upcoming marriages and other festive ceremonies. In contrast, men and boys engage in a minimal amount of household-related work. They do, however, take weekly trips to the town market to purchase fresh fruit and other food and will for short periods of time supervise their own young children or siblings. When not working as seasonal migrants or laboring during the peak farming season, men (along with some young boys) spend many of their days or evenings in the local coffee shop. This is a location only males frequent, since it is considered socially unacceptable for women and girls to be in the company of unrelated men.

The availability of wage and migrant labor, however, not only brought about a remarkable alteration in the gender division of labor but also new moral views concerning the status and perception of men's and women's work. With seasonal migration accelerating until the 1970s, the overwhelming majority of village households today have (or have had) predominately male members who work as wage laborers outside of the community (see Ilcan 1994c). While this wage labor is viewed by villagers in highly valued moral terms, as previously discussed, the same cannot be said for the work that women do in subsistence agriculture. Prized by women as traditionally significant and essential to agricultural production, labor-intensive farm tasks are currently viewed by men as work inherently suited to women. In fact, younger and older men do not consider women's work as embodying much skill or expertise. Often when men talk about those who work with agricultural machines, they refer to the skill and experience that this type of work requires, contrasting it with the lack of skill involved in labor-intensive agriculture. As one male peasant says,

Our women work in the fields and this is the work that they are accustomed to. Our daughters, too, are there with them and they learn how to work the land. Men don't do much work in the fields the way they did before. . . . Yes, I sometimes help my brother with his harvest and work the threshing machine with him and deliver the wheat to the flour mill, but this is more difficult than just working in the fields. . . . Women can't do that kind of work.

The moral judgment that women are not suited to a particular kind of work only attempts to circumscribe arenas of duty and obligation for women, not fully disclosing the underlying power contests between men and women or the fact that the primary target of masculinist power has been the subjugation of women. The fact that women's attitudes toward agricultural labor are different from men's reveals their location in the battleground of power networks. Women claim that it takes a great deal of training to become a good farmer and many older women express their desire someday to have a physically strong (*kuvvetli*) daughter-in-law (*gelin*) to teach and take over their farming chores. As in other parts of rural Turkey, and unlike the situation in earlier periods, older married women in Sakli gain more social status and respect when they withdraw from agricultural work and become more restricted to performing tasks inside the home (see also Kandiyoti 1984: 25). This newly acquired status is, however, an effect of power since it derives from the devaluation of women's farm work by wage-earning male kin.

Other new cultural changes have been generated in this local community. One important development has to do with the emergence of a new discourse, referred to as "tradition" (*adet*), which defines the permitted and forbidden by linking current social relations to those of the past. However, the contemporary meaning of tradition in Sakli does not simply refer to ways of acting and behaving that derive from conventionally established practice or from the sanctity of age-old rules and powers. Tradition has been transformed from the way it operated under the landlord-peasant regime to its present exercise, as a technique of power, administered under different economic and gender conditions.

Prior to the onset of seasonal male out-migration, village life was envisioned in slave-like terms, since much of what the peasants did was done under the watchful eye of village landlords. During this time period, there was little conception of a well-established peasant tradition since the landlord regime regulated and influenced the major aspects of social ties and relations, including property and distribution networks, work ethics and labor processes, marriage negotiations, arrangements, and bride-price payments. As one older peasant woman said, "We served and worked for them [landlords] and then, later, we worked for half of the yield. This work had to be done under any circumstances, even if there was a death in the family. We even had to carry their drinking water. With the way it was, our life was really in their hands." The sentiments expressed here speak to a way of life that was very much ordered and governed by a landlord tradition of sorts, where peasant voices and social preferences were just beginning to alter relations of power. Nevertheless, the discursive emergence of tradition today builds from, yet breaks with, the distributions of power associated with the landlord-peasant tradition.

The current discourses of *adet* reveal not only an exaggeration of the links to the past (or the "original")[12] but also the transmission and production of new power relations.[13] Especially after the slow decline of the landlord-peasant regime and the availability of male migrant work, the importance of tradition became a specific point of discussion in Sakli because relations of power (particularly between men and women) started to establish it as a possible object of investigation. During the initial period when a large proportion of male peasants seasonally migrated to urban centers for work, one of the most significant developments emerged when the practices of *adet* became tied to a moral concern over village women. With the seasonal absence of men, the moral behavior of women was called into question by men and it was at this point that women's activities came under closer scrutiny and were subject to new forms of moral regulation.

The discourse of tradition is an especially dense transfer point for uncovering relations of power between men and women and for guiding people's possibilities of conduct in the sphere of gendered activities. Male villagers, in particular, speak about their tradition in a gendered fashion, emphasizing women's roles in household and subsistence agriculture and men's roles outside the household and in migrant work. Even some older women see it as their obligation to carry on this tradition, attaching much prestige and status to their roles as wives, mothers, or daughters. As one married woman said, "It is our tradition for women to look after their husbands and their children. . . . We are proud to work the land the way we do . . . yes it is hard work and long hours, but what else can we do. . . . Our sons work hard too and when they marry, their wives will do what we do now. This is how it is in our village." This discourse on tradition is cloaked in positive and functional terms, and while it is made to seem as if "things have always been such and such a way," its most profound effect is that it masks its success in organizing and imposing constraints upon women's lives. In providing a way to render community life amenable to certain kinds of actions, the discourse on tradition serves as a point of support for the idea that women are the main transmitters of tradition and village values. Because of their reproductive capacity and their confined location within the village, women's roles as workers or citizens are not as important as their perceived roles as wives and especially as mothers. Their responsibilities of caring for and socializing young children are viewed by both women and men as morally superior to those of the urban world, where women dress and travel openly, working in public places alongside male strangers. In their attempt to strive toward traditional ideals, women in Sakli take on the bulk of agricultural work, household maintenance, and child-rearing duties and are responsible for training future daughters-in-law for home and farm labor. They are also involved in morally training sons and male kin toward a life of migrant work, expecting daughters to marry migrant laborers over male farmers. In fact, the women's responsibility for labor-intensive subsistence production is taken as if it is a safeguard of family tradition, even though families themselves are characterized by paternal authority, gendered property and inheritance, virilocality, and power relations, and by separable, often competing, interests, rights, and responsibilities. Therefore, the deployment of traditional values is an effect of power since it confines women to certain social spaces and enmeshes them in relations viewed as traditional.

Aside from being an effect of power, traditional discourse also becomes "naturalized" or "normalized" as it is used to act upon people's lives and to provide a way to make the domain in question (gender, family, work) susceptible to evaluation, criticism, and intervention (Foucault 1979: 184–85). This is particularly the case when the discourse of tradition is employed as an instrument of power, most especially by men, to explain women's inability to travel by themselves from one village to another, to speak to unrelated men, or to engage in wage labor. It is thought that women should be shielded from unknown or untrustworthy men, since these men have the potential to take sexual advantage of them and cause much shame to husbands and male kin and to village tradition. Even when women enter the forest to cut, collect, and carry wood, they are thought to be in need of surveillance so as to protect village tradition. As one young married man said, "*Kadin yalniz gitmez, yaninda birisi lazim: ya erkek kardeşi, ya kocasi, ya da komşusu*" ("A woman cannot go [to the forest] alone as someone must be with her: either her brother, husband, or neighbor"). More specifically, the discourse on tradition permeates the nondiscursive domains of travel and movement by constituting them as gender specific. That is, women are expected to work and visit within the geographical boundaries of the village, travel in groups rather than by themselves, and speak with more deference to others in public than men do in similar circumstances (such as among strangers or people physically near but morally remote). In contrast, most men travel both within and outside of the village, engage in both wage and nonwage work, and participate in a variety of urban consumption practices that are socially prohibited to women (for similar parallels see Delaney 1991: 237).

Making use of moral values, together with their mechanisms of discipline, is an important cultural strategy for regulating women's movement in other areas of rural Turkey as well. Morvaridi's (1992: 580–81) study of economic and cultural development in northeast Turkey, for example, highlights how certain moral sentiments attempt to seclude and subordinate women, by regulating their dress, mobility, and interactions with community members. In his words, "Only when accompanied by a male member of her household can a woman move outside the village. An unaccompanied woman caught talking in public to a man from the village would find it difficult to marry, as she is seen as dishonoring her family" (Morvaridi 1992: 581). Likewise, Sirman (1990: 45–48) highlights the interrelations of state, village, and gender in a western Turkish village, illustrating how men (as household heads and providers) represent the politics of the state within the village, and how women remain under their moral rule. This kind of moral regulation has the potential to subsume women, in this case, into systems of governance by making them "subjects" to these meanings and seducing them to believe in its goals, and to speak and act its claims. And, when they come to believe in these moral values and to identify themselves as agents protecting or enhancing a group or tradition (as in Sakli), then moral discourses serve as clever disguises and subtle expressions of the forces of domination (cf. Abu-Lughod 1990: 47).

In order to understand local community politics and its links to rural transformation, we must take seriously the significance of cultural strategies, such as the uses to which morality is put. For it is morality, as a microeconomy of knowledge and power, that explains why development or social change is not simply a matter of state initiation, technological diffusion, market rationalization, or capitalist penetration. In other words, and as I have shown above, there is a relationship between moral regulation and other forms of economic processes (see also Valverde 1994: 213–14; Morvaridi 1992: 580–84).

However, while microlevel forms of power in Sakli attempt to morally regulate women's work and behavior, they should not be thought of as having a totalizing effect that resolves all differences and contradictions through a masculinist or traditional discourse. Poststructural analysts of power remind us that we are not entirely encapsulated by a prevailing discourse. Discourses can be both instruments and effects of power, as well as points of resistance. I have shown how both women and men are involved in supporting the existing system of power through the deployment and naturalization of tradition. What I will illustrate below is that women, as one of the most marginal groups, also resist these forms of moral regulation and, in this way, we cannot ignore their attempt to overcome the totalizing incentives of a dominant and often masculinist morality (see Diamond and Quinby 1988: 201–2; Hennessy 1993: 92). It is essential, therefore, to document how women themselves engage in acts of resistance to prevailing discourses. In what follows, I will briefly describe two main forms of resistance undertaken by women, showing how these intersect with the techniques of power or moral regulation outlined above.

Sakli women engage in a variety of resistance efforts that work against the dominating effects of traditional discourse. The first arena of resistance, one I have described elsewhere (Ilcan 1994a), is one in which women attempt to overcome their perceived subordinate status as household and farm workers through the use of magic. Women use magic (*büyü* or *muska*) as a way to change daily working conditions and demands within their virilocal households, alter conflictual relations with family members and local residents, and subvert moral expectations surrounding arranged marriages, spousal sexual demands, and home and child-care duties. This form of resistance indicates one way power is exercised by women through a range of spiritual strategies that attempt to transform traditional relations and aspirations. *Muska* not only exposes the contradictions of women's lives but it also creates an avenue from which they can disembody themselves from the confines of moral regulation (similar to *zar* spiritual possession discussed by Boddy 1991: 129–30). In this regard, *muska* has the potential to transform, reverse, or undermine forms of moral regulation because it seeks to change all sorts of power relations by arresting their strength, such as when women arrange to have spells cast upon husbands who demand too much from them or upon in-laws who restrict their social mobility. Within power domains—such as those between women and men—there is resistance, and the use of magic permits women the possibility to mobilize themselves and others and to control certain types of behavior and expectations. Furthermore, women's engagement in magic (in comparison to men's) is considered by most men to possess less transformative qualities, thus revealing how power struggles culminate in the production of new knowledge around women's activities.

A second and widespread form of resistance is the manner in which women engage in clandestine activities to ensure that incoming brides meet women's own needs as well as their household's. One of the most popular ways that married women attempt to control future working relations within their households is by exerting their influence over their sons' choice of spouse. Women, and their informal networks, are extremely active in bride searches, in that they try to seek out women with whom they can get along. This works to their advantage, especially when they find a bride who is reputed to be a hard worker, looks physically strong, and has the potential to take responsibility for a large segment of farm and household tasks. These women also play an important role in occasionally preventing their daughters from marrying men arranged for them by older, male kin. In such cases, women and their female friends search actively for any information on a prospective groom and his family that would raise doubts about his suitability including any immoral activities affiliated with a household or its members. Furthermore, contemporary young women oc-

casionally resist arranged marriages by eloping with another man, a traditional activity that was once a form of resistance to landlord taxation,
still referred to as *kiz kaçirma*. Overall, these practices reveal that women
can resist the decisions of their husbands or fathers in marriage arrangements and negotiations and, as such, can influence changes in their status,
and in some cases, alterations in their work and household schedules.

The acts that I have just described are not exhaustive of all female sites
of resistance to traditional discourses in Sakli. Women have also been
known to resist prevailing standards of appropriate femininity by secretly
engaging in extramarital relations, selling homemade goods to local towns-
people for cash, and traveling to areas outside the village. No matter what
the extent of these forms of resistance, they indeed demonstrate sites of
struggle and power relations and have implications for the way in which
they operate through women's work and status in the community. Moreover, these resistance efforts provide a context out of which women can
pluralize meaning by breaking presumably established constructs which influences their social, economic, and political domains.

Contrary to the view that new economic efforts completely transform
old forms of community relations and domination, processes of cultural
change in this community mediate development regimes. This chapter has
illustrated that the moral values associated with male migrant work were
central in overcoming landlord-peasant relations, creating new gendered
fields, and in producing modern perceptions and judgments of work and
responsibility. Together and in line with these changes, I have demonstrated
how the emergence and discursive invention of tradition plays a role in
guiding people's possibilities of conduct and in regulating more directly
women's work activities. While the exercise of this form of moral regulation masks its success in confining women's movement and work patterns,
it also culminates as a point of resistance by women through their informal
participation in magic and marriage practices. Instead of conceptualizing
moral relations as strictly rule-bound or as devoid of conflict, this chapter
has revealed that the genealogy of these relations necessarily draws from,
and impinges upon, a multiplicity of power regimes and resistance efforts.

## CONCLUDING REMARKS

In this chapter I have examined how new economic and social changes
in industrializing societies like Turkey are underscored and influenced by
the exercise of moral regulation as a technique of power. In the context of
Sakli, the transition from subsistence production to varied forms of work
and relations also becomes part of a transition to a new and different disciplinary society (where people discipline themselves in distinctive ways
from each other and from the past). What is interesting about these processes is that we can identify how unique social relations unfold for various

gender and work dynamics, and how the forces of development articulate with local cultural meanings and disciplinary techniques. What is to be understood by disciplinary techniques, such as the uses to which morality is put, is not that individuals or groups who become part of them become more obedient, but rather that an increasingly invigilated process of adjustment is sought after by those who attempt to transform others in the field of social activities and through the play of power relations. A relationship of power is a mode of action that does not act directly and immediately on others; instead, it acts upon their actions, in the present or the future, and consists of guiding people's possibilities of conduct, including the manner in which they may be regulated and the forms of resistance they may embrace. Therefore, in any hierarchically ordered society, power is not simply centralized (in the state, in Islam, or in the global economy), but dispersed in a multiplicity of sites, continuously directing people's potentiality of comportment. This is why the analysis, elaboration, and the bringing into question of moral regulation is at the heart of understanding local rural transformation.

## NOTES

1. A revised version of this chapter was presented at the Middle East Studies Association of North America (November 1994). I would like to recognize and thank Gülen Coşkun for helping in the production of survey data, Yakin Ertürk and Nükhet Sirman for providing important suggestions for this research, and Parvin Ghorayshi and Lynne Phillips for contributing valuable insights and critical comments on an earlier draft of this chapter. Financial support was provided by the Social Sciences and Humanities Research Council of Canada, a Heritage Fund grant, and a University of Windsor research grant.

2. See Valverde (1994), Fraser (1992, 1989), and Foucault (1983) for more on the relationship between discourse and power. I understand power not simply in the macropolitical terms of class and state, but in the micropolitical terms of the networks of discursive relations within local economies and institutions.

3. The task of the genealogist is to trace the lines of connection between similar and disparate meanings, as relations of power not relations of meaning (Foucault 1980: 114). Genealogy does not trace the development of unities or the development of cause or origins (see also McNeil 1993: 149). What makes the history of human relations intelligible is not their connection on the level of meaning, but "the intelligibility of struggles, of strategies and tactics" (Foucault 1980: 114). As Bevis, Cohen, and Kendall (1993: 194) suggest, genealogy offers an understanding of the process, not a snapshot, perspective on the web of discourse.

4. For an elaborate discussion of moral relations, see Ilcan 1993.

5. This marital practice is no longer thought of as an act of resistance against landlord domination. The practice today is perceived as a strategy used by the young to resist familial authority.

6. However, given that migrant work is low paid and seasonal, it does not

enable migrant families to completely remove themselves from subsistence agriculture altogether.

7. For example, in central Turkey, there are pockets of rural populations that have developed into capital-intensive areas of cereal farming and have retreated from subsistence production altogether (e.g., Kandiyoti 1990: 190). In some southwestern regions of Turkey, high levels of landlessness exist and many household members participate in seasonal cotton work for the world market (e.g., Sirman 1988, 1990). These areas are characterized by an increasing separation of production and reproduction and the concomitant rise in strict gender divisions of work, as well as alterations in family arrangements and marriage patterns. And still, in some northeast regions of Turkey, especially those governed by the government's intensification and regional development program (i.e., Turkish Sugar Factories Corporation), farming operations are market oriented and regulated by the state's control over crop cultivation, production, marketing, and processing. Such cash cropping operations not only replace animal husbandry and subsistence farming, but also create the need for family and wage workers among large landholders and the demand for female family labor among small landholders (Morvaridi 1992: 571–72). In this regard, state-initiated developments attempt to organize and order rural populations, by forcing them to generate new forms of work patterns, household schedules, and labor forces. These techniques of power are dedicated to making laboring populations grow and expand, rather than impeding or destroying them.

8. Obedience is simply the inability to exert power and so one is made subject to the purpose of another (or subject to a set of purposes or aims, i.e., morality). Furthermore, obedience is an effect of a process of compulsion in which subjects are constituted in a discourse of purposes, aims, ends, or reasons. In obedience, one is subjected to a purpose or an aim that is interpreted either as duty or choice. Therefore, power relations compel action, not obedience or duty.

9. Of Sakli's eighty-four households (excluding the three landlord households), only a few (10.7%) are nearly landless (under six *dönüm*), some have marginal landholdings (between six and ten *dönüm*), and the majority (66.7%) have small-scale landholdings (eleven to fifty *dönüm*) (Ilcan 1993, 1994c).

10. The average household in Sakli owns, or has access to, approximately fourteen *dönüm*. One *dönüm*, equivalent to just under one-quarter of an acre, is considered the amount of land that one person can work in a day. The average-sized household (containing between six and eight members) requires at least twelve to sixteen *dönüm* for basic subsistence needs.

11. For instance, some major household demands include: pickling, collecting wood or corn cobs for heating and cooking, preparing daily meals, tending to children, and sewing, knitting, and repairing clothes.

12. See Butler (1990) for an excellent discussion of the parodic repetition of "the original."

13. It is common for villagers to make use of the term *adet* to explain and uphold the prevalence of arranged marriages, patrilocal inheritance practices, virilocal residence, and many other endorsed features of village life. However, its utility in demarcating women's and men's work as distinct and separate and in creating a basis from which to order and regulate women's lives is of particular significance.

# 10
# Filipino Women and the Work of Mothering
*Delia D. Aguilar*

## FAMILIES AND WOMEN'S ROLE

That families continue to constitute a central force in Philippine life is indisputable. From ordinary people whose daily survival hinges on sustenance by family members to popular writers and newspaper commentators whose columns inveterately link nepotism and government corruption to kin ties and the patronage system (Roces and Roces 1985), and to textbook writers who view the family as the "basic unit of social analysis" (Medina 1991), there is common agreement that family and kinship exert an influence in Philippine society as yet unsupplanted by any other institution.

Women's location at the heart of the family is also widely accepted (Nelson 1968: 100; Mulder 1990–91: 78). But what is now subject to debate is the precise character of that role. Researchers of the sixties and seventies, analyzing empirical data using paradigms borrowed from the United States, replaced earlier notions of matriarchy and female dominance with those of gender complementarity and equality (Aguilar 1989). More recently, with the inception of feminism and women's studies programs, the existence of gender parity is being sharply questioned, as is the supposed egalitarian household division of labor upon which such a conclusion was based (Angeles 1990; Lopez-Rodriguez 1990; Israel-Sobritchea 1990; Tiglao-Torres 1990; Eviota 1992). Following this line of interrogation, activists and feminist theoreticians are seeking ways of assessing the value of household within the political economy (Ybanez 1992). Domestic work performed by housewives is now beginning to be recognized as vital to the smooth functioning of Philippine society and extends beyond purely cultural considerations. Curiously enough, however, mothering is cited as only one of many activities subsumed under the general rubric, "household work," instead of being understood as its main ideological underpinning.

When social researchers studied mothers and children in the 1960s and 1970s, and even through the 1980s, attention was focused exclusively on child-rearing practices and their effects on children (Guthrie 1961; Flores and Gomez 1964; Guthrie and Jimenez Jacobs 1966; Domingo 1977; Arellano-Carandang 1979; Minoza, Botor, and Tablante 1984). Recent feminist inquiries have questioned the absence of the father in these studies (Tiglao-Torres 1990), but the experience of motherhood itself and the impact of maternal ideology on women has so far escaped examination. There is some irony in this despite the enduring view that children are "gifts from God" (Hollnsteiner 1984: 98). For it is also the case that the mother is thought to occupy center stage in the family, the power she wields being presumed to reside in her disbursement of household funds (Alvarez and Alvarez 1973; Roces 1985; Medina 1991) and in her control and influence over her children's behavior, even when they become adults (Lapuz 1977).

## INTRODUCING THE STUDY

This chapter, then, is intended as an initial exploration of this particular lacuna, laying the groundwork for further research. It is also an offshoot of an earlier inquiry made by the author in which mothers' accounts of the household gender division of labor and their largely unquestioning acceptance of it revealed the ways in which their assumption of housework as a natural concomitant of mothering prevented them from disentangling one activity from the other (Aguilar 1991).

To the author's knowledge, this is the first study looking into Filipino women's perspectives on motherhood. Collected in the late 1980s, this set of partially structured, in-depth, open-ended interviews with nineteen mothers in the Metro Manila region sought to elicit these women's perceptions of their experiences as mothers, along with their conceptualizations of motherhood. Representing a cross-class sample, the group interviewed (ages 26 to 43, having from one to nine children) consists of a bank officer, a pediatrician, three unemployed squatter dwellers, two garment factory workers, an executive secretary, two college instructors, a schoolteacher, a community organizer, four full-time mothers (one working-class, two middle-class, and one upper-class), a home-based small garment factory owner, an office administrator, and a college personnel office head.

The following is a schema of the questions I posed to this sample. At the outset the women were asked about their views on marriage prior to becoming wives and what part children played in the picture. Did they ever, even for a moment, consider not having children? They were asked about family planning, childbirth, postpartum depression, and how the coming of children affected their lives in and out of the home. They were asked to describe their everyday schedule of motherwork and the supporting structures, if any, that assisted in the conduct of this task. For example, what specific child-care chores did husbands engage in? Who else was called upon in the household or in the immediate vicinity and what role did these people play in the care of the child or children? What did having children mean for these women and what were the benefits and difficulties? What experiences as mothers could they cite as making them the most happy and the least happy? What regrets did they have, if any, about having children? What were their ideas of a good mother? Was self-sacrifice part of it? As mothers, what was their most important function?

## THE WOMEN RESPOND

### Marriage and Children

None of the women departed from conventional expectations regarding marriage and children. Indeed, a few thought it strange that such a question would be posed at all. When 26-year-old Benardita, a garment factory worker with a 3-year-old daughter, replied simply, "Isn't it when you get married, you want children?" she was voicing the sentiment of every single woman in this group. Milagros, a humanities instructor, echoed cultural dictates similarly: "I know you don't go into marriage simply for companionship. Sooner or later you'll have a baby." To be sure, the reasons for desiring children differed according to class and access to resources—material and social. Popular wisdom and social scientists rightly interpret the notion of children as "gifts from God" as predicated on the economic utility of offspring in a social system offering its members little or no public assistance (Yu and Liu 1980: 218; Sevilla 1983). Amalia, a squatter dweller with six sons, expressed her concerns directly: "What would happen to us when we're old?" She had only wanted three children, but kept hoping for a girl. Earlier studies, too, have documented women's wish for a daughter as their first born for reasons of expedience, the belief being that girls can be trained to look after younger siblings (Licuanan 1979). Speaking to the mutual aid function maintained by family members regardless of age, marital status, or stage in the life cycle, Amalia projected her thoughts to the future when, with her own parents gone, she would need her children when roles became reversed.

All except one woman (a former biologist, now a full-time mother, whose family history included a hereditary disease) automatically associated marriage with bearing children. But, as already stated, the nature of the responses to this initial question was class defined. Belen, a college math instructor, repeated my question: "Ever consider not having children! No, no! That's out of the question. [*Laughs*] That's something natural." Tess, a well-heeled bank officer living in an exclusive "village," said as much: "It was very natural for my husband and me that we'd want children. It was just assumed—we didn't talk about it. My God, I cannot imagine life without children!"

In fact, talk of the naturalness surrounding motherhood permeated much of my conversations with these women whatever language it was conducted in (the women with college educations spoke in English and Tagalog, the main language spoken in Manila, while the others used Tagalog), a point I shall return to later. Moreover, to state that class distinctions differentiated arguments in favor of parenthood does not mean that the poorer women saw their offspring solely in instrumental terms. For example, Teresita, a garment factory worker with a 9-year-old boy, saw her child as "an inspiration," someone who "gives me energy to wake up in the morning." This motive for having children, in fact, punctuated the women's utterances, regardless of their class niche. Consuelo, a squatter dweller with nine children ranging in age from 2 to 21, told me that she wanted children "*para sa kaligayahan*" (for happiness), implying by her tone that surely, since I am a mother too, I would understand that.

Given the conflation of marriage with children, all of the women, except two whose first few years of marriage were spent overseas, practiced either no birth control or relied on rhythm. Amalia, with the six sons, now planned to take birth control pills; others of her class expressed fears that the pills cause women to lose weight and grow tumors, while fearing that tubal ligation weakened the body. On the other hand Marina, a 38-year-old schoolteacher, underwent ligation after her fourth child. Tess, who likewise had four children, was considering the same; but even she, who could readily solicit experts' opinions, was anxious about how the process might hasten aging. This corresponds with findings that Filipino women normally employ family planning only after having borne three or four children, not before (Sevilla 1983).

### Experience of Pregnancy and Childbirth

It is perhaps not unusual that, because of the naturalization of motherhood in general, these women's accounts of their experiences with pregnancy and childbirth are marked by a calm acceptance of pain and suffering. Marina had difficulty conceiving and carrying her pregnancies to term. Belen, pregnant at the time of the interview, admitted that were she not hoping for a girl, she would not want another child; she went through an excruciating twenty-seven hours of labor and a cesarean section with her son. Bernardita lost the use of her legs for four months after her baby was born. These were some of the major problems reported and, to reiterate, expressed with tranquility. A statement from Manuela, a former secretary whose husband was stationed in a commercial vessel off the coast of Japan, provides a possible explanation for such composure: "I had a difficult labor and a painful episiotomy. But it's good to experience these things to appreciate the rewards later."

Few had heard of postpartum depression, except for the highly educated. The poorer women interpreted the phenomenon, after I explained it, as a matter of *nerbiyos* (nerves), and began to communicate their anxieties about their younger children's illnesses and their inability to purchase medicine. Tesing, a squatter dweller with five children, asserted that she was nervous before childbirth, but not afterward. For Amalia, who tried to deliver her children by herself ("I sometimes called my sister to assist"), *nerbiyos* did not apply. Despite her incapacitation after delivery, Bernardita explained that she did not have *nerbiyos* because she lives with her mother who looks after her child. It appears from these narrations that *nerbiyos* is believed to be unwarranted when the aid of others is within close reach. Tess rendered this with clarity. Familiar enough with life in the industrialized West, which she contrasted to the women's situation in the Philippines, she explained why she herself never had postpartum depression: "Here, after childbirth, there are lots of people helping you."

It seems that a philosophical attitude, combined with the presence of supportive kin, mitigated the discomforts (albeit magnified in those too poor to afford medical care) attendant to biological reproduction. Even the five women who had heard about postpartum depression and had experienced it themselves remarked on the shortness of its duration or clarified the circumstances (that the husband was away, for instance) that may have been its cause. In a setting where motherhood is naturalized, the postpartum phenomenon was oddly deprived of a biological foundation.

## Childcare

Class differences emerged rather clearly as well in the task of caring for the child or children. When asked about who does what in childcare, this is how Jinky, full-time mother of two and wife of a corporate executive, responded: "During the first month I breast-fed and changed diapers. My husband began changing diapers during the second month. We expose our children to music and books. We never, never babytalk. When Boyet was 1 year old, he had a vocabulary of 300 words, and was able to read quite early. According to my sister, this is quite unusual."

I asked Jinky, "And what is the role of the *yaya* [nursemaid]?" She replied, "The *yaya*'s care is inversely proportional to the age of the child. Up until Liza was 6 months old, I was at home with her. Beginning the eighth month, I started getting involved in political activism again, so there were times when I wasn't home; the *yaya* took care of her. But in terms of quality time, since I'm older and more relaxed, I can be more creative in the way I react to Liza. My primary concern is that she have a wealth of material that will mentally stimulate her." Contrast that account with the starkness of the following account by Tesing, a squatter dweller: "Everything that has to be done in the house is done by me. [*Laughs*] I wake up at five and cook breakfast. At a quarter to six, I take the children to school. Then I clean the house and wash clothes. I buy water at twenty-five centavos a gallon. But there's also a well farther away. I usually go there to do my laundry. My 9-year-old [a girl, the eldest of five] looks after the 2-year-old."

Or consider the response of Rose, a 35-year-old community organizer with two children, as she describes her role: "In the evening when I get home between seven and eight, I play with my 5-month-old baby. She stays with us in our bedroom, but in her own crib. I fix her bottle. Benjie [5 years old] sleeps in his own room, but comes to join us in bed early in the morning. I feed the baby at 6 A.M., give her a bath, and then leave for the office."

When I asked whether it would be accurate to state that childcare is shared by her and the *yaya*, Rose replied: "Yes, it's important to say that," but emphasized that after 7:30 in the evening she and her husband Fred take over, and that it is she who wakes up for the baby at night.

It must be noted that, of the nineteen women interviewed, twelve had at least one housemaid or *yaya*. Of these twelve, five also had their mother or mother-in-law either living in the house or visiting regularly to help out. Of the seven who had no maids, one (Manuela, whose husband was at sea) had her mother-in-law move in; another (Feliza, a garment worker separated from her husband) lived with her father and sister; still another (Bernardita, who could not walk after childbirth) lived with her mother. Out of the nineteen women, five were living apart from their husbands: three temporarily separated by work and the other two separated permanently. Of these five, three had maids, one lived with her father and sister, and one lived with her mother-in-law. None of the women who were also employed dispensed duties without some form of help, either by a hired live-in maid or by a family member living in the house.

It was only the three squatter dwellers who had neither maid nor family member in the household; they also had the largest numbers of children— five, six, and nine—and were full-time mothers. Life for these three was a strain all around. In the words of Amalia, "If I pondered over every bit of work that I do, maybe all my hair would have turned gray a long time ago." It must be remarked, however, that they too had family living in the vicinity. Interestingly, one woman (Carmina, the biologist turned full-time mother) deliberately elected not to hire household help on principle: "It is a feudal arrangement and I don't like the idea." Needless to say, this is a point of view one seldom comes across in the Philippines.

The availability of household help, however, must not lead to the assumption that the majority of these women relegated mothering work to *yayas*. For the women with successful careers outside the home especially, the heavy weight of maternal ideology seemed to compel them to prove their compliance with the charge of motherhood. This was clear in the narration bank officer Tess gave of her household tasks. She described how she woke up at night for her first two children, how their cribs were in her bedroom, how she "did everything" for them, and continues to do so now.

The case of Milagros, who was on a fellowship and on leave from teaching at the time of the interview, similarly confirms this. The most maternally bound of this sample, she refused to turn over childcare to her maid, made sure to sterilize bottles herself, and washed the floor daily with Lysol ("every nook and cranny") so the child could crawl freely without worry of infection. Household help, then, does not obviate the need felt by these women to perform the job of mothering when they can, which is not to say that the availability of *yayas* does not lighten the responsibility considerably. It also relieves the husband of having to pitch in any more than he cares to. It is obvious from the majority of their reports that husbands actually did very little, and that neither traditional arrangements nor the women themselves demanded more. It is equally obvious that most of them tended to exaggerate the extent of their husbands' involvement.

Marina, the schoolteacher, whose husband operated a business at home, spoke of her husband's attentiveness to the children. But when asked about his routine childcare tasks, she failed to come up with anything more substantial than: "He tells them before he leaves the house not to quarrel. When he comes back, he asks what they did all day." Bernardita, a garment worker who lives with her mother, lauded her husband's talents in cooking and washing ("He does laundry even better than I do"), yet his weekend routine did not seem to include these activities: "On Sundays when I'm at work and my mother is in church, he looks after our daughter at home."

Because convention does not require husbands to partake in housework and childcare, these women may well not have been meaning to exaggerate at all, but simply voicing appreciation for their husbands' slightest involvement. Only the situation of the squatter dwellers strayed from this pattern, in which the husbands (one was a habitual drinker) failed to function even as providers. These wives manifested great frustration concerning the provider role.

## Impact of Children on Life at Home and Outside

On the whole, the responses to the question about the impact of the first child on life at home centered on positive aspects. It would have been surprising had it been otherwise, since children are regarded as a natural accompaniment of marriage. Violy, an executive secretary whose husband was in Saudi Arabia when her child was born, recounted how happy she and everybody in her mother's household was and how she chose not to get a maid during her forty-five–day maternity leave in spite of what she called her "body exhaustion."

Bernardita reported that when she had her daughter (recall her resulting inability to walk), "I became an even happier person. I didn't give a thought to how difficult life was. I just thought about her." She succumbed to tears, however, when she thought that she might never walk again. Tesing admitted that having the first child was hard, especially when her family didn't have money, "but children also take your mind off worries." Besides, she added, her mother-in-law was around to take care of the baby, which allowed her to go out and do some sewing in a nearby bag factory.

When negative, the responses stressed schedules that had to be drastically altered to accommodate the new round of responsibilities entailed by caring for an infant. The garment factory owner, Elvira (28 years old), gratefully recalled how good health enabled her to withstand the endless routine of "childcare, cooking, cleaning, laundry, supervising employees, everything!" At that time her family had no maid and she did not feel ready to have a baby. But being the eldest of nine children gave her the experience of caring for her younger siblings, which now held her in good stead.

For Carmina, who chose to reject the practice of hiring yayas, the baby's arrival had a "big, big impact." She remembered feeling harassed and, thinking of those days, doubted that she would wish the experience repeated. She was not entirely on her own, it must be added, since her mother lived across the way and provided meals for her and her husband. Angela, head of a personnel office, spoke of her new baby as "an inspiration" for both herself and her husband. Her paid maternity leave of three months, along with the presence of maids, gave her ample time to recuperate from her cesarean delivery and to reflect on the entire situation as "a trial that makes the family stronger."

With Milagros, the question had to be rephrased and pursued as she appeared not to grasp the point. Observe the following exchange:

How did the coming of the baby affect life at home? "We had maids the first few months. It was my recuperation that was a priority. By the way, I breast-fed for one year and two months."

Did you have to get up at night? "Yes. I did lose weight, too, perhaps because of that. But my mind was already set on breast-feeding because of the benefits to the child."

Did the baby's arrival mark a crisis at all? "No. Financially, maybe, but breast-feeding saves a lot. She's taking my milk from a bottle now."

It is only when the naturalization of motherhood is taken into account that Milagros' reaction makes perfect sense. She starts by talking about her recuperation, a priority that the maids were to ensure so that she could perform the maternal function of breast-feeding. Note her emphasis on its benefits for the child, its duration and continuation in bottle-feeding (the daughter is now 2 years, 4 months old), and its practicality as a saving scheme. As for the suggestion that the child's arrival might precipitate a crisis at home, that was comprehensible only on financial grounds.

When asked about the impact of the child on life in the public sphere of paid work, on the other hand, Milagros did not hesitate to say yes, it has affected her profession. Fortunately, a five-year fellowship has freed her from teaching, but mothering and the priority she has accorded it may prevent her from meeting the deadline for her dissertation. The choice between a Ph.D. and her children was put more bluntly before the other college instructor, Belen, by her 11-year-old son: "A Ph.D. or us?" Belen gave up the Ph.D.

Angela discovered that when she took her sick children to the office rather than miss work, her female supervisor, also a mother, was not so sympathetic: "She was well-off, and couldn't understand what I was going through." Marina declined the urging of her colleagues to go for the master teacher award, a title she held before marriage, knowing that it would detract her attention from her children. The ensuing raise in pay it would have brought mattered less. The impact on Zenaida, a pediatrician, was circumstantial; required to undergo a six-month rural internship, she left her 10-month-old child with her mother and found herself unable to concentrate on medical work. Because of the demands of breast-feeding, Rose (community organizer) felt as though she was being pulled in several directions, yet acknowledged that having a *yaya* to help was "one of the luxuries in the Philippines."

Once more, the acceptance of mothering work as natural, coupled with the presence of helping hands, alleviate the disruption that the coming of a newborn might cause at home. But the world of employment is not as hospitable and it is in this arena where the women with careers felt some ambivalence.

## Good and Bad of Motherhood

When the women were asked about the disadvantages of motherhood, only Carmina refused the question, reiterating her equation of marriage with children: "When you marry, you have kids, that's it. You can't look at it from a negative point of view." But the majority weighed the question carefully. A few of the career women underscored the restrictions imposed by children on their mobility, outside involvement, and on their time in general. Rose's longest separation from her children was four weeks when she was in the United States, in contrast to her husband who had spent three months in Canada. Lea, an office administrator with a master's degree, confessed that she often wondered how much she would have accomplished if she did not have five children, quickly adding that she was "not working for herself, after all, but for the family."

Those with less means spoke of the cost of bringing up children (food, milk, medicine) and the maintenance of their health. Young children, in particular, kept poor women from going out to earn a livelihood. Tesing admitted that when really hard-pressed, she wishes she did not have children at all, playfully quipping, "But then you think about the impossibility of putting them back where they came from." Still others spoke of the tremendous responsibility of "teaching the children well," a meritorious concern when offsprings' misconduct is seen to tarnish the family's reputation (Medina 1992: 196).

None of the women were reticent about mentioning their occasional frustrations with their children, such as when the children are quarrelling, rowdy, or stubborn. To the question, Did you ever have any moments of regret about being a mother? several of the women who answered "yes" referred to "moments when life is really hard," again referring to lack of money or employment or both. For Rose, it was one particular moment that stood out. After having stayed out late for three consecutive nights doing lobbying and then being refused a kiss by her son, she asked herself: "Is this right? Maybe I shouldn't have children. And I was pregnant with Maya then! I think it has to do with thinking you can be an A-1 mother, A-1 wife, and A-1 professional." Amalia's concerns bore slight connection with those of Rose and she had no room for regret about motherhood: "I wouldn't consider life without children. Look at my oldest; in a little while he can help us out."

Whether or not Amalia's children actually end up helping out as she hopes is for the future to disclose, but statistics bode well for her. Figures indicate that in 1986, urban poor children, aged 10–19, represented 16.1 percent of the labor force (*Situation of Children and Women in the Philippines* 1987: 75).

Predictably, it was when the women were asked about the advantages of having children and the pleasures of motherhood that they were the most effusive, energized, and voluble. Most of what they reported was touching, precisely because of their utter simplicity and dailiness. Many were unable to focus on a specific incident. Carmina referred to "the everyday rewards of motherhood." Lea expressed her fascination with the process of watching her children's development: "I think of the little joys of life, like their growing up, as magic. I feel it's magical, their growing up. You never know what your children will learn to do the next day." Beten said that she was happiest "when spending time with the family. I thank God for those moments when there are just the four of us, all in one bedroom, enjoying each other's company."

Delight in togetherness emerged as a pervasive theme in the women's responses, regardless of where they were situated in the social hierarchy. From Jinky who said she "felt alive when with my children" to Tesing who said, "I'm very happy when we're all together and I can kiss the children," to Amalia who described herself as being particularly happy "when my children are laughing and dancing, especially my fifth who likes to dance when he hears music from the neighbors," everyone concurred in "the everyday rewards of motherhood." Sometimes for Amalia, physical togetherness was not even necessary: "When you're alone by yourself and you think of your children, you feel very good. That's especially so when they're happy and not sick—there's no feeling like it."

Several women who singled out a particular event summoned memories of the delivery itself. Lilia, a former airline stewardness married to a Canadian, recalled her first view of the baby. Milagros remembered "the beauty of being fully conscious and holding the baby as soon as she came out." Others spoke of an occasion that demonstrated their achievement as mothers. Carmina was happy when her daughter delayed gratification by holding off on a soda when they were out together one day. Feliza spoke with pride about her son who topped his kindergarten class and of the day she was asked to march up to the stage with him. The awarding of her degree was a proud moment, too, for Lea: "I was receiving my master's, getting a promotion at work, and had these very cute children. I was so happy, too happy, that sometimes I think that was why my first husband died."

Bernardita distinguished between her feelings about marriage and about motherhood: "When I got married, I couldn't really say that I was happy. But as a mother, I'd stare at my child and observe her closely. I thought, this is what it's like to be a mother. I can't explain the happiness I felt."

The same sentiments were captured by Rose in the following portrait of maternal bliss. "When I was breast-feeding, I felt that my baby and I were both in our own little corner of the world together. I have a rocking chair upstairs. I was sitting there nursing Maya; Benjie was also on my lap. I thought to myself, this is really a picture of happiness and contentment."

## Ideal Mother

To draw out their conceptualizations of a good mother, I posed to the women a variety of questions, including what they thought a mother's most important functions were and whether motherhood entailed sacrifice. I discovered that I had to do this because, as encapsulated as they all were in maternal ideology, few had previously reflected on the subject. Several openly stated that, in truth, they had not thought about the status of motherhood at all; this included Tess, the bank officer, and Milagros, the college instructor. Indeed, why ruminate over what comes naturally? Consequently, a few of the statements elicited were initially abstract in character, such as, "a good mother is one who gives love and does everything" (Manuela), or, "a good mother is someone who sees to it that children are well directed in keeping with Filipino values" (Milagros). When asked about a mother's most important functions, however, the replies assumed a more concrete shape: "give enough to eat, even though life is hard"; "attend to them, not leave them by themselves"; "not delegate the care of sick children to the husband."

This turn of thought inevitably led to the subject of motherhood and self-sacrifice: were the two necessarily linked? The majority of the women believed that this was indeed the case, with no one feeling constrained about revealing her own sacrifices, large or small. Elvira defined motherhood as "a major test in life" and proceeded to detail how she has had to surrender dreams of travel and of further education ("Whatever you desire for yourself has to be set aside"). Marina referred to mothers' reproductive work, both biological and social ("conception, childbirth, and child-rearing"), as already a sacrifice. Tesing declared that "you really only know hardship once you have children," a rendition of motherhood with which I had become familiar through prior interviews with slum dwellers. Bernardita and Feliza both cautioned that to be a mother one must be prepared for problems—to meet the child's needs for money, love, and attention. The illness of children was specifically cited as extracting sacrifice from mothers. Belen and Amalia both recollected stressful experiences with their children's hospitalizations. For Belen it was an "emotional drain"; in Amalia's case, poverty forced her to run frantically from one hospital to another until she found one that would admit her son. Jinky negated the view of motherhood as an institution demanding sacrifice, claiming instead that "it's a win-win situation." But she comprehended the situation of mothers who, unlike herself, had to work outside the home from nine to five: "If I have to stay up for a sick child one night, I can sleep the following day."

For some women the subject of motherhood and sacrifice evoked thoughts of their own mothers and the never-ending job of mothering. Rose mentioned that she has not ceased to depend upon her mother for support and advice, and for help in childcare. As a community organizer concerned with forging new values, she was also aware of feminism: "I don't call my father to ask, can I leave my child with you?" The continued reliance of many of these women on their mothers or mothers-in-law made them acutely conscious of the endurance, indeed permanence, of the obligations they had embraced with their assumption of motherhood. When Tesing wept in response to this question, recollections of her dead mother, not her own motherly sacrifice, drew the tears: "How hard it is to raise children! So you really feel *utang na loob* (a debt of gratitude) to your mother because it is she who actually nurtured you."

While the women responded to the earlier set of questions with relative ease, discussing the topic of the good mother in many cases induced guilt feelings in those who also had active lives in the public sphere. Thus, Violy (executive secretary), Bernardita (garment worker), and Belen (college instructor) all declared that there were times when they fell short of their own ideas of good motherhood because employment detracted from the spontaneity of the loving that they could otherwise offer their children. Violy illustrated this by describing mornings when leave-takings were consistently hurried and children's patter silenced because of the mad rush for the office. No one was oblivious of perquisites passed up (promotions, bonuses, trips abroad) on behalf of the children, but each made certain to declare that if tensions ever mounted to a point where choices needed to be made, she would choose to abandon her career. Luckily for Violy, she is not confronted with that dilemma at the moment (her husband sends money from Saudi Arabia, but it is not sufficient): "Of course you can go to work and be a good mother, too. Some say you give quality time, not just quantity. But I think, to be honest, you can't really be a good mother when you have little time for your children and you're so tired. Of course I don't want to stay home all the time. You can't watch Betamax all the time or you'll get fat."

## CONCLUSION

In reviewing the above data, it must be stated that the repertoire of responses given by these nineteen women falls squarely within the conventional categories of thinking about marriage, motherhood, family, and children in the Philippines. That marriage is the most normal state for women and men and that children are an essential part of that union (Tiglao-Torres 1990: 110; Illo and Polo 1990: 104; Medina 1991: 193); the primacy of reproductive work over women's other roles (Israel-Sobritchea 1990: 32; Lopez-Rodriguez 1990: 22); self-sacrifice as the woman's, not the man's duty (Medina 1991: 133); the extension of parental obligations after children's marriages (Illo and Polo 1990: 80): all these are commonplace assumptions in Philippine society. In this sense, the representatives of this cross-class sample is validated.

Exactly how do these and other ideas expressed by the women shape their lives as mothers and also their experiences of mothering? I should repeat here that I undertook these interviews for the express purpose of uncovering how maternal ideology functions to oppress women; as a result of an earlier collection of life stories, I had assumed that women's acceptance of the household gender division of labor was undergirded primarily by maternal ideology. With this in mind, in the current study I attempted to probe women's perceptions of motherhood and the ways in which these affect their experiences of the work of mothering. The resulting interviews give me no reason to doubt my previous assumption that maternal ideology holds the key to women's acquiescence to cultural expectations of appro-

priate gender behavior. It also ought to be clear from the foregoing discussions that it is the naturalization of motherhood to which all the women
subscribe that profoundly affects their conduct and molds their thinking
about themselves and their performance as women and as mothers. Now
whether, and to what extent, this essentialism operates to subordinate
women is a more vexing issue in light of the women's narrations.

Above all, the genuine pleasure felt by the women in the task of mothering cannot be ignored. For the poor women, the lack of other sources of
satisfaction magnifies these pleasurable moments, despite the fact that joy-
ful events are always tempered by memories of suffering, as when children
are ill or there is no food. For the women with means, the work of mothering can shift more readily from an emphasis on the instrumental to the
affective. In all cases, the value placed on children by Philippine society as
a whole and the mutual dependence marking parent-child relations creates
an atmosphere for mothering that can only be described as favorable. When
mutual parent-child obligations that are the societal norm are taken into
account, notions of maternal sacrifice acquire a practical slant and traditional sermons that preach the sanctity of family ties become demystified.
Thus, the assertion that "you only begin to know hardship when you become a mother" begins to take on a multitude of meanings.

At the same time that essentialism pervades their thinking, these women
have not been deprived of a strong practical sense that daily life must be
managed; to manage, after all, is their chief assignment. The naturalization
of motherhood, then, combines with a keen cognizance of social reality and
causes mothers with careers to perform an intricate "juggling act" (Tess
and Rose). This act of balancing mothering work with paid work, while
exerting stress, needs to be recognized as a finely honed skill that also
provides gratification. Belen, who gave up her Ph.D. and claimed willing-
ness to abandon her career if necessary, also comprehended that home life
alone would stultify her—and so did her husband, who urged her to hold
on to teaching. In short, the internalization of maternal ideology gives
women pleasure in mothering work; but satisfaction derived from talents
exercised elsewhere (as well as in the balancing act itself) belies declarations
that their outside employment is undertaken for their families and not for
themselves—ironically, an assertion typical of patriarchs. An uncritical sub-
scription to maternalism, without a doubt, can only perpetuate women's
subservience, as in the advice Belen would offer her daughter in adulthood:
"Know your duty or function—do it to avoid conflicts in the house." But
commitment to the movement for social transformation fashions new view-
points and forces Rose to discern the challenge in the imperative to bridge
private and public worlds: "The movement for social change is really so
demanding—I wish it were not so. We want to reshape our society for our
children, but we have to be very conscious about balancing the time we
spend with them and with our work because they could grow up in a

changed society and not know the values of fairness, honesty, and justice because we were not there to share these values with them."

The world of mothers we have glimpsed is thus far removed from that of the industrial West where the practice of mothering in isolated, nuclear, middle-class households invariably fosters feelings of dependence, alienation, demobilization, and loss of control in women (Minturn and Lambert 1964; Comer 1974; Oakley 1980; Boulton 1983; Rich 1986; Lewis 1981; Dally 1982). The presence of kin or household help and a set of values that places a premium on social interdependence (Lopez 1991: 3), or family centeredness versus a focus on the individual (Guthrie 1961: 44), need to be acknowledged as resulting in an environment congenial to the work of mothering. Such a statement is by no means intended to gloss over conflicting gender interests that underlie conceptions of family unity inscribed in the popular consciousness. It is merely to assert caution in uncritically adopting feminist paradigms imported from the West, particularly as applied to a neocolonial formation like the Philippines. That feminist theories of motherhood do not have universal validity (Hill Collins 1994) and that women themselves are engaged daily in social constructions of mothering (Glenn 1994) should be seriously considered.

To conclude, in spite of the material pressures that the raising of children exerts on the great majority of women in a developing country, the work of mothering is at once burdensome and yet an unequalled source of joy. This is not to deny the impact of class standing; but whether a poor squatter dweller or an executive wife, the women in this sample seem to experience, in their own peculiar ways, genuine pleasure in mothering. Here the presentation of social constructions like family and motherhood as natural in a society with feudal features has to be accounted for. Indeed, the women's vocabulary surrounding mothering reflects this naturalization. Perhaps the fact that all these women subscribe in varying degrees to popular mythologies that romanticize and idealize motherhood attenuates whatever hardships they actually experience. In other circumstances the force of this maternal ideology, as documented by feminists in the industrial West, has proven quite oppressive. But in the Philippines, maternal ideology is articulated in salutary fashion, with the material and moral support of kin (and, in the middle class, household help) and women's own grasp of social reality, making motherhood and mothering their own rewards.

## NOTE

I wish to thank the nineteen women who graciously shared their accounts of mothering with me, along with my generous feminist friends in Manila who led me to them. Names and occupations have been changed in order to protect these women's identities. This study was aided by a grant from the Faculty of Research Council of Bowling Green State University in the summer of 1991.

# PART III

# A Challenge to Capitalist Development

# 11

# The Case of Mauritania: Women's Productive Activities in Urban Areas—A Process of Empowerment

*Gisèle Simard*

## INTRODUCTION

More than being a part of the monetary economy and an important source of revenue, urban microenterprises are becoming a way of life for African women as they learn to live with and from them. In fact, microenterprises are places of multiple apprenticeships for women—socially, politically, and economically—where they experiment with autonomy, negotiation, and transformation of the social contract. As a result, they learn to become entrepreneurs, discover the power of solidarity, and reconstruct ethnic and gender relations.

In this chapter, I argue that the classical studies, inspired by neoliberal models and economic notions of productivity, are limited and disregard this type of activity as being productive. I show that the fluidity and complexity of the reality of women small entrepreneurs must be understood within the perspective of a cultural rationality[1] rather than of a strictly economic one.

This research focuses on the urban tradeswomen in the field of beauty, which includes the veil, pearls, and henna, in Mauritania. First, I discuss the limits of the productivity model. Second, by revising both Barth's model of entrepreneurs and the analysis of gender relations, I develop a multidimensional framework to understand the reality of the tradeswomen. In the third section, I present an analysis of the findings from the case study.

Finally, I conclude that women's productive activities are an efficient means of establishing equilibrium in gender relations.

## WOMEN'S URBAN MICROENTERPRISES: A REALITY THAT ESCAPES THE PRODUCTIVITY MODEL

### Reductionist Logic

For the analysis of the informal sector,[2] economic rationality has, in many ways, demonstrated its limits. Within the linear and binary framework, the informal economy is seen as a transitional phase in economic development. This is reductionistic logic and does not reflect living reality. In fact, far from disappearing, today's informal economy is widespread in all types of activities, not only in developing countries but also in the Occident.

The articulation, evaluation, and measurement of the informal sector, much like its conceptualization, also have been deficient. The econometric model was a failure, given its view of urban work as a closed system, cut from "outside-production," and detached from social relations and new experiences in the city.[3] Furthermore, this model categorizes workers in the informal sector according to a number of inapplicable criteria. These criteria include: using wage earners as the base; resorting to national census and sectorial statistics; and employing long questionnaires and complex mathematical equations. The use of these criteria created major shortcomings and, in particular, ensured the invisibility of women.

### Women's Invisibility

Women's presence in the urban informal sector was barely noted in the seventies (Sethuraman 1981: 166). It has only been since the eighties that statistics have been divided by gender, that methods of data collection other than macroeconomic indicators have been used, and that qualitative approaches based on case studies or microanalysis have given women the right to speak. As a result, the large proportion of women working in the informal sector, and their contribution to the economy, began to appear as a bursting phenomenon. In fact, it is estimated that hours of work for women are 28 percent to 33 percent higher than those for men (Bisilliat and Fieloux 1983; Tinker 1987). Small trade is the principal occupation of women in the urban African centers south of the Sahara, accounting for up to 95 percent of the women in the labor force (Coquery-Vidrovitch 1994: 171–77).

It is difficult to grasp and evaluate women's production in small African enterprises whose survival is linked to communities' solidarity, offerings, barter, auto-consumption, and social transactions. In these enterprises "symbolic relations, professional rituals, and non-productive socializing"

(Bouvier 1989: 7) are as important as economic transactions. In such typical contexts the rigidity of the economic rationality, which tends "to restrict the merchant's dynamic to a given time and the highest possible return" (Gorz 1968: 168) becomes more apparent. Within the framework of the neoliberal model, one is forced to conclude that women's work is characterized by low productivity, lack of return, and deficiency in management, which is, in a pejorative sense, seen as "social management of excesses."

To avoid this pitfall, we require a multidimensional approach that grasps women entrepreneurs' situation, seeks to understand their cultural rationality, and takes into account all aspects of their lives within a global perspective.[4]

## A MULTIDIMENSIONAL PERSPECTIVE FOR UNDERSTANDING THE CULTURAL RATIONALITY OF WOMEN ENTREPRENEURS

Microenterprises are a way of life for African women. They are a creative fusion of the social and economic elements based on women's productive work. They present themselves like the market of social and kinship relationships constituting a "mode of production" and solidarity that generate "surplus value." These productive activities also constitute a space for negotiating the identity of women and are a means of establishing a new equilibrium of gender relations.

In order to grasp the fluidity and complexity of this reality we can use Barth's model of entrepreneurs from his anthropology of work (1972), together with the analysis of gender relations in feminist anthropology. However, both of these models are rather theoretical and nonoperational, and are ill-adapted to field studies. In order to compensate for these problems, it proved necessary to develop a flexible multidimensional tool that adopts a feminist-biographical approach, starting from tradeswomen's views and favoring women's subjective life. That is what I hope to have accomplished through my doctoral research and I think it will be an appreciable methodological contribution, useful not only for researchers, but also for practitioners in the field.

According to Barth, goods obtained through entrepreneurial activities are not restricted to monetary or material domains; they also take the form of power, social rank, experience, and ability. Barth uses the term *profit* to represent all these forms of reward. This model gives priority to the observation of the entrepreneur in his community, where individual actors are engaged in a series of transactions in a dynamic of social change. This model was used only for men in small ethnic communities of northern Norway working in agriculture and fishing. It was neither applied to women entrepreneurs nor to an African context. Given its holistic character and its relevance, I attempt to complete and adapt this model to my case study.

Barth's model combines three elements of observation: (1) the ecologic situation (the entrepreneur's position in his environment); (2) the social structure (mapping social costs and systems of exchange); (3) the strategies and conditions of success. Barth's model, however, has three weaknesses: (1) it is difficult, if not impossible, to operationalize; (2) the concept is not well articulated and no means of data collection are suggested; and (3) the strategies and conditions of success are vague and do not question relations of power.

## Barth's Model Adapted and Completed

Keeping the above comments in mind, I have adapted and completed Barth's model. I have constructed four profiles of trading women: The first two, sociological and economic profiles, are quantitative and replace Barth's ecological environment, and the last two, anthropological and gender profiles, are more qualitative and have been elaborated to articulate gender and social structure, as well as help to operationalize the strategies.[5]

This research, which took place over a period of four years (1990–1994), combined several techniques of data collection: nonsystematic observations and a diary (referring to various stages of the social reality of the trading women); systematic observations of women on production sites and within their families; repeated in-depth interviews lasting from two to six hours each (I met with each woman three times to create a trusting bond and to increase the information collected); photo albums of women; a double polling of the verbal exchanges; and focus groups (group discussions with trading women on controversial subjects such as the wearing of the veil, beauty, seduction, and the power of trading women).

To construct a representative sample that was coherent and in which subjects recognized themselves (Bertaux 1980: 216), technical folders containing quantitative information and keywords were developed while collecting data. In more than two-thirds of the cases, the contents were validated by our sample of trading women during several meetings with them.

The sample of my doctoral research contained sixty women entrepreneurs. They were involved in the trading of the veil, henna, and pearls. These three strictly feminine activities bring added value and constitute the triad thread of beauty at Nouakchott, the Mauritanian capital.

## CASE STUDY IN MAURITANIA

### Context

Mauritania is a little or little known country that is difficult to approach without a preconception. It is a country of paradox, located both within and south of the Sahara. It is Arab and white while geographically located in black Africa. It is part of both Sahel, a Muslim country where the women are lightly veiled, and Maghreb, an Islamic republic that gives priority to liberal democracy and is in the process of implementing social consensus.[6] It is also a country with a long history, ascending from the Paleolithic era (20,000 years before the Christian era), marked by tribal wars as well as by cultural or religious hegemony. This country, which somehow shows little influence of colonization, can best be summarized as "the administration of emptiness and of teacup politics" (Balans 1979: 280).

With an area as big as Mali,[7] the population of Mauritania (2,311,000 inhabitants)[8] is approximately four times less than that of its bordering state. Its population distribution, with 90 percent of the country desert, is very uneven: one-third of its area is uninhabitable.

The majority population group in Mauritania, estimated at 80 percent, includes the Beidanes or white Moors and the Haratines or black Moors. Both groups are from Arabic-Berberian[9] and speak the Hassanian dialect (PNUD: 1991). The minority group (20%) is composed of African blacks[10] (Peuhls, Toucouleurs, Soninkés, and Wolofs). Almost 35 percent of Mauritania's population is concentrated in two urban areas (Nouakchott and Nouadhibou). The informal sector represents approximately a quarter of the working force and more than three-quarters of the urban population. In the business sector, 80 percent of the transactions are conducted by women.

Colonial penetration in Mauritania differed from that of other African states since it originated from the south (De Chassey 1984: 48). Until its independence in 1960, the administrative capital of Mauritania was Saint-Louis of Senegal. Colonization came late and was slowed by persistent resistance,[11] and thus its impact was minimal.[12]

The traditional Moorish society was nomadic, stratified, and very much influenced by its trading customs and pastoral way of life. However, since the major droughts of the 1970s the population has become mostly sedentary: In 1965, three out of four persons were nomads, while today, we can count only one out of ten,[13] resulting in deep sociological changes and rendering the description of this society generated in the 1950s and 1960s obsolete.

## Mauritanian Women, None Quite like Them

The social position of Mauritanian women has always been recognized as particular and privileged as cited by several authors (De Puigaudeau 1992; Tillion 1966; De Chassey 1977; Tauzin 1982, 1988; and Caratini 1993). The power of the Moorish women, which is not always revealed in the macroeconomic statistics, shows itself in the observation and analysis of certain zones of freedom (Simard 1990). We can particularly cite:

- *Monogamy*: Moorish women, despite the fact that the Muslim religion allows polygamy, demand and receive monogamy as a condition of marriage;
- *Young girl's names*: a woman who marries keeps her maiden name and does not adopt her husband's name;
- *Divorce*: the divorce rate is 37 percent, twice as high as that of other Arabic-Muslim countries (Tunisia, Morocco, Syria), with divorce often initiated or requested by the woman, even though Islamic law concedes this privilege only to men;
- *Nonexistence of conjugal violence*: the occurrence of conjugal violence is either rare or nonexistent among Moorish couples, where a certain tenderness emerges in the man-woman relationship probably due to the fact that the preferred spouse is a cousin who is considered like a loved and protected sister. In cases of physical or even verbal aggression from her husband, the wife can demand a divorce;
- *Redeeming of the dowry*: in instances of divorce, the wife's family is not compelled to reimburse the dowry;
- *Remarriage*: the rate of remarriage is 72.5 percent: 20 percent of women remarry twice, 6 percent three times, and 3 percent four or more times. The divorced and remarried woman is not ostracized by society, as is the case in the majority of Muslim and African countries. On the contrary, she appears more seductive in men's eyes. The example of an ideal wife is not that of the mother but, instead, that of the "Chebiba," a star that every man would like to court;
- *Women as family heads*: 36.5 percent at the national level and 38.7 percent in Nouakchott indicates one of the highest rates in Africa. Even though this responsibility is recognized in reality but not by law, Moorish women as heads of households are not forced to accept the guardianship of a man (clan's elder). Considering the long-term absence of their spouses, they can make major decisions, such as approving the weddings of their children;
- *Right to speak in public*: young or old, women, in the same manner as the elders, can speak in public even in the presence of men. In addition, it is well accepted that a woman might contradict her husband or an older woman.
- *The possibility for women to accumulate wealth*: women can assume autonomous control over wealth, including the land they inherit. As a rule, Moorish women have no obligation to contribute to housekeeping;
- *Privileged status of young girls*: contrary to most countries where one observes the double weight of being born a girl and poor, the status of young Mauritanian girls is privileged. The family gives them food before the boys, tending to spoil them while encouraging austerity for boys, and the girls are not compelled to do hard labor. Girls are socialized to resist men whereas boys are taught to please women.

In Moorish society, the capacity to manipulate men's desires is recognized as proof of feminine intelligence (Tauzin 1988: 34). In a similar context, beauty and seduction, besides often being associated with the Arabic culture (Couchard 1994), assume a particular importance.

Moorish men are, in general, slim, but this is not the case for women, whose round bodies are appreciated. There are many Hassanian proverbs that link women's beauty with being round.

In their daily lives and despite changes inherent to modernity, women always accord a great importance to beauty and seduction. That is why their presence is prominent in certain types of commercial activities such as the sale of women's clothing (the veil, in Mauritania), makeup (henna), and jewelry (pearls). These activities constitute the production of added value, almost entirely at the hands of women, and they appear as an extension of their identity rather than as simple consumption goods.

### The Veil

Moorish women wear the veil (*melehfa* in Hassania). It is a light and transparent fabric, six meters in length by one and one-half meters in width, embellished by geometric patterns and multiple coloring. Women tie it first on their shoulders, much like a tunic, in order to drape their bodies and cover their heads. It is their daily garment and it assumes multiple meanings:

- *Religious meaning*: the *melehfa* responds to the Islamic requirement demanding that a woman cover her body;
- *Sign of beauty and seduction*: women believe that the veil embellishes them and makes them more seductive. As opposed to the *chador*, whose objective is to homogenize women, thus making them all look alike, the *melehfa* allows women to keep their specific characteristics by adding their personal touches through the choice of colors, designs, and the gestures to which they associate;
- *Ecological meaning*: the *melehfa* is an appropriate garment for the Saharan climate as it ensures protection against the heat and sand winds;
- *Political meaning*: women say that the *melehfa* is their nationality. In this respect, they neglect the fact that 20 percent of the Mauritanian population is of black African origin and women of this group do not wear the veil, even if they are Muslim. This is an example of how ethnicity is confused with nationality;
- *Economic meaning*: the veil has an economic importance, since all Moorish women wear it from adolescence and must often replace it, given its short durability, after two or three washings. I have estimated its economic impact, and for the city of Nouakchott alone, based on three hypotheses, it would yield one to three million Canadian dollars monthly.

The three most prosperous veil traders at Nouakchott are, at the same time, fashion designers. Like the best French, British, or American designers, they launch many fashions that are then copied by the smaller trading women who do not have either the money or the creativity of the bigger traders. They derive their inspiration from the sociopolitical life of their country; we might even claim that they eventually outline its history.

Overall, it is estimated that women manufacture and commercialize about 95 percent of the veil.[14] Men intervene as wholesalers in the purchase of the basic fabric (imported from India or Pakistan), as creditors for merchandise, and as laborers employed by the trading women for various operations linked to sewing and dying (soaking, ironing). This is a women's field, where men traders are considered intruders, incompetents, or employment thieves. Mauritanian women have strongly denounced, and even boycotted, men who tried to have veils manufactured in Pakistan by copying the designs conceived by Mauritanian fashion designers, and who, by selling them at reduced prices, created unfair competition for women traders.

More than being a women's business, the veil trade has other rules that are respected by everyone: the quality of the product, customer satisfaction, the absence of advertisement,[15] and agreement on established rates.

### Pearls

Pearls[16] constitute the second part of the triad of Moorish beauty, where the symbolic value is often converted into commercial value, given all the meanings women have invested in it since its origin.

Precious or semiprecious pearls were amassed during wars and tribal conquests. Warriors looted the pearls from each conquered tent and camp and brought them back home; it was the women, mothers or wives, who shared the precious pillage. Often, women of the conquered tribes would hide their pearls in pottery vases or small caskets and bury them in the sand to prevent their discovery by enemies. The legend of pearls found in the sand was born fifty or one hundred years after these tribal wars.

In traditional society, pearls represented a prestigious asset and served as an exchange currency: one could trade a palm grove for pearls and give a *buzrada* to buy a slave. One could resell pearls and regain one's money. It is customary to say that in reselling, one would get double the original price. Although the commercial value of pearls is recognized in Mauritania, this does not appear to be the case outside Mauritania. Given that there is no universal standard to evaluate pearls, as in the case of gold and diamonds, their commercial value might not be agreed upon by foreign financial markets. We could buy a pearl necklace, valued at $10,000 in Mauritania, and discover that its trading value in Canada, the United States, or elsewhere is close to worthless.

The world of pearls in Mauritania is a mythical universe whose multiple symbols, at times, vacillate between the registers of conservation and the changing of the system.

Pearls contribute, in part, to mark ceremonies in the passage of women's lives, as inscribed in the customs of beauty and seduction. In fact, it is quite customary to offer pearls at significant stages of a young girl's development: birth, first teething,[17] puberty, wearing of the veil, wedding, and in the life of the married woman: entrance into the conjugal household, birth of a child, husband's return from travel, and so forth.

Furthermore, the trading of pearls confirms the power of women's ability in the men's universe, like that of the cadi and that of the marabout. When it comes to litigation and testifying in court concerning pearls, the opinion of a single pearl-lady suffices; there is no need to consult another woman or man, as stipulated in Sharia. If a pearl-lady gives a pearl to a person, she can also transfer her "baraka" or chance, as a great marabout has the same power by other means (gift of saliva or benediction). This knowledge, highly valued in Moorish society, is transmitted from mother to daughter.

### Henna

Henna is the last of the triad thread of beauty that inserts itself in the spiral of seduction. It seems that no man can resist the combined effects of a nice veil, pearls, and henna.

Henna is an arborescent shrub. From its bark and dried, pulverized leaves, a yellowish powder with various properties is prepared, of which the dye is the best known. This shrub grows in the shadow of date palm trees. Mauritania is a culture dominated by women who control the entire process, up to the sale in plastic bags displayed on tables at the market.

The henna treatment is generally given in parlors, operated by five or six women who are specialists in this occupation. The treatment involves decorating hands and feet[18] with geometric patterns resembling a fine lace or rich illumination, cleverly sheared. The process, which includes preparation and drying, can last two to seven hours, depending on the complexity of the chosen design.

Henna's origin dates back to the "Book."[19] It is said that the prophet Brahim (Abraham) had two wives, one of whom was black. The first wife was jealous and had her co-wife wear braids and put on henna to make her unattractive and unpleasant to her husband. She discovered, on the contrary, that her husband's love for the black woman with braids and henna was increased because he found her pretty and desirable. Therefore, jealousy is the origin of henna.

Henna is also referred to in the history of Joseph, who was sold by his brothers to an Arabian caravan. The king gave this slave to his wife who fell in love with him, as he was extremely beautiful. Other women would tease her and reproach her for not showing them such a handsome man. One day, while the female servants were preparing vegetables, she asked Joseph to drop by. They all saw him and were so astounded by his beauty that they began to gash their hands instead of cutting the vegetables. It is from here that the legend of the lines on the hands originated and how the putting on of henna started, following the contoured lines of the hand.

Since then, designs and techniques have evolved considerably. The use of thin strips of adhesive plaster helps to achieve all kinds of creative prowess (snake, fish, mosque, tam-tam, etc.). Henna reveals the Arabian identity of the Moorish women as well as the vitality of the central motherly cell composed of the mother, her daughters, and nieces. At the production level, the mother-daughter bonds are valorized for many reasons: (1) the knowledge of the elders of the central motherly cell (mother, grandmother, or aunt) is transferred to the young woman who recognizes its value and technical nature; (2) the trust and complicity sought are easily put in place, whether in a professional exchange (replacement in case of sickness), mutual aid (affective support in case of afflictions, loans, children's care after school), or mutual understanding (love, relaxation, enjoyment of being together); (3) all income and profits remain within the family and are used to improve the living conditions of its members.

From the four profiles (sociological, economic, anthropological, and gender) that were addressed, based on the approach described earlier, three salient elements surfaced: the cleavages between the groups of trading women, the fullness of the social redistribution, and the importance of nonmonetary transactions.

### Economic Cleavages among Trading Women

A distinct economic cleavage can be observed between the more prosperous and the smaller trading women, manifested in the potential profit per month. Profit is eight times higher for the first group (private shops in the market) than for the second one (public stalls at the market). When compared with the poverty level as defined by the DSA (adjustment of social dimensions) project of 32,800 ouguiyas or UM[20] yearly, per person, in a household, it appears that the trading women of the second group barely earn 37,299 UM, while those of the first group make at least 297,000 UM. Therefore, we can state that the activities of the trading women with private shops produce the wealth, while those from the public stalls in the market do not generate profits and remain at survival level. This is the case for those conveniently called "informal sector shelter." This cleavage can be explained, in part, by three factors:

1. Level of education and on-the-job training. Women in the first group have almost three times the education and have benefited from a basic apprenticeship (initiation into the business by the father, mother, sister, or cousin) four times more often than women in the second group.

2. Starting capital. The most successful trading women invested an initial amount three times that of the smaller traders ($702 as opposed to $201) and nearly

doubled their initial capital, whereas the profit for the others falls below their starting capital. Given that the monthly volume of business for the women of the first group is eight times that of the second group and that the inventory of the first group is twenty times that of the second one, we can assume that a starting capital, leading to a profitable level, must be much higher than $150 or $200 and should be close to $500 to $700.

3. Extension of social networks. The more prosperous trading women have extended social networks. They have relatives and friends in public positions and in the business world who guarantee them regular customers from within and outside their tribes. In this way, they can rely on a steady income. This is not the case for the small traders who are supported by a limited kinship network and who have to be satisfied with casual customers in fluctuating numbers.

### Extent of the Social Redistribution

This research provides evidence that the income of the trading women increases as their number of dependents grows; it is almost twice as high for the more wealthy women entrepreneurs as for the others. This shows that the importance of social transfers increases with growth in wealth. However, it is difficult to measure the extent of this social redistribution since the notion of a dependent has not been defined in terms of expenses, as was the case for the national poverty level. Although we can certainly assume that the trading women of the first group, who claim to have eighteen dependents, are not fully, but partially in charge of their expenditures (food, clothing, medication, education, gifts for birthdays, and special events). Two potential hypotheses were carefully developed indicating that the expenses of this social solidarity can reach a proportion varying from 40 to 53 percent of the potential profit of the trading women. This is equivalent to a high income tax. It is an approximate average, but nevertheless provides evidence of the extent of the social redistribution, confirming, therefore, the reputation of the legendary solidarity of Mauritanian men and women.

In the case of the smaller trading women who have a very narrow operating margin (approximately 5,000 UM above the national poverty level), we can postulate that the solidarity expenses, which they assume for the benefit of their declared dependents (totaling 9), force them below the poverty level.

The power of solidarity, acquired by the redistribution of their wealth, has two opposing positive elements for the trading women: (1) a regular clientele, as seen before, that guarantees a stable income; and (2) a group of followers, more and more widespread, that creates prestige in this world of seduction where the rule is to please the largest number of, preferably influential, people.

### Importance of Nonmonetary Transactions

Nonmonetary transactions are a strong means of transforming a business exchange into a social relation. Whether it is a gift, loan, or commercial transaction, the trading women avoid at all costs concluding a transaction that could endanger their social links. They prefer to prolong the interaction, under a number of conditions, and to create links. They provide: credit[21] for refundable merchandise and voluntary renewal at a later time; acquisitions in foreign countries for services rendered in Mauritania; and profit-sharing loans, as opposed to immediate repayment. The highlight of these transactions is the negotiation that combines three forms of exchange: barter, cash, and profit (in kind or its equivalent).

As Sahlins' model (1976) postulates, the trading women avoid negative reciprocity (impersonal economic exchange, perceived as a form of non-sociability), seeking instead, balanced reciprocity (exchange with equivalent benefits). To achieve such a goal, they proceed tentatively and often release a large sum of money before they perfect their system. This is the case with nonrefundable credit for customers judged to be reliable; giving rebates, in vain, to relatives who had to demonstrate their loyalty to the trader; and giving gifts to women who do not need them (because they have money), or who do not display their gratitude by bringing in new customers. In other cases it is more difficult to reach an equilibrium, as with used merchandise, in which the evaluation stands on hazy criteria and could be detrimental if hidden faults are later discovered.

Nonetheless, general reciprocity, as Sahlins defines it, is not frequent. In extreme cases (only one woman mentioned it), the goods rotate unilaterally, favoring the impoverished population. The pure, altruistic gift appears to be rather rare and compensation is usually expected; or it is the unconditional support of the poorest that can be perceived as courtier's actions (visits at birthdays, weddings, births or deaths, gifts of little value, small services rendered); or it is God's benediction which, in reward for this generosity, will spread its goodness on the family and tribe.

### Formalize or Not? A Debate to Overcome

In summary, all the trading women's behaviors ascribe to a coherent and articulated logic, tending to set up a "credit notoriety" (Bourdieu 1972: 239), which forces them to abandon the dichotomy of economic versus noneconomic, theory versus practice, and, instead, leads them to subscribe to the total compatibility of symbolic profits (individual, familial, and ethnic), regardless of its material components.

However, it is difficult not to ask the classical question, Must this informal business by women, which has such a considerable economic potential, be formalized or regulated? My analysis suggests that we must resist this temptation for two main reasons: First, the field of beauty is strongly engraved in the Moorish culture and the entrepreneurial women assert themselves as the guardians of the values of Mauritanian society (beauty, seduction, tenderness, solidarity, tolerance, greeting, philosophy, and joy of life), and second, the field of beauty serves as a societal anchor for the trading women and as a means of affirming their autonomy. It is the opposite of the virilocal, endogamous, and patrilineal system that leads to a principle of equality amid unequal relationships.

If we were to formalize the beauty business, the actual products that are an extension of women's identity would become ordinary consumer goods, not only making this ritual ordinary, but also affecting women's condition. Women could, in fact, become excluded from these activities and men could totally take over, forcing women to return to their private world, as in certain other Muslim countries.

## CONCLUSION

This research conducted among the woman entrepreneurs of Mauritania has demonstrated that in the urban environment their productive activities are an efficient means of establishing equilibrium in gender relations. Although these activities are totally dominated by women, an incursive pheonomenon in the men's world arises in parallel, where the conditions are negotiated in a perpetual fashion in the renewal of the social contract.

The wealth or opulence that provide access to economic power and the notoriety that allows for the assertion of political power are two important societal stakes. In the competitive struggle to have access to them, the trading women dispense major assets, such as their personal work, their generosity, and their wealth or richness of heart. They attach great value to these assets and to the different solidarities that ensure them support and popularity. Their initial capital and basic training complement this list.

To attain their economic goals, the trading women make use of men as means of access to certain resources that are hard to obtain or control: credit, raw materials, hard labor. As for their political goals, they are recognized for their competence as women and their contribution to the community, provided that they remain guardians of the tradition and nurturers of the system. In this manner, the women small entrepreneurs are both the agents of conservation and of change in the society, where only a subtle dosage of traditionalism and innovation is the guarantee for the maintenance of their influential power.

The various strategies that women develop, throughout their production activities, are engraved in the affirmation of an identity process, enabling them to grow as persons and to expand their autonomy. In this way, they become an effective means of struggle against Islamic fundamentalism. The Mauritanian women can describe themselves as social actors who play

against power and reestablish the balance between all types of power relations.

## NOTES

1. Cultural rationality is a holistic concept, as opposed to the concept of economic rationality, that limits the rationality of human beings to utilitarian terms
(calculation of maximization), for individual benefit in isolation of the social actors
(De Romana 1989).

2. One can index a long string of studies in the formal sector since the 1970s.
It amounts to the same for the definition of this concept. In this case, refer to Ilenda
Mbemba's synthesis, of the Centre Sahel de l'Universite Laval (1989: 4–12). In this
chapter, the term *informal sector* is used for reason of convenience, as proposed by
Charmes (1983: 94).

3. Several authors have dealt with this problem, in particular, De Seve 1982;
Boulding 1983; Michel 1985; Mignot-Lefebvre 1985.

4. See Simard 1994.

5. The sociological profile includes ten variables: age, ethnicity and tribe, region
of origin, education, civil status, number of marriages, length of marriage, number
of children, number of dependents, and residential pattern.

The economic profile also contains several variables: number of years in business,
import-export activities, tontine (informal credit) membership, starting capital and
its source, monthly sales (by number), inventory, prior work experience, and trading initiatives. Finally, I provide a newly designed index: the monthly potential
profit which will be compared to the national poverty level in order to understand
the wealth produced through trading women's activities.

Barth's social structure was revised and simplified into a new anthropological
profile composed of four indicators: (1) perceptions and anticipations of the community: the importance of women's small trade, differences between the trading
men and women, meaning of the feminine production (origin, evolution, problems,
solidarity network linked to the production, and reproduction); (2) wealth and
expectations of the community: the perception of wealth and its manifestations,
expectations resulting from the wealth and poverty at the family and tribal levels;
(3) forbidden and successful models: denials to the trading women by their husband, family, or religion; successful models of business related to women entrepreneurs and their ethnicity; and (4) exchange systems: importance of nonmonetary
transactions, search for reciprocities, objectives, conditions, and concrete examples
(gifts, presents, rebates, credits, trading of services, and other forms). The triple
way diagram of Sahlins (1976) was used here as a reference point.

Assuming that women's identity is a constantly developing evolutionary process,
a gender profile was outlined. This shed light on the strategies that women developed to increase their spheres of power in relation to men, women, and children.
After multiple attempts, more or less satisfactory, a method was adopted and titled
"album of marriages, divorces, and remarriages." Based on the biographical approach, the trading women were invited to describe their first marriage and divorce,
their second marriage and divorce, and their subsequent marriages, while identifying the changes they experienced in their choice of spouse, space of freedom, and

the pattern of seduction. Through these accounts, questions were inserted on the importance of the marriage (husband, child, single or multiple marriages, single or multiple divorces, denial of marriage, denial of divorce), relationship between men and women (image of ideal husband, ideal wife, criteria of beauty for a man and a woman, expression of love), and the importance of child (desired sex, status of young girls, changes in the life of the mother and in the lives of her daughters, children's custody in case of divorce).

6. A democratic government was elected in 1991, with one parliament and two chambers, and an opposition made up of approximately fifteen parties. In parallel, the free press, which *Jeune Afrique* (No. 1672, January 1993: 57) qualified as "the most free Maghreb," progressively set up its influence. Almost two hundred titles are registered from which we can count about twenty regular publications.

7. Mali: 464,373 sq. miles; Mauritania: 452,700 sq. miles.

8. "La Mauritanie en chiffres." National Statistics Office, 1993, p. 6.

9. Hassania is a dialect closely related to Arabic. The white migration, Berberian or Arabic, came from the north: North Africa (Maghreb and Egypt) and the Orient (Arabia and Yemen).

10. The black migration came from the south, with the movement of the first great empires of Occidental Africa, which controlled the gold trade: Ghana, Mali, and Shongai.

11. Mauritania is the only country south of the Sahara where Christian missionaries did not venture.

12. Independence took place in a state of destitution of equipment and qualified personnel without equivalent in the other French colonies of the African continent. We even say that the Independence was signed in a tent, given that no administrative building had been constructed by the French.

13. "Rapport national de la Mauritanie pour la Quatrième conférence des femmes: Lutte pour l'égalité, le développement et la paix, Pékin, septembre 1995," Islamic Republic of Mauritania, October 1994, p. 3.

14. No veil-trading women appear in the repertory of small enterprises (no registration) and, to that effect, are neither registered at the national accounts department nor at the national social security register. Even if the number of female traders has not been officially counted, it is estimated that it has substantially grown since the 1980s. It is even said that all women sell veils either at home or at the market.

15. Women pretend that Mauritanians do not like publicity and are even wary of it; in fact, they tend to believe that publicity is necessarily unique in the case of foreign or poor quality products. The trading women prefer to be known for the quality of their work and their greeting, "Satisfied customers will tell others."

16. Several types of pearls have been registered in Mauritania: stone, glass, herring-bone, metal, shellfish, and odorous (Delaroziere 1985). The pearl ladies, after appraising the value of precious or semiprecious stones, of which "the best quality ones were given by prophet David" (those found in nature), cut them with a file, polish them with a grindstone, and pierce them with a darning needle to make necklaces and bracelets.

17. A nice set of natural teeth is a seduction criterion.

18. If we decorate the hands and feet of women, it is because they are the only

parts of the body not covered by the veil. There is, of course, the face, but the Sharia forbids makeup to Muslims.

19. I am referring to religious books.

20. The ouguiya is the local currency, also called UM (Unité Monétaire). To ease exchange, 100 ouguiyas are worth about seventy-five cents U.S.

21. Since it is practically impossible for Mauritanian tradeswomen to acquire a sufficient amount of foreign currencies, they rely on their families abroad to provide them the merchandise they want to buy. When they come back to Mauritania, women reimburse this debt by giving the equivalent in ouguiyas to children of these families.

# 12

# Women Traders as Promoters of a Subsistence Perspective: The Case of Juchitán (Oaxaca), Mexico

*Veronika Bennholdt-Thomsen*

This chapter is based on a year-long field study of Juchitán, a small, rural town in the south of Mexico. In this town, women are traders, while the men are peasants, fishermen, craftsmen, and wage earners. The traders sell mostly what they themselves have produced, that is, prepared dishes and processed foods, making them traders, craftswomen, and housewives at the same time. Seventy-five percent of the merchandise these women sell is food, mainly originating from this region. Through the market, the women of Juchitán control the town's economy. Juchitán has a subsistence economy and remains this way insofar as the items and goals of the transactions serve to provide for the daily needs of the inhabitants. Trade in this rural town is considered nothing less than an art, and a natural gift most women are born with. The specifics of trade nevertheless have to be learned, and the senior market women are proud and more than willing to pass on their special knowledge. This perception prevents the skill of trade from becoming the duty of dependent employees, thus preventing this economy from transforming into a capitalist business enterprise. Any surplus is accumulated and used for *fiestas*. This type of conspicuous collective consumption hinders the spread of capitalist accumulation. Despite massive modernization programs and the introduction of a large irrigation system, (male) agriculture also remains dominantly subsistence-oriented. This can be attributed to the mechanisms of the female-dominated trade in this region. The question that automatically comes to mind is, How is this possible in such an unisolated area with mediums of good communication at the end of the twentieth century? This chapter analyzes the most important structural reasons as well as the theoretical and practical implications concerning changes toward another economic model in overindustrialized countries.

## JUCHITÁN—A TOWN OF WOMEN

Juchitán is a town of 80,000 inhabitants in the tropical lowlands of the Pacific coast in the province of Oaxaca, Mexico. It lies on the Isthmus of Tehuantepec, the second narrowest part of the American continent, after the Isthmus of Panama. Even in precolonial times, the region was a passage for trade from central Oaxaca and Mexico-Tenochititlan to Guatemala and Central America. A railroad was constructed in the late nineteenth century across the isthmus to connect the Atlantic and Pacific Oceans, and to act as an alternative route to the Panama Canal. Today, the port of Salina Cruz, 50 km from Juchitán, is recovering its earlier importance due to the presence of petroleum. A pipeline from the oil fields of Tabasco runs across the Isthmus of Tehuantepec to the refinery and port of Salina Cruz, where 15 to 20 percent of Juchitán's economically active male population are employed. The central government considers the region of this isthmus to be of primordial economic importance to Mexico, as it should serve as a connection between a new Europe and the Pacific Basin.

Juchitán is a small town with the outlook of a village. Half of the economically active male population works as agricultural laborers and another 10 percent as fishermen, mostly in combination with other seasonal occupations.[1] The remaining 20 to 25 percent are craftsmen: weavers of hammocks, carpenters, and goldsmiths, while others work in the professions and in administrative jobs.

The women of Juchitán are principally traders. In fact, every second woman earns her living by selling and producing, even when working in other professions such as teaching, medicine, or banking. Women engage in both professional areas because, in this society, Juchitecas are traders by birth and are famous throughout the Mexican republic for this unique trait. There exists no marketplace where Juchitecas are not found with their export items, whether they be *totopos* (a sort of corn cracker), dried shrimp or fish, cheese, coffee, clothes, or jewelry. In Juchitán itself, 2,300 traders, or 15 percent of women above 15 years old, work daily at fixed market stands in the marketplace. The rest of the trade is done in the *callejones* and *barrios* (sections of the town), and between the town and the surrounding villages inhabited by other ethnic groups. In addition, the stores surrounding the central market belong almost exclusively to the women, despite the fact that the sexual division of labor is less rigid. Any man working in the market area is either a foreigner, or a *mushe* (a "woman-man," normally a transvestite or a homosexual). With women's work being held in high esteem and because it renders a good income, the effeminate man is socially well situated in this society.

The fact that every woman is engaged in marketing stems from the high division of labor among the women themselves. Comparably, in the industrialized centers of the north, the social division of labor ascribed to women has decreased remarkably. The one-woman enterprise "household" has been created, burdening one person with a multiplicity of tasks. In Juchitán, the privately working housewife does not exist. The production of a household economy remains public and socially necessary, it is the economy *tout court*. For example, when the fruit of the tree on her patio is ripe, a Juchiteca does not prepare jam and store it for her own consumption. Instead, she sells the fruit or prepares a sweet from it for sale.

In Juchitán, one woman cuts the lettuce for a salad while another prepares and sells the dressing. In the same manner, the work of cleaning, washing, and caring for children is divided among different women and remunerated with money. The expertise of a person in any one of these tasks is recognized and rewarded, because it is a necessary form of social labor.

## THE TRADESWOMAN AS ARTISAN

Trade in Juchitán is not considered a secondary activity, nor does it have the aura of being something morally inferior as observed in most of European history. On the contrary, items and the process of their production is valued because these items can be sold, appearing similar to the value system of modern Western society, where only work in exchange for money is considered a valid form of labor. However, important differences exist. In Juchitán, money does not act as a dividing line between the public and the private work sphere. As private and public spheres are not separated, neither is circulation separated from production for a woman, since men are excluded from circulation as vendors and also as buyers. However, women do not translate this fact into a question of ranking or into a hierarchy as men in modern society are prone to do.

Despite the fact that trade is consistently linked to some form of production and processing, Juchitecas consider themselves not craftswomen but traders and tend to frown upon the *regatona* or the trader who is only engaged in buying and reselling, without any additional processing. Trade is considered productive work, above all when it is combined with traveling. The buying of dried, salted shrimp from the neighboring ethnic groups of the Huaves or coffee from the Zoque for resale in Juchitán implies being in possession of a special kind of knowledge. Knowing the trade routes and knowing how to deal with foreign people are recognized as important skills.

Juchitecas are traders, or more precisely, businesswomen by birth. This ability is thought to be a special gift of the women of this area, but even when the career is clear, the skills still need to be taught and learned. The girls learn the tricks of a certain trade from their mothers or other older women. The recipes of many dishes are handed down from generation to generation and are held as family secrets. Girls are taught where and how to sell their merchandise, how to present and offer it, how to measure, count, and haggle. Juchitecan traders are well known for their straightforward approach to trade and for their lack of timidity and fear. The aim of a Juchitecan trader is to conduct all of her business transactions *con gracia*—gracefully. She not only concerns herself with the presentation of the merchandise, but also with her own appearance. Great care is taken in the Juchiteca woman's appearance. Before going to the marketplace, a woman showers, dresses up, and adorns her hair with flowers.

A Juchiteca is proud of being a good businesswoman. To become successful means achieving self-fulfillment in her profession which, in turn, is her life's vocation. Therefore, trade and commerce are much more than just matters of business and are elevated to the level of an art. With this ethos, no trader would ever think of hiring dependent workers to do her job. This is why the trading transaction alone, like the whole production-cum-trade, continues to be artisanal. Even long distance trade is done by the tradeswomen themselves, mostly traveling by bus with their merchandise. Even the three women brokers of dried shrimp who own trucks (one even owns two) don't simply send the loads to be delivered, but always go themselves. This prevents trade from becoming a mere accumulation-oriented, capitalist enterprise.

Readers may have already asked themselves why I do not use the term *petty commodity production* to describe the Juchitecan market economy. There are three reasons why I refrain from using this term. The first is because of the evolutionist connotations associated with this concept. It is normally understood as the phase that precedes generalized commodity production or, contemporaneously, as a remnant that will soon disappear. But this assessment does not apply to Juchitán. Here, the integration of crafts, including trade as a craft, into the capitalist market economy exists and follows its own pattern—a pattern throughout which the trader's own social and cultural traditions define the rules.

One could nevertheless argue that the actual situation in Juchitán is still a remnant that will eventually be swallowed up by the mechanisms of an accumulation and growth-oriented economy in the future. This, of course, could happen since the future is unknown. The question still left to answer is how else can this economy and culture make sense, if not to prolong the nearly religious faith in the logic and forces of the free market economy. In reality, the well-connected location and geography of Juchitán, as well as the low impact developmental efforts and projects beginning from the last century onward have had, contradict the idea of survival in a traditional niche. We, on the other hand, place emphasis on the astonishing fact that the described structures that, according to evolutionist faith should have disappeared long since, still exist in Juchitán and are still going strong at the end of the twentieth century.

The second reason why I do not use the term *petty commodity production* derives from the special position the women of Juchitán hold in their society and culture as the main acting participants within the craft-based merchant economy. Furthermore, products of a typical female household production are commercialized, which separates the Juchitecan market economy from those economies traditionally referred to in terms of petty commodity production. In the European tradition of guilds, *craftsmen* and not *craftswomen* have been dominant. This fact implies an aggressive, antiwoman policy in the creating of male institutions as in a public male and private female sphere that has been interpreted as one of the historical pillars of capitalist development (Wolf-Graaf 1981; Knapp 1984; Hall 1980). Historically, where women's households were dominating the economy described in *das ganze Hause* ("the whole house," the peasant women economy of the sixteenth to the eighteenth centuries, Brunner 1968), commercialization was only marginal.

Third, the practice of employing the term *petty commodity production* in describing the recent phenomenon of artisan production, this time in a more structural sense, more accurately identifies such production as seen in modern informal sector activities. However, the Juchitecan female merchant economy cannot be compared to either Latin American informal sector production (where women also outnumber men) or to the artisan production of indigenous women. Juchitecan woman do not produce for the world market, nor do they depend on entrepreneurial capital as is often the case in the production of textiles for the tourist industry typical of the artisan production of indigenous women.

In conclusion, questions arising concerning the Juchitecan example are different from any that may arise in connection to situations usually described as petty commodity production. Through direct market control and the modes of exchange employed, Juchitecan women rule their economy. As with the items of exchange, the division of labor and production are geared toward immediate needs and the whole economy is subsistence oriented. The crucial question is, How is it possible that, at the end of the twentieth century, a highly commercialized economy such as the one observed in Juchitán, can be centered around use-value? How has this economy transcended the concept of mere subsistence and yet not developed into an economy of growth as is seen elsewhere? Geographical isolation or economic marginalization cannot be the reasons, given the opposite characteristics observed. Thus, the reasons must be some built-in mechanisms of this society.

## CONSPICUOUS CONSUMPTION OR WOMEN'S HONOR

As elsewhere, the aim of the economy is to achieve sustenance, prestige, and security for the future. In Juchitán, however, prestige is not obtained through accumulation or through the power gained by material wealth. Instead, a person's wealth is spent through collective consumption. Juchitán's is a prestige economy. The achieving of prestige is accomplished not through saving but through spending money and goods at fiestas. And the social web woven by money and goods being spent and consumed in fiestas thus provides security.

In comparison to other prestige economies, namely those analyzed by Bourdieu (1979) or Peristiany (1966), which typically share certain parallels to the Juchitán case,[2] one significant difference merits close inspection. In Juchitán, the women themselves are the subjects and achievers of social prestige and not the objects of male honor. It is this difference that prevents the Juchitecan prestige economy from being displaced by the competitive pattern of the economy of scale as occurs in the circum-Mediterranean area. Capitalism, after all, is patriarchal and this is why patriarchal societies are more easily transformed into this form of economy.

In Juchitán, the main goal or aim of a women's career is to act as a *mayordoma* at a *vela*. This means to be an organizer for a cycle of fiesta events during the course of a year. A *vela* is always celebrated in honor of a saint, but is centered around a clan, a neighborhood, or a group of crafts-people, and acts to reaffirm social cohesion. The main feast at most of the *velas* takes place in May and is clearly connected to the beginning of the rainy season and agricultural fertility. The main celebration lasts four days, opening with a gala night ball in the streets attended by approximately 1,000 to 4,000 people followed by a *misa* and its fiesta, celebrated also in the street but in front of the house of the *mayordoma*. On the third day, the procession known as the *regada de frutas* (pouring forth of fruits) takes place and the fourth day is marked by another ball held in the afternoon called *lavada de ollas* (washing of the dishes). Juchitecan has thirty-five *vela* cycles in the course of a year and the *mayordomas* in charge must spend a considerable amount of money, goods, and time performing their duties. Even when responsibilities and expenditures are distributed among several households, the main burden still falls upon the *mayordomas*.

*Velas* are not the only fiestas held in Juchitán. Following the same basic model, the cycles are of three days (no procession), with shadow-thatched streets, two or three musical bands, dancing, beer, and specially prepared dishes. The occasions meriting a fiesta include a baptism, a girl's fifteenth birthday, the fiftieth birthday of a woman, a wedding, the passing of exams, and inaugurations.

Because the location of all greater fiestas is in the streets of Juchitán, the town's administration must be notified.[3] According to administrative records, 628 fiestas take place in the course of an average year. And, since anybody who wishes may attend a fiesta, it is said that, in Juchitán, nobody could ever starve because there is always a fiesta somewhere at which to go and eat.

The fiestas are basically female affairs. Women are responsible for the organizing of every detail (except for the constructing of the shadow thatch, which is done by the men). After the cooking for the fiesta is done, the women dress like queens, with skirts of velvet and finely embroidered blouses. At the fiesta, the women occupy the front seats around the dancing square and dance together. The next day, they will comment on the event at the marketplace. Men also participate in the fiestas but take on secondary responsibilities such as the role of *mayordomos*. It is a recognized fact that if a man is aiming at a post in political administration, he needs to have female relatives with strong social ties and connections in the community. It is through women that men can become important members of Juchitecan society. Through the honor of choosing and inviting the guests for the fiesta as well as by dedicating time and goods for the benefit of the community, women have the means of achieving ascribed *presencia social*, or social presence.

The frequency and high number of fiestas is a result of the combination of a strict sexual division of labor, the high esteem placed in one woman's subsistence work, and the social action of rewarding females with public prestige. The fiesta also acts as an effective mechanism in maintaining an equalizing model in Juchitecan, versus the competitive hierarchical model.

## RECIPROCITY AS A PRINCIPLE OF FEMALE INTERACTION

Social cohesion in Juchitán is based on the principle of reciprocity. Normally, this principle disappears when the modern market economy appears. Even though Juchitán is a member of the modern market economy, reciprocity is still present. How can this phenomenon be understood?

If we define the modern market economy as the generalization of commercial exchange, with money as the means of exchange, and if, in such an economy, the local economy is embedded in a national and world market, then this system is, without a doubt, reigning in Juchitán. However, commercial relations here are also part of a network of reciprocity, rather than being separated from it, which is what has occurred in the dominant economic model. Prices and the terms of trade are fixed according to the social relation of the person engaged in the commercial transaction. How much and when one is asked to pay for merchandise depends on each individual's reciprocity account. In short, money has not been abstracted or detached from social relationships and remains a mere unit of measurement. Therefore, the conclusion that can be made is that the modern market economy in Juchitán has been molded and shaped by its woman-centered culture and value system.

An example of this system is the preparation of dishes for the fiesta, which forms an intrinsic part of the social function of the entire event. The high prestige of the hostess is first proven by the number of helping hands she has at her disposal for fiesta preparations. These helping hands only attend when the hostess has helped others with the preparation of past fiestas. Help cannot be hired or paid for with money. If a hostess does attempt this, her prestige will be seriously damaged. Therefore, the town's shopkeepers, despite having the financial means to take over a *mayordomia*, in reality cannot accomplish the task because of fixed business hours that hinder them from assisting their neighbors in fiesta preparations. By not assisting, they cannot expect any assistance in their own preparations. A market woman will prefer not to go to the marketplace for an entire day in order to help her neighbor. As a reward for her help, she receives enough food from the hostess to feed her family for that day of missed work. Because of this, the amount of food prepared for those who help equals the amount prepared for the numerous guests. Consequently, the shop-owners who prefer to open their shops rather than to help with another person's preparations are considered strangers or are socially marginalized, which in turn proves unproductive for business.

The fiesta itself is a mystery or a puzzle, constituted by innumerous acts of reciprocity. First of all, the number of persons who attend depends on how frequently the hostess herself has visited other fiestas. Furthermore, every guest is expected to contribute something. Men bring along a case of beer, women a prepared dish and an offering of money called a *limosna* or charity. Some of the women take upon themselves the responsibility of one area of input for the fiesta. For example, a friend will act as a *madrina* (godmother) of the musical band and be responsible for its hiring, while another is responsible for the birthday cake, and so on. The hostess mentally registers all the different contributions in her memory because one day she will have to pay each individual back accurately. Some hostesses will put off their own fiestas until they have earned enough help and material contributions in advance.

Day-to-day attitudes are also impregnated with the principles of reciprocity. The people of Juchitán visit each other frequently and spend—or better said—*give* each other their time. Visitors come bearing gifts, helping to create a relationship of mutual liability. As the acts of reciprocity are practiced by all members of the society and have become internalized, future social security is accomplished with each individual's acts, lying in the principle of communality itself.

Reciprocity is also dominant in the relationship between parents and children, above all between mother and child and between husband and wife. Female work rendered gratuitously as unselfish love is unknown to

Juchitecas. Within the realm of the sexual division of labor, each woman is responsible for the giving of food, housing, and clothing for the day-to-day care of her family. She is also responsible for the education of her children and for her own individual inclusion in the social network of prestige. Women are the members of this society who keep the daily lives of their families going. Children, therefore, are socially and psychologically indebted to their mothers (see also Tanner 1974). In exchange for all these family contributions, men give women the raw materials necessary for their households and for their businesses. Wage earners hand over their salaries to their wives since the task of managing the budget is a woman's responsibility. The house is always "mother's house," considered hers even when occasionally the man of the house has inherited it. Normally, the youngest daughter, or the one who looks after her mother into her old age, will inherit the house. And the first task of any woman is always to construct and strengthen her house and household.

All of the above examples indicate that this town belongs to its women. Within this setting, a man comes to need a woman to earn his living—whether he be a peasant, a fisherman, a craftsman, or a wage earner. As a peasant, he will need a woman to sell his fruit, which she will accomplish in quite an elaborate form to heighten its market value. A man also needs a woman to provide him with a roof over his head, for his meals, and for the administration of his farming enterprise. A fisherman depends upon a woman to dry or smoke his fish and then to sell it. In exchange, he will receive everything he needs, including access to the *vela de los pescadores* (the great fiesta cycle of the fisherman). Through a woman, a goldsmith will sell his jewelry and she will be able to buy the raw materials he needs at a better, lower price. The wage earner will earn his living and obtain additional financial security through the trade activities of his wife.

Observing the content of this culture from this perspective, it becomes evident how and why women, through trade, contribute to the continuing subsistence orientation of agriculture. For a peasant to hand over his produce to a woman consists of more than just tapping into a channel of marketing. By doing so, a peasant earns his social and economical livelihood. He will be less likely to become entrapped by the agents of agroindustry by means of the abstract channels of marketing, a situation evident since 1964 in the sphere of production as well. Despite the fact that more than one-third of the arable land has been integrated into an irrigation scheme, two-thirds of the corn domestically consumed comes from local fields. Eighty-three percent of the soil under seasonal tillage and 40 percent of the irrigated land is still being cultivated with maize (Holzer 1994). This high degree of regional self-sufficiency is very unusual for areas with this type of agricultural structure tending to lean more toward industrialization. Even on plots under irrigation, the old maize variety, *zapalote chico*, is grown despite its low productivity per hectare because it corresponds to the unique requirements of taste and texture for many locally prepared corn dishes and it is grown specifically for this purpose. Because of this fact, locally grown unprocessed corn is not sold in the marketplace. Any raw corn found unprocessed in the marketplace is imported from somewhere outside the region. The *zapalote chico* is well adapted to the extreme climate of the isthmus, but this advantage still does not make it competitive against higher-yielding varieties in other regions.

The business needs of the women in the isthmus region for corn processing has proved stronger than the state's demands concerning industrialized agricultural production imposed by developmental projects. This strong arm of the women of Juchitán is far-reaching. Juchitán was the first district in all of Mexico to oust the mighty Pri-Party and replace it with a local socialist-populist political group. This group, the COCEI (*Coalición obrero campesino estudantil del Istmo*), was founded amid struggles concerning property rights on land taken over by the construction of the irrigation system. This opposition proved effective as the people of the region fought against giving up communal land rights in exchange for state-controlled *ejidos* or private property rights. This struggle should be viewed in relation to the singular sex-based systems of exchange and the production patterns of this region. Communal land rights translate into local autonomous social forms of production and exchange maintained against the developmentalist pressures of the centralized power of the state and of monopolized agroindustry. As a result of these struggles, 75 percent of Juchitecan land today consists of irregular property forms, meaning that this de facto situation defies official registration. Access to land, inheritance, and the logic and principles of production still remain under local mechanisms of control.

## ETHNIC IDENTITY OR SELF-WILL

Seventy-three percent of the inhabitants of Juchitán speak *Zapotec*, the native Mexican language. Even though the percentage of those who speak Spanish is at a high 83 percent,[4] Zapotec is still the dominant (mother) tongue. Politicians, for example, must know Zapotec and deliver speeches in Zapotec if they have any desire for reaching a higher political post. Juchitecans are extremely proud of their ethnic identity. Unlike most other indigenous Mexican nations, Juchitecans do not identify themselves as *indios* (Indians). They are Juchitecan or Isthmic Zapotecs. An evident pride in culture is seen in the maintaining and celebrating of their language, music, painting, fiestas, and their prepared dishes. Their loyalty to local products furthers their regional economy. Pattern of consumption is another example of how the women of Juchitán, through their regional-based commercial activities, maintain their local economy. This contradicts all theories that maintain that the industrialization of agriculture and the globalization of the market is necessary for economic development and for the well-being of the people. On the contrary, Juchitecans are well-off and live in relative wealth in relation to inhabitants of any other comparative region of Mexico. There is no starvation or malnourishment seen in Juchitán. The average degree of nutrition in children of preschool age is better than that seen in the United States. In other indigenous regions of Mexico, 80 percent of preschool children are affected by malnutrition (Oswald 1994). This high degree of nutrition can be attributed to the nonglobalization of the market, the maintenance of regional production and circulation, and the fact that the agriculture and economy of the region remain subsistence oriented.

Given the picture of scarcity drawn by the developmentalist ideology for situations of economic "disobedience," we have to underline that Juchitecan wealth does not just mean living above the subsistence level, but, on the contrary, it means enjoying the abundance of food, of *convivencia* (sharing and living together) and well-being concerning daily needs. The Juchitecan idea of beauty goes along with this subsistence philosophy. It is a sign of beauty for a Juchitecan woman above 20 to 25 years to be corpulent. After all, she is the breadwinner or, better said, the "tortilla giver" and the fact that she cooks and provides her house with good food, shelter, and social warmth is a source of pride and recognition. All this is expressed through her body and her body language. With her head held high and her commanding shoulders, straight back, and prominent belly, she makes herself seen wherever she is walking.

The secret of maintaining a subsistence-oriented value system in a world where the overwhelming majority of people believe only in economic growth, lies in the self-confidence and self-will of these unique people. Their attitude toward a developmentalist attack from outside is not a defensive one, but more resembles an independent conviction of the superiority of their own lifestyle. New ideas, things, or people are never rejected, but quite to the contrary, are accepted with curiosity. Juchitecans are eager to assimilate all that is useful and to transform it into something of their own (see also Tutino 1993). This specific strength is rooted in the high esteem in which the mother is held, both symbolically and in everyday practice. What has been called *malinchismo* in other regions of Mexico, is absent in Juchitán. *Malinchismo* is a double-bind view held of the mother in which she is both beloved and, at the same time, detested; detested because she has been raped by the conqueror, the father (Giebeler 1994). Juchitecan sons and daughters are proud of their origins and therefore can also be proud of their culture and stubborn in preserving their own way of life.

## MARKET AND SUBSISTENCE

A widespread misunderstanding of subsistence leads many people to believe that subsistence orientation and trade are mutually exclusive (see Bennholdt-Thomsen 1994). Subsistence is also often confused with autarchy. In reality, there has never existed a social group that did not engage in regular exchange with other groups, except perhaps in extremely isolated situations. Although not every exchange involves trade, not even pre- and nontrade forms of exchange amount to autarchy. The fact that subsistence is confused with autarchy is a typical outcome of the ideology of the modern market economy.

Many people, impressed by the magnitude and extent of the domination of commerce over social structures, tend to ignore the presence of commerce in other conditions and incidences. The ideological background of the modern market economy is based on evolutionist theory. According to this pattern of thought, a high level of social complexity has been reached through the generalization of commodity production. Earlier historical situations are interpreted as less complex, with a lesser degree of exchange or no exchange at all. Instead of letting evolutionist theory blind our interpretation of other realities, be they historical or contemporary situations, a more cyclical and comparative view is needed. In our epoch, the prejudice or belief in the superiority of the free market system is very common as is the opinion that there is nothing or, at least, nothing of value if this system is absent. This prejudice should be counteracted for its invalidity.

At the same time, modern economics and sociology tend to ignore the persistence of subsistence production in cities as well as in the countryside—in the north as well as in the south. Homemakers, mothers, or parents are involved daily in subsistence production, by cleaning, cooking, and washing, and at night, while watching the baby. Different subsistence activities may include: the growing of vegetables for household consumption; feeding a pig, or some hens; constructing a hut in a slum; fetching water, and so forth. Yet all these forms of modern subsistence production are not considered work and are very often neglected, particularly if these activities are being performed by women and housewives. Such activities do exist and are, without a doubt, growing with the globalization and monopolization of the markets, leading inevitably to more and more unemployment (see Mies, Bennholdt-Thomsen, and Werlhof 1988).

The alternative to neglecting subsistence production is to improve it and make it more beautiful and satisfactory out of our respect for the environment, as just one of many reasons. At the other extreme, development and the economy of scale need to be rejected for a better, alternative subsistence perspective (see also Mies 1986).

Juchitán is not a universal model of this subsistence perspective, since the idea of one model for the entire world is unrealistic and impractical. Yet, Juchitán gives us hope! From it, we can learn that the destructive forces of the free market economy are not almighty and that a market economy need not be destructive even under modern conditions. Juchitán has proven that a strong mother/woman-centered culture can counteract even the mechanisms of patriarchal capitalism.

## NOTES

*Translated from Spanish into English by E. Soto.*

1. Figures concerning the economic structure are based on our own research and are related estimations. Official statistics have proven unreliable.

2. Similarity stems, last but not least, from the imposition and infiltration of Spanish culture in American colonies.

3. This administrative act cannot be called "permission," as there exists no way for the town's government to prohibit a fiesta despite the fact that it blocks and hinders traffic for at least three days.

4. In comparison, of the 9 percent of all Mexicans who speak an aboriginal language, 71 percent of them speak Spanish.

# PART IV

# Social Change Through Empowerment and Self-Organization

# 13

# Turning Acts of Borrowing into Acts of Empowerment: Self-Organization of the Annapurna Women of Bombay

*Dina Abbott*

## INTRODUCTION

Over the past decade, there has been an increasing awareness of women's income-generating activities in the developing world, particularly those of poor women who make a living through informal sector activities. As the importance of these activities to both the household and the economy become more clear, there have been differing attempts at enabling women to improve their chances of income generation.

One of the most important moves has been in the direction of credit facilitation for women. Banks, for instance, can be sources of larger loans at fairer interest rates, replacing the meager sums available from money-lenders who charge extortionately.

But, as studies (Lycette and White 1989; McKee 1989) have shown, women often face discrimination within financial systems that do not recognize their economic activities as legitimate. Thus, it is often impossible for individual women in informal sector activities to get access to formalized loans.

However, as women in India have proved, it is only when they have approached the banks in organized groups that they have been able to receive working loans in their own right. As the now famous examples of the Self-Employed Women's Association (SEWA) and the Working Women's Forum (WWF) have proved, group formation, initially only meant to achieve credit facilitation, has had far-reaching consequences for women in poverty. Women who have often been thought of as "unorganizable" and "invisible" have now arisen in resistance to many other systems that have regularly undermined their livelihoods (Bhatt 1989; SEWA 1984).

By taking the example of a similar organization, that of the Annapurna Mahila Mandal (AMM), I will attempt to show how this radical change has been achieved, and how women have turned acts of borrowing into acts of resistance and empowerment.[1]

## WHY DISCUSS CREDIT FOR WOMEN?

There is now a large array of literature on how poor women in developing countries make a living, particularly in the informal sector. And, while there is strong disagreement as to how to define these women and their livelihoods, one thing that has become less obscure is the fact that poor women are in need of working capital to initiate and continue with their income-generating activity (call this microenterprise, petty commodity production, self-employment, or whatever).[2]

Even if their activity provides the main source of household income, women often find it extremely difficult to obtain access to feasible amounts of money for working capital. There are several reasons for this, including household circumstances of poverty, hierarchical power and gender relationships within the family, societal interpretations of the worth of women's economic activities, and so on. There are a number of studies (Abbott 1993: 119–22; Savara 1987: 61; Tinker 1985: 13) backing the suggestion that men carry out more lucrative activities within the informal sector simply because their larger share of working capital allows them to do so. Women, on the other hand, have to constantly borrow daily amounts from relatives, friends, and moneylenders in order to continue with their crucial but undermined income-generating activities.

The recognition of this fact has led both academics and development planners to furiously debate interventionist strategies of providing "credit injections" for women from within formal financial systems (see for instance Berger 1989; Vyas 1992). While in other developing countries, such strategic intervention has been provided by program planners and development agencies, in India it has become a part of the national development policy. In a unique and extraordinary gesture, the Indian government decided that one way to assist the masses of its poor would be by opening up formal financial systems to them. Therefore, to the world's amazement, the Indian government decided to nationalize its banks. The first bank to be nationalized was the State Bank of India in 1955, followed in 1969 by fourteen of the largest banks. By 1980, 91 percent of deposits were held in public sector banks (Everett and Savara 1983).

## FROM ELITISM TO POPULISM: SOCIAL BANKING FOR "WEAKER SECTIONS"

In order to develop a mass banking system that both the rural and urban poor could access, the Indian government ordered banks to make radical changes, replacing their elitist image with a populist one. Recognizing that even among the poor there are people who are clearly more disadvantaged than others, the government targeted what it called the "weaker sections." These included scheduled castes and tribes, the disabled, and women.[3]

The policy of social banking was backed by a variety of weaker section lending programs (Government of India 1986), of which the Differential Rate of Interest scheme (DRI) is of primary concern to this chapter. The DRI is an urban scheme allowing the poor access to Rs 1,500 for working capital and Rs 5,000[4] for fixed assets at a minimum interest rate of 4 percent per annum compared to a much higher and fluctuating rate for other borrowers (sometimes 20 percent). Eligibility depends on the ability of the person to prove that family income falls below Rs 5,000 per annum.[5] In order to enforce the policy, each urban bank branch is ordered to meet certain DRI targets checked by government auditors. Thus, banks are forced to dispose of their DRI money by increasing their lending to the poor.

However, banks have not always responded positively. Bank managers, used to dealing with large transactions, do not consider it worth the administrative annoyance that is involved in lending and recovering the smaller weaker section loans. Often, the transaction cost to the bank is greater than the amount lent. Furthermore, the borrowers do not fit with the conventional image of business lending. Weaker section borrowers are often illiterate, sometimes having no fixed abode or proof of family income and self-employment. Also, in a caste/class ridden India, higher status bank employees can show overt prejudice against such poor, lower caste/class clients. The banks half-hearted attitude to weaker section lending programs is reflected by the minimal level of resources allocated to these programs by some branches. The clients themselves are fearful of bureaucracy and officialdom and are often frightened by the implications of non-payment. Altogether this adds up to a reluctance on behalf of the clients to borrow and the banks to lend. Many such schemes therefore remained paper schemes in the early 1970s and still do today in some banks (Everett and Savara 1986).

But while the weaker section loan may be cumbersome to banks, for some targeted groups these loans can make a difference between survival and ruin. Loan schemes such as the DRI can, in theory, provide a major positive intervention for thousands of women in poverty. But, as pointed out earlier, what was written on paper was not always put into practice until women began to get together to demand their right to access the DRI money so that they could borrow in order to live. SEWA, WWF, and the AMM all have their beginnings and successes in this ability to turn paper credit schemes into workable schemes, and the story of how this happened is illustrated by the case study below.

## THE AMM STORY

The story of the AMM is the story of one group of women, known as the *khannawallis*. The khannawallis are women who makes a living by cooking meals for male migrant workers in Bombay.[6]

Simply told, the story of the khannawallis began in colonial times when Bombay began to develop rapidly as an important port and industrial base. Its labor requirements were at that time largely met by rural migrants and still are today. Although patterns of migration now include family migration by landless families, Bombay's history is dominated by single male, seasonal migration from agricultural backgrounds. Usually one or two males migrate to the fast-growing city to supplement agricultural income (see also Dandekar 1986).

Bombay is notorious for its lack of housing, and historically it has been unable to provide adequate housing for its expanding industrial workforce. The migrants have developed many systems to cope with this and it is common to find large numbers of men (sometimes thirty to forty) sharing single-room tenements. The overcrowding, congestion, and lack of facilities mean that these men are unable to cook for themselves.

Some of the women who joined their husbands in Bombay during its founding days saw an opportunity to earn income in this situation. For an agreed upon sum, they began to provide the men with daily meals, giving rise to the khannawalli activity: a form of income-generation that is passed on from mother to daughter and that continues to operate in a similar form today. For generations, therefore, the khannawallis have met the needs of Bombay's industrial workforce (particularly the dominant group of textile workers) by either packing meals for them in "tiffins"[7] for consumption at the workplace; or if the men prefer, they can eat at the khannawallis' homes. Some khannawallis also allow men to board with them, although they themselves live in the already crowded slum areas.

The activity is hard and the resources inadequate. Many khannawallis live in single-room tenements or in shacks. There is usually no running water, electricity, or proper sanitation. The women cook twice daily for up to thirty people in these shacks, without adequate raw materials because stoves, fuel, and basic ingredients such as rice and oil are rationed.[8] The khannawallis have very little access to cash (working capital) with which to buy raw materials and often the whole operation is carried out on borrowed money. There are real difficulties if the men do not make their payments on time. The activity is therefore very stressful and the khannawalli's day is extremely long, made even more so by endless queuing for water and other raw materials. Most khannawallis I spoke to said that they did not make any real cash income, but they continued with the work because the activity guaranteed regular meals for their families and their children.

Yet the service they provide for scores of workers is essential and has enabled industrial workers throughout the history of Bombay to live and work in conditions that would otherwise be unacceptable. The khannawallis' contribution is taken for granted and is of little interest to most people. In fact, because the activity is associated with poor, illiterate, and sometimes single women, the khannawallis are seen as common and undesirable.[9]

The following quote perhaps sums up the image of the khannawallis held by most people: "The very term 'khannawalli' has a derogatory meaning. It insinuates a socially ignorant woman, plying for a trade, looked down upon. . . . Her work is not recognized. After all, what is so special about a woman cooking? Contributing to the family income? What a fancy idea! She is only feeding herself and her children. As a mother, it is her moral duty to do so." (Annapurna Mahila Mandal [AMM] Annual Report, 1990)

## HOW THE KHANNAWALLI BECAME THE ANNAPURNA (A GODDESS OF FOOD)

In 1974, there was a major textile strike in Bombay, lasting some forty-two days. The length of the strike was devastating for most families, since for people in poverty who lead precarious lives, even two days without income can cause severe problems.

It was during this period that one of the full-time textile trade union officers (and a cadre of the Communist Party), Mrs. Prema Purao, realized that despite personal money crises, the strikers were turning up well fed for strike duties. Upon talking to the women, she found out that the khannawallis had continued to feed the strikers, deferring payment. Yet, because they themselves did not have any money to buy raw materials and so on, they were being forced to pawn their possessions and take on extra work (such as domestic service). It would appear that the striking textile workers were receiving crucial, but silent, invisible support from the khannawallis (some of whom also joined the men on picket lines and in demonstrations). Prema Purao also discovered that this trend was a general one not only confined to the localities in which she worked.[10]

This realization had a strong impact on Prema Purao and she decided to leave her trade union job in order to work with the khannawallis. From talking to the women, two points began to emerge: first, that the women were desperate for working capital; and second, that they were getting themselves deeper into debt due to the high interest rates charged by moneylenders. With the help of her husband, a Communist Party member and a banking official, Prema Purao thought of approaching the bank for a DRI loan. This idea was frightening to the women, not only because of its novelty, but also because of the perceived consequences of nonrepayment. Already there were rumors of imprisonment started by moneylenders who foresaw a decline of their lucrative business in slum localities.

In order to overcome the initial psychological barriers, considerable organizational skills were required and Prema Purao's political background gave her a good grounding in this area. Adopting a Ghandian strategy in which the first approach to social reform is through the challenge of negative images, the khannawallis changed their tradenames to that of the *Annapurna*. According to folklore, Annapurna was a self-reliant woman who, when her husband deserted her, not only fed her household but also the whole world, earning herself the name literally meaning "the goddess of food." She represents an "organized, socially aware, and economically independent woman" who is clearly strong enough to bear the burdens of the whole world (AMM Annual Report 1988). While the khannawallis had been isolated, the Annapurna gained strength in coming together, and in 1975 the women officially registered their organization, the AMM, as a *mahila mandal* (women's organization). The AMM (like SEWA and the WWF) was to be a women's organization run by and for poor women, unlike previous mahila mandals that had been run by rich women on a social welfare basis on behalf of their poorer sisters.

AMM's immediate aim was to acquire credit (working capital) for its members, which could be done through the DRI scheme. However, as discussed earlier, despite government efforts to give poor women loans, there was little hope of individual women obtaining these loans because their work was not seen as business. Despite her negotiating skills, not even Prema Purao could convince the banks to lend money to khannawallis. Eventually, however, with the help of her husband she met with the Bank of Baroda, which agreed to pilot a scheme under one condition: that if Prema Purao could gather a group of up to twenty women, they would consider administrating a group loan. They refused to consider individual loans for the khannawallis (Mahtre, Bhrame, and Kelhar 1980).

The bank's stipulation proved very difficult in practice. Women were reluctant to come forward for fear of officialdom and of getting their families into debt and into formal situations that they did not understand. Also, envisioning a decline in their trade, the moneylenders in the locality began to spread rumors to frighten the women, even resorting to physical violence, with Prema Purao herself being stabbed on one occasion. Eventually, fourteen women came forward. These fourteen women were special in that they, and some of their family members, were already active members of the Communist Party. Therefore, unlike other women, these women received active support from their families, especially from the men.

In view of their limited literacy, the women took four days and nights to complete their first DRI application, which was submitted to the bank in 1975. Six months later, the women received Rs 1,500 each in their own names as working capital for their businesses. For the first time in history, the khannawallis were officially recognized!

In slum localities, where people are generally under the thumbs of moneylenders, the news of low interest rate bank loans spread quickly. Poor people began to think of banks as real alternatives. Other khannawallis now came forward asking if they could be included in the second group, which was formed soon after the first. There were already some forty women who had now come together. The banks' stipulation of group formation inadvertently achieved what others had thought was impossible, that is, the bringing together of isolated women involved in "invisible" activities.

The rest is history. As groups multiplied, informal gatherings became more formal and each woman began to contribute Rs 50 from her loan toward a building fund for the organization. Within two years, the Annapurna women had increased their numbers in the thousands and were strong enough to buy a building for themselves in the center of Bombay right in the heart of the textile localities. To the women who still lived in shacks and run-down tenements, this building was a major landmark. From these first steps, the AMM has grown from strength to strength, today occupying at least three buildings and in 1991 claiming a membership of 51,000 Annapurna women.[11]

## FROM CREDIT TO SELF-EMPOWERMENT

While credit facilitation continues to play a major role in the organization, the AMM strongly views itself as an instrument of empowerment. In order to combine these two roles, the proviso of credit programs has been ingeniously exploited to raise awareness and to produce a grassroots leadership. Figure 13.1 illustrates that what lies behind a large and ever-increasing membership is, in fact, a very simple and straightforward structure that is not only functional for credit purposes, but also allows each individual involved to develop along the way.

As the original group of fourteen women gained experience at credit facilitation, they became the group leaders for new groups. The group leader is responsible for filling out the loan applications and collecting weekly repayments from borrowers. Although the group leader, like the rest of the Annapurna, is often illiterate, these duties mean that she has to teach herself writing, along with numerical and organizational skills. In turn, this builds her self-confidence.

The group leader is assisted by the area leader whose role is perhaps the most pivotal in the organization. An area leader will look after the several group leaders as well as identify possible new groups. This gives area lead-

Figure 13.1
The Organizational Structure of the AMM

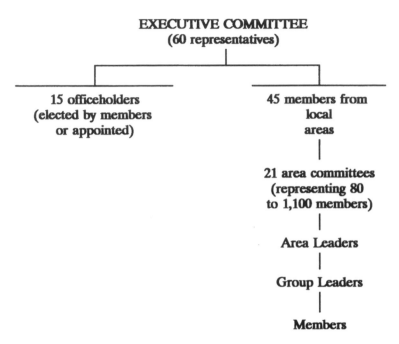

*Source*: Adapted from AMM handout.

ers considerable responsibility requiring and developing organizational and leadership experience.

Area leaders, in turn, elect an area committee responsible for ensuring that the area leaders are carrying out their tasks and for communicating the needs of the area to the organization. The area committee then feeds into the executive committee in order to make decisions about the organization as a whole.

What is important to remember is that all of the women are taking on these responsibilities voluntarily, in addition to their already heavy burden of unpaid and paid work. There are only two or three paid workers, such as an accountant and a lawyer. Both membership and leadership therefore derive from the same roots.

But while they may have come together initially to obtain credit, the Annapurna have learned that as a group, they have the strength to address several other challenges. For instance, one of the first actions that the AMM members took (and one they still recall with pride) concerned a particular moneylender who was harassing one of the women. Instead of arguing over accounts that they could neither read nor decipher, in a public show of defiance the Annapurna women beat him with their sandals and dragged him to the nearest police station. I personally witnessed an incident in which the women forced a ration-shopkeeper to empty a truckload of food that he was trying to divert to the black market.

The women also give each other the strength to deal with personal problems. For instance, husbands who have been violent in the past are now fearful because their wives' AMM friends might come around demanding an explanation! One woman told me that the only safe place that she can save money in the house is in an AMM moneybox because none of the male members of the household would dare to break into this box.

By coming together, the Annapurna have also been able to assist each other in their income-generating activities. For example, now when a woman is bearing a child or is ill, she does not necessarily have to give up her clients. The clients will be provided meals by other women with the understanding that the clients will return back to the original supplier as soon as possible. Furthermore, the women now set standard prices for localities in order to eliminate undercutting, communicate with one another, and bar clients who do not meet their payments.

In addition to credit facilitation, there are several other areas in which the organization has now entered. There is a large catering section where women learn new recipies and cook food for new types of clients (such as government employees, student hostels, and so forth). There are medical facilities where women receive regular health checks and literacy programs for all members. The AMM has just opened a new center to train the daughters of the Annapurna (whose only previous job opening would be their mother's trade) in new vocational skills so that they can broaden their income opportunities and their futures.

But perhaps the major change of recent years is the opening of the AMM cooperative credit society in March 1986. Because of this society, women no longer have to wait six months before receiving loans and they can also receive loans for crises instead of working capital only. Also, the AMM, like SEWA and the WWF, is now in a position to offer membership to other, non-Annapurna women who are equally vulnerable. Third, the AMM is currently seeking DRI quotas directly from the government, rather than from the banks.

All of the above tells a story of women who have found strength by getting together and addressing issues where previously they may have been powerless.

## CONCLUSION

After researching the questions of credit facilitation and self-organization, I have come to the conclusion that small amounts of working capital do not always bring dramatic changes for the Annapurna women. There are several reasons for this. First, the women simply cannot afford to wait six months for credit from the DRI administration. Any radical changes occurring in the business activity will have already taken place by the time they receive the loan.

Second, although women receive DRI money as a working loan, they do not necessarily use it for that purpose. In the standard situations I encountered, the first loan went toward any outstanding familial debts; the second toward housing repairs or other crises; the third toward children's dowries, and so forth. It was only a sixth or seventh loan that was perhaps allocated to the activity.

Also, despite the fact that this loan is given to the woman, within familial power hierarchies, it is usually men who control how it is utilized. An example of this is when I accompanied some women home after a very public, grand loan-giving ceremony (attended by an MP, a famous film star, television crews, and so on), at least two of their husbands were waiting at the entrance of the locality and immediately took the money away.

Nor does the small amount of money allotted free women of moneylenders as has often been grandly claimed by many, including the AMM because this is usually impossible in vulnerable circumstances in which the situation can worsen at any time, such as when illness strikes, for example. The family is then forced to turn to the moneylender, who despite his high rates, at least makes the money available immediately.

Thus, credit facilitation has to be understood within a context of both poverty circumstances and power relationships within the household. As Berger (1989: 1030) suggests, credit should be treated with some caution because it "cannot be regarded as a panacea to cure the ills of all self-employed women in the informal sector."

Credit, therefore, provides an on-off loan to women, which is no doubt valuable to the individual concerned. However, what is more important perhaps is that organizations such as the AMM have proved that institutional mechanisms, such as credit facilitation, can be exploited for other purposes. The Annapurna women may not be free of moneylenders, but now they certainly feel more able to challenge their interest rates and to read their accounting! Equally, they may not be able to have complete control over how the loans are utilized within the household, but they now have a better say.

What self-organization has done for scores of Annapurna in Bombay is far more than single credit loans could ever have achieved. And also, a group of women who have remained "invisible" for generations are now able to speak at international meetings (such as ILO conventions); recount their experiences in small business management at Western universities (such as the Cranfield Institute, U.K.); take trips to New Delhi to seek parliamentary representation; and organize group holiday visits to places all over India when some of them have not dared to step out of their localities before (AMM Annual Reports, 1991–93).

As one member of the original group of women told me, "People say that I am alone now that my husband has died. I need a man to look after me. But I do not need a man." And pointing to the AMM logo tattooed on her arm, she said, "This has given me more protection than any man."

## NOTES

1. The AMM is chosen as a case study because I carried out research on the khannawallis for my Ph.D. and it is a lesser-known example (see Abbott 1993).

2. For debates on Indian women, see Government of India 1989 and Sharamshakti 1988.

3. Scheduled castes and tribes are those disadvantaged groups declared under articles 341(i) and 342(ii) of the Indian Constitution. In the state of Maharastra where this case study took place, there are at least fifty-nine castes and forty-seven tribes so defined.

4. In March 1996, 32 Rs. was equivalent to one U.S. dollar.

5. The differential rate of 4 percent was set in 1972, but continues to be applied today because of the way the then-finance minister, Mr. Chavan, worked the decision. For a more complete explanation see Abbott 1993: 177; Everett and Savara 1983: 18.

6. Fur further detail on this section, see Abbott 1993, chapter 4, pp. 61–94.

7. Tiffins, also known as *dabas*, are metal foodboxes consisting of three to four round containers clipped together.

8. Under the Essential Commodities Act (1955), the Indian government controls the public distribution of what it classifies as essential commodities. Depending on the country's needs, these items can include anything. Items are then distributed through Government Fair Price Shops and only rationed amounts can be purchased. See Abbott 1993: 156–60.

9. Single khannawallis are usually widowed or deserted women and will take on this activity because it is home-based. However, they face considerable social stigmatization because of their association with their men clients.

10. For a more complete story, see Abbott 1991; and Abbott 1993: 170–98.

11. There is some confusion here because the AMM may have counted people more than once in these figures if they have received several loans. The figures are presently in the process of being computerized and should become clearer.

# 14

# Working for Social Change: Learning from and Building upon Women's Knowledge to Develop Economic Literacy

*Mary Morgan*

## INTRODUCTION

The gradual change from family production of goods and services to specialized production has occurred simultaneously with the evolution from an agricultural base to a technological and manufacturing base supported by a service sector. The roles of both men and women in society and in the workplace have changed radically as a result of these transitions. In many parts of the Third World, changing from an agriculturally based economy to a market economy has forced men, women, and children to exchange labor for money with which to purchase basic necessities. Subsequently more women are making the transition from the home to the workplace to supplement family incomes. The nuclear family unit is also evolving as many women are becoming the sole family income earners or as their spouses migrate to look for work or leave them for other women. Between 18 percent and 38 percent of all households surveyed in Latin American cities in 1982 were headed by women, with the highest rates apparent among the lowest income groups (Berger 1989). With limited work skills, low levels of education, and doors closing in the formal sector, women are having to create their own employment in the informal sector (Peebles 1984).

Paid employment is a key issue for women. Women's social and political status is closely linked to their economic status; as their incomes increase, women in most societies have more political and social value attributed to them. It suffices to say that women's access to income-generating activities is an essential step toward achieving economic independence. Economic independence can provide an opportunity to become more aware of the workings of the larger economic, political, and social structures of the society. Economic literacy is a means of empowerment for women in a world where capitalism is predominant.

Adult education is an approach that can be used to develop a curriculum that enhances this aforementioned step. In looking at improving economic opportunities for women, the educational process can only be understood if it is located in the context (geographical setting, economic and political system, social stratum, and community group) of the learners or the participants will not engage themselves in the learning process because it will have no place in their lives. It is therefore critical that local experiences be utilized as curriculum for the participants in any program that facilitates a learning process assisting women to move into the public sphere of the economy.

In this chapter I draw from my field work[1] with a group of women in Petén, Guatemala. With these women I developed a methodology for developing economic literacy using popular education techniques. Although the field work was conducted to develop and work with a specific educational technique, I engaged in this field work in the spirit of exploring and defining possibilities and venues for promoting social change with the women I worked for and with. An educator is someone who draws knowledge out so that an individual can recognize her or his knowledge. Whether one professes to be a researcher, policymaker, scientist, or social scientist, listening to people and then reflecting clearly back to them what they have said is one way to encourage and support social change. Popular education techniques are a means to do this.

This chapter is comprised of three separate, but related parts: the first draws our attention to the importance of identifying women's reality, and the obstacles and risks involved in a transformatory educational process; the second identifies three major components in developing a popular education curriculum while cultivating economic literacy; and the third discusses lessons learned while implementing a transformatory educational process. The conclusion pulls together the key factors necessary to promote self-determination in any activity that is initiated with group facilitation.

## PART ONE: IDENTIFYING WOMEN'S REALITY

### Mapping the Life and World of Women: Their Social, Economic, Cultural, and Political Reality

This study generated insight about how popular education techniques can be used to assist rural women in Latin America in starting microenterprises. Using popular education to develop economic literacy for women, an educator has to tailor it within the political, economic, and social structure of the society in which she or he is working. One of the major components of popular education is decoding, which means re-presenting themes that learners describe to the educator. Within this field study, demystifying the economy by using daily examples of economic activity and taking an objective stance to analyze the activity was the decoding mythodology I used. Facilitating a process that allows women to decode the economy is necessary if women are to place themselves as active participants in it. The process I chose to facilitate responded to the needs of the women; they wanted to learn how to start microenterprises so that they could generate income. If the microenterprise operations were going to provide an income for them, then the basic concepts of profit, price determination, market, and potential clients had to be understood. Otherwise, the scarce resources—human and monetary—could be exhausted.

In order to *develop* economic literacy for women while teaching them how to initiate microenterprises, the curriculum content has to be based in the learners' social, economic, political, and cultural context *if* the educational program is going to address the women's life experiences. Incorporating learners' experiences is a big factor in monitoring their learning (Brookfield 1987, 1990; Freire 1970b). Thus, the educational program required that my instructional process facilitate the involvement of the women in developing the curriculum content so that it fit within the context of their reality.

I discovered that the content needed to include a description of the functioning of the local economy as a basis from which to develop the curriculum. In order to make my description of the economy have meaning for women, I had to use their own words. And in order to develop a description using their own words, they had to verbalize their experiences in, and with, the economic sphere of their society. I used brainstorming, discussions, role playing, and popular theater as strategies to encourage the women to share their experiences and to participate in the learning process. As the women shared their experiences and knowledge, I used these experiences as examples to teach economic concepts. For example, in the first class, when I used drawings, the women told me how the lack of employment for men was forcing women to look for work. They all had experience selling baked goods or tortillas on the street, or had taken in washing to do by hand to earn money. Sometimes this supplemented their income and sometimes it was the family's sole income. When I asked the women what their profit had been, they had no idea. So I used the example of producing and selling piñatas, which one woman in the class had been doing, to determine the costs and profit that she gained from one piñata. To do this we determined all the materials needed to produce one piñata, the amount of time it took to make the piñata, and then calculated the total costs. The woman told us the price she sold the finished product for and we were able to conclude that she did not make a profit. I used other examples that the women had given of possible microenterprise operations to teach them to calculate costs and profit. As the women recounted their experiences, I was able to assess their knowledge of the economy. These activities provided a window through which I saw the cultural, political, and social restrictions that enveloped them. For example, they informed me that they were the ones who were responsible for the children so they could only engage in economic activities that did not interfere with child care or preparing family meals. Street vending, making tortillas, or washing clothes at home allowed them to continue with their family duties because they had control over their "working" hours (Berger 1989).

The women then learned to name their knowledge base, and in doing this discovered that their work in the private and public spheres had value. For example, they considered making tortillas and washing clothes to be menial jobs that had no value. When they verbalized and named the reason that they were engaging in these menial tasks, which was to earn an income, they recognized the cultural limitations that they were operating within.

### Decolonizing the Minds of the Learners

A colonized mentality is one symptom of oppression and can be detected within the social, economic, political, and cultural context of the learners' lives. It manifests in general low self-esteem and a grave inferiority complex (Memmi 1967). My previous experience in Guatemala had taught me about the level of fear that Guatemalans in general live with; fear of neighbors who might turn them into the authorities, fear of the military, and fear of authority. When I first met the women in the classroom session they were reluctant to talk despite the fact that they were all familiar with each other and were from the same community. I was a stranger to them, and being a white woman from an industrialized nation gave me authority, which made me intimidating. Therefore, I wanted to include personal growth in the curriculum. This began with communication of empathy and continued through honest dialogue. Facilitating an environment in which the women could express their experiences and could gain support for what they knew ultimately gave value to their life experiences and developed their feelings of self-worth. For example, I gave them the opportunity to share their experience and knowledge about street vending operations that I then used as examples to teach the calculation of profit. I operated from the assumption that they knew more about street vending than I did. Freire (1970b) calls this a "dialogical" relationship between the educator and learner instead of a "banking" style of teaching.

A supportive environment builds trust, and trust encourages deeper communication, which becomes realized in mutual support (Bopp 1985; Peck 1987). As the women became stronger they became more self-sufficient and depended less on me (Barndt 1980; Bopp 1985; Freire 1970b). For example, in the fifth class when the women were presenting the projected weekly profit of a sample microenterprise, which they had calculated in small groups, they had asked me not to intervene in their presentations until all the information had been presented. They had confidence in their ability to do their own calculations, which they had done without my help. In the home visits they changed from cowering individuals afraid of being "stupid and slow," which they themselves said they were, to self-assured individuals who took pencils in hand and wrote their own calculations without me prompting them to do so.

According to Freire (1970b) and Tilakaratna (1991), to break down the colonized mentality, the curriculum in a transformative educational program should aim at eventually replacing the outside educator so the learners can continue with the educational program on their own. In this program, I enabled the women to assume their own leadership after I had gone. For example, they were able to obtain credit even though the arrangements I had made fell through. Moreover, they were able to debate conditions and assume leadership when the community organizer who was my initial contact person tried to take over the collection of the loan money so that she could have access to it.

Networking with community resource people, developing communication skills, and developing mutual support are all means by which to achieve having the learners assume responsibility for their continuing education (Roberts 1979). These were all factors in enabling the women in this study. For example, networking with a respected community member and bookkeeper was a key factor in their continued efforts after I had gone. And their ability to meet, discuss, and collaborate about the lending conditions of the money and the local community organizer, who wanted to take advantage of her position in the community, were also results of the networking, communication, and mutual support I had encouraged.

## The Risks of Transformational Pedagogy

Within most social, economic, political, and cultural contexts there are restrictions of some sort for women. The objective of an authentic educational process is to develop a critique of the society and then to transform it (Barndt 1980; Freire 1970a, 1970b, 1977). In some contexts, critiquing and/or attempting to transform the oppressive reality could lead to reprisals. To alleviate this possibility, I had to be cognizant of the fact that it was the women who knew best the possibilities of reprisals and the limitations imposed upon them in their reality. My dialogue with the women had revealed some but not all of the ugly aspects of their contextual environment. By being sensitive to the women's messages, expressed in body language or/and in words, I was able to more effectively base the curriculum content on the women's analysis of their situation rather than imposing my ideas of what they *should* be learning. For instance, I believe that many of the women's economic problems were caused by the militaristic state, which impeded economic development as one of its means of controlling the population. The guerrilla activity in the area demonstrated the support of the communities for the guerrillas and the inability of the military, even with their advanced technology, to quell the armed struggle. The military was (and still is) obstructing the constructing of roads to discourage the armed struggle's access to communities and this is turn has hampered the movement of goods to the marketplace. However, I avoided developing antimilitary rhetoric during the class.

During the class I had to listen with my heart as well as with my ears for the issues that the women raised, often in a confused form. I then re-presented these themes in an organized and challenging form. For example, when the women began itemizing production costs for a piñata in the first class, they did not include labor costs. This was an indication that they devalued their labor, implying that their labor was free. I then asked them to itemize the costs of a table constructed by a carpenter and they included the labor costs. I asked them why they had included labor costs in the selling price of the table made by the carpenter and not in the selling price of a piñata. When they saw the comparison, they recognized the way in which they devalued their work. We then talked about the way we as women devalue our work. This approach agrees with the findings of Freire (1977) who points out the importance of listening for ideas, reorganizing the ideas into themes, then re-presenting these themes to the learners.

By allowing the women to formulate their own questions, I facilitated a process that allowed them to answer their questions with their own words. For example, in the sixth class when we were writing the group's constitution, the women had concerns about how the repayment of the monthly quotas were going to be monitored. As they verbalized their concerns, I wrote them down. We then brainstormed as to what sort of disciplinary actions would be appropriate. These actions were discussed and then added to the constitution. This is consistent with Bopp's (1986) findings that to be a responsible educator requires that one is respectful of the parameters in the learners' learning processes within their context. Bopp reminds educators that the participants' learning processes have evolved over time and in response to the learners' contextual realities.

## PART TWO: CONTEXT, PROCESS, AND CONTENT

The key finding of this study is that the factors of context, process, and content are interrelated. This interrelationship is a complex process and forms a network, rather than a relationship of hierarchy or order. In Figure 14.1, I present a schematic diagram showing these interrelationships. The

**Figure 14.1**
**A Schematic Diagram Showing the Interrelationship among Content, Process, and Context**
The interplay between the three dimensions of intervention is constant and complex. Each dimension affects the other and all are mediated by the dialogical process.

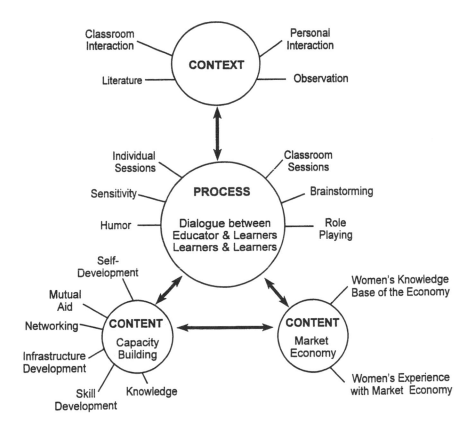

following description of the schema helps explain the interrelationship of factors for carrying out effective educational intervention in the lives of women for the purpose of improving their economic literacy.

### Context

Having a basic understanding of the learners' contextual environment provided a framework within which to present the curricular content. When I entered the Santa Elena community I did some preliminary research by going to the literature, doing some interviews with community contact people, and speaking with people that knew the community of Santa Elena. In the community, I learned through observation about the dynamics between men and women, the nature and relative strength of the religious elements in the community, and who had which kinds of power in the community. In the classroom sessions through the dialogue and the activities that I facilitated, I learned about the women's context through the interactions that ensued. The individual sessions also provided an opportunity for me to enhance my awareness of the community, especially because these sessions were conducted in the homes.

From these interactions and observations, I deduced the cultural and political restrictions on women in the community and better understood their social and economic functions. These were the points that guided me through the development of the curricular content. This is consistent with findings as to the importance of the educator's immersion into the learners' reality in order to better understand the context of the learners. This is a critical aspect of a transformatory educational process (Brookfield 1987, 1990; Lehmann 1990; Macy 1985).

## Process

The key component of the process was a dialogical relationship. Dialogue was the medium that enabled the process to occur. Dialogue opened up communication and built trust (Bopp 1985; Fessler 1976; Freire 1970a, 1970b, 1977; Hope and Timmel 1984; Peck 1987). To make the learning environment fun and enjoyable, to break through shyness, and to eliminate the fear of not wanting to make mistakes, I used humor during the dialogical process. The activities selected to encourage dialogue were brainstorming, discussions, and role playing. Individual sessions were good opportunities for me and each participant to develop a personal relationship. I strongly believe that the core of the educational program was this dialogical relationship, my dialogue with the women, as well as dialogue among the learners. This dialogue enabled me to ground the educational program in the women's reality. Dialogue can only occur *between* people as they name their world, not with one person telling the other person what their reality is (Barndt 1980; Brookfield 1987; Freire 1970a, 1970b, 1973; Lehmann 1990).

## Content

The field work was comprised of an educational program that was intended to improve the economic literacy of eight women. The content was twofold, including an aspect focused on the market economy and an aspect focused on individual capacity building. These two aspects were not mutually exclusive, but rather complemented each other during the program.

Essentially, the development of self cannot be separated from the learning process because it is an integral part of any learning (Barndt 1980; Bopp 1985; Brookfield 1990; Hope and Timmel 1984).

Through the process of dialogue, implemented during various strategies, I became aware of the women's context and their social and economic functions in the community. From these experiences I was able to determine the women's knowledge base of the economy. The women's experiences then were used as examples for developing economic literacy. For example, one woman sold used clothes from the United States in small rural communities having no clothing stores. She had to go to the capital city to purchase the clothes in a warehouse and then have them shipped back to Petén. She had recognized a need that was not being met by anyone else and hence had targeted her market segment. By using this as an example for targeting potential clients, an important economic concept was conveyed to the women.

At the same time that the women were learning about the economy, they were building their capacity to develop skills and to obtain further knowledge about microenterprise development. Because the process medium was dialogue, communication was a constant focus of mine. My facilitation activities promoted a safe environment for the women to express themselves and to share their experiences and knowledge; this in turn gave value to their lives and encouraged self-development and mutual aid (Briskin 1990; Fessler 1976; Peck 1987).

I prepared the women to take control of their learning process so that the educational program could continue after I had gone. Capacity building incorporated the development of an infrastructure, which supported the ongoing learning of the women. This infrastructure was comprised of their advisor and their collaborative approach. This preparation entailed my assisting the women in organizing themselves and in creating their own democratic and nonhierarchical approach (Tilakaratna 1991). Acquainting the women with group-building skills while strengthening communication skills were means to develop mutual aid among the women. My effort to familiarize the women with community resource people enabled them to learn how to network and to benefit from local knowledge, which, in turn, contributed to their effort to become self-reliant and to break out of the colonized mentality of dependence.

Referring back to Figure 14.1, the educational process was centered on dialogue. This ensured that I responded to the women in their own environment and promoted the transference of knowledge and skills in a manner that responded to their learning processes. Constant self-evaluation on my part was essential to ensure that I was not imposing my learning objectives on the women.

The content dimension of the educational program used the women's life experiences as teaching examples for transferring skills and knowledge specific to microenterprise development. Acknowledging the women's experiences gave value to their lives and work and promoted their self-development.

I found that being aware of the interplay of the three dimensions of context, content, and process during my field study provided me with guidelines for effective intervention using popular education methods.

## PART THREE: LESSONS LEARNED

### Context and Critical Consciousness

*Webster's Dictionary* (Random House 1991) defines critical as "finding fault." Critical consciousness or being critically aware can be described then as finding the cracks or faults in one's perception of reality and realizing that what has been accepted as truth, is not truth at all, but rather *one* explanation of reality from *one* perspective.

Critical consciousness makes is possible for learners to see that their poverty, deprivation, and/or abusive relationship is not an outcome of their deficiency or fate, but is the result of cultural and social constructs embedded in dominant values and the prevailing social and/or political systems. Thus, if the learners realize these values are social constructs they can also learn that they can change them.

The sociopolitical constructs of the existing world order have created an unequal relationship between those that *have* and those that *do not have*. Structural inequalities based on gender have managed to restrict the participation of women in the formal economy. These structural inequalities are entrenched in the social, political, economic, and cultural dimensions of all societies. If the objective of an educational process is to develop critical consciousness, the learners in such a program are going to be encouraged not only to find fault with the existing world order, but also to name it and act upon it to transform their reality.

The *haves* in the world have access to power embedded in the *metastructure* of society (the overarching political aspects of a society's governmental, military, political, and social organizations) and the *infrastructure* (the overarching economic aspects of a society's means of production and distribution). Although gender analysis is incomplete outside of class and race analysis, it is women who are most often marginalized. Therefore, I categorize women as *have nots*, as a generalization.[2] Being a have not implies vulnerability because a have not does not have access to power. When a have not questions structured inequalities and begins to act to transform her reality, she will have to rebel against the established structures. And, as Heredero (1978: 13) aptly states, "History shows that few people give up their privileges voluntarily."

Ethically, educators should be fully aware of this reality because as they bring the learners to critical awareness of their world and encourage them to take this new knowledge and transform their reality, they could also be setting the learners up for reprisals. Essentially, as women become more conscious of their situation at the microeconomic level they will move toward an awareness of the macroeconomic level on their own. As they progress at each step they will garner the skills needed to cope within their actual environment, even with the imminent threat of domestic violence or of state reprisals.

Thus, in entering an educational process, it is important that the educator have faith in the learners' capacity to define the parameters of their own contextual reality. Learners know the existing cultural and social restrictions operating in their communities; they live this reality. This knowledge will be conveyed to the educator through informal discussions, local jokes, and even body language. If educators are sensitive, listen, and are in constant dialogue with the learners, they soon will become aware of the contextual reality. And if obvious activities affecting the learners, like wife battering or military reprisals, are not openly discussed, this is a good sign that the issues are much too volatile for analysis. Educators must respect this reality. Ultimately, educators will leave the community, while the learners remain.

Learners will indicate when they are ready to confront the apparent obstacles impeding their personal growth and their abilities to live their lives with dignity. The individual cannot be separated from the collective society, so an authentic educational program should start at the place of the individual and move outward to the society. Therefore, any effort that is made toward self-development should move to the macrolevel as an evolutionary consequence, but the educator should not force confrontation.

### Facilitating a Self-Reliant Educational Program

It is very easy for educators to impose their words and analyses on learners. Freire (1970a) talks about the culture of silence that results when people have been denied the right of self-expression. With little experience in self-expression, it is common for the women who are participants in an educational process to adopt the educator's explanations as their own. It is difficult for them to formulate the new knowledge they have gained from the educational program with their own words, their own convictions, and their own rationales if they have not had the opportunity in the classroom to develop these rationales. In many cases learners parrot and imitate the educator.

It is therefore necessary to dedicate time in the educational program for learners to formulate their own questions and to find their own words to answer these questions if the new-found knowledge is going to be adequately transferred. When this knowledge is worded in the learners' terminology they are much more prepared to transform their lives. They are not merely imitating the order of the day with some cosmetic differences in the material world while feeling better about themselves. They are more prepared to take responsibility for influencing the future and creating what is possible and desired. Brookfield (1990) talks about learners developing the capacity to create their own values, meanings, and environments, which also discourages a co-dependent relationship between the educator and the learners. When learners can speak for themselves, they do not have to depend on the educator to speak for them.

Continual learning does not have to occur in the presence of educators. Conscious measures should be taken by educators to make their role progressively redundant in order to pave the way for the self-reliant capacity of the learners themselves. This phasing out requires assistance in developing the group's own facilitators. To encourage a continuing educational forum for the learners, the fostering of mutual aid and networking should be part of the content of the educational program. Communication and group-building skills, along with creative problem solving, are means used to create mutual aid. Knowledge of and access to local resource people can also be part of an established network so that learners can continue in their pursuit of knowledge. The accessing of resources in a community is a vital skill in any educational program. These measures can assist people in organizing themselves, giving them the skills to create organizations that are nonhierarchical and that can be effectively used as instruments of action to create change.

However, popular education techniques can only be applied if educators are willing to immerse themselves into the very lives of the learners in the educational program. Working within the praxis model of action/reflection—practice/theory—I have discovered that the three dimensions of context, process, and content required that I immerse myself in the learners' world and open my heart to hear their voices and feel the pulse of their lives. This kind of relationship has assisted me in developing a curriculum that responds to the women's needs of developing microenterprises as a response to desperate social and economic situations. Effective adult educational intervention in a socioeconomic setting occurs best when educators engage in mutual learning with the learners.

## CONCLUSION

"Women who live poverty" (Lehmann 1990) are not "poor women" but in fact are very rich in humor and understanding, and have a great desire to learn new things if they are given a chance. Facilitating a group experience that allows women to learn from one other provides positive reinforcement of each individual's abilities and knowledge. When individuals have self-confidence they will look outward to others with confidence and trust. Breaking down isolation is key to achieving social change for women.

Educators should encourage critical thinking that objectifies the learners' reality as they verbalize and analyze it. When the learners are able to see their reality differently, they begin to recognize that it can be transformed. However, it is critical that educators do not push learners toward changing their reality. Rather, educators should allow learners to take their own steps toward change, because in some situations effecting change when the time is not right can have grave repercussions.

Educators should promote independent learning, not dependent relationships. As popular education is a methodology that encourages transformation, learners are inspired to continue their learning. Therefore, any educational program that promotes transformation must include personal growth, healing, and group building. The educator should also include in the curriculum content, through a dialogical process, the development of an infrastructure that will sustain continued learning.

When women are able to realize their ideas, then visioning is possible. The culture of survival, which I define as struggling on a daily basis to meet basic survival needs, absorbs all of one's energy. Until the next day's needs are met, it is impossible to create a future. When women have the experience of making a profit and have cash surplus, and understand how to manage this surplus, they can start to think about the next week, month, year. With the knowledge that we can create a future, we then have choices. Creating a future is an act of resistance to the structured inequalities based on gender that constrain women in the economic sphere and a realistic means to mobilize women to make substantial changes starting at the grassroots level with individuals acting collectively. At no juncture, however, would I encourage capitalism as an answer to the alleviation of poverty. The reality is that women are living in poverty, children need to be fed, and capitalism *is* predominant. To tell a woman who has a sick child needing medical attention that capitalism is bad is redundant because she already knows that. Her interest is in getting cash so that her child can live. It is not for anyone to tell any woman what her needs are. And if a woman has no experience in voicing her needs, popular education is a means to assist her in recognizing them.

With the globalization of the economy, cash is needed to sustain families and this need can be a means of bringing women together to learn how to access and manage credit. It is important to realize that microenterprises can be another face to the ghettoization of women if they do not have the knowledge and access to credit to expand their enterprises within the context of their own communities. This theme needs to be researched and developed. But at the same time, in this sociohistoric moment, when microenterprise development and access to microloans for women is in vogue, there is a space to work within. Developing economic literacy using popular education techniques that encourage individual and community economic development can now be used as a stepping stone for women who live in poverty to become conscious of the market economy and move from being objects of history to its creators and subjects.

## NOTES

1. This field study was conducted within the broader socioeconomic context of Petén, Guatemala. My contact person was the local representative for the National Organization of Women (ONAM—Organización Nacional de Mujeres). Women had identified to her the need to start microenterprises as one response to their social and economic situations. Credit was a major problem in starting microenterprises and acquiring, using, and repaying credit was critical to the success of implementing their income-generating ventures. A total of six group sessions were presented over a six-week period between December 13, 1991, and February 4, 1992. After the second group session, I began to meet with the women in their homes individually between group sessions to do individualized sessions that reinforced the activities in the weekly group sessions. There were eight women in the program ranging in ages from early thirties to sixties. Six were married with children, one was single, and one was a widow. Their formal educational backgrounds varied. Four of the women had high school diplomas, three had advanced through Grade 3 or Grade 4, and one had never been to school. They all had ideas for microenterprises, but were not sure how to start them. This dream is what brought them to the first class. I was able to identify a nongovernmental organization, Compañeros de America, which provided the seed capital for a loan fund.

2. I am aware of the diversity of women and that there are women who would be considered *haves* in this world. For the purpose of this chapter, I use a universal notion of women as *have nots* to locate the discussion within the sector with whom I worked.

# Bibliography

Abadan-Unat, N. (1991). "The Impact of Legal and Educational Reforms on Turkish Women." In *Women in Middle Eastern History*, ed. N. R. Keddie and B. Baron, 177–94. New Haven: Yale University Press.

Abbott, D. (1991). "Utilizing Bank Loans as an Organizational Strategy: A Case Study of the Annapurna Mahila Mandal." In *Development Perspectives for the 1990s*, ed. R. Prendergast and H. Singer. London: Macmillan.

Abbott, D. (1993). "Women's Home-Based Income Generation as a Strategy Towards Poverty Survival: Dynamics of the Khannawalli Activity of Bombay." (Unpublished thesis available from the British Library.)

Abu-Lughod, L. (1990). "The Romance of Resistance: Tracing Transformations of Power through Bedouin Women." *American Ethnologist*, 17(1):41–55.

Achola, A. Milcah. (1991). "Women's Groups in Siaya District: Objectives, Constraints and Achievements." In *Women and Development in Kenya: Siaya District*, ed. Gideon S. Were et al., 24–43. Nairobi, Kenya: Institute of African Studies.

Acker, J., K. Barry, and J. Esseveld. (1983). "Objectivity and Truth: Problems in Doing Feminist Research." *Women's Studies International Forum*, 6(4):423–35.

Aguilar, D. D. (1989). "The Social Construction of the Filipino Woman." *International Journal of Intercultural Relations*, 13:527–51.

Aguilar, D. D. (1991). *Filipino Housewives Speak*. Manila: Institute of Women's Studies.

Akande, J., and K. Awosika. (1994). *Women in Trade and Industry in Nigeria*. A Study Report Submitted to UNIFEM, Nigeria.

Akgündüz, A. (1993). "Labor Migration from Turkey to Western Europe (1960–1974)." *Capital and Class*, 51:153–94.

Aleta, I. R., T. L. Silva, and C. P. Eleazar. (1989). "Women in Rural Areas." In *The Filipino Women in Focus: A Book of Readings*, ed. Amaryllis Torres, 110–25. Bangkok: UNESCO.

Alonzo, Ruperto. (1991). "The Informal Sector in the Philippines." In *The Silent Revolution*, ed. A. Lawrence Chickering and Mohamed Salahdine, 39–70. San Francisco: ICS Press for International Center for Economic Growth.

Alvarez, B. C., and P. M. Alvarez. (1973). "The Family-Owned Business: A Matriarchal Model." *Philippine Studies*, 20:547–61.

Alzona, Encarnacion. (1934). *The Filipino Woman*. Manila: Benipayo Press.

AMM. (1988–93). *The Annapurna Mahila*.

Amos, V., and P. Parmar. (1984). "Challenging Imperial Feminism." *Feminist Review*, 17 (Autumn).

Ancheta, Rufina. (1982). "The Filipino Women in Rice Farming." Occasional Paper No. 4, NFE/WID Exchange-Asia, University of the Philippines, Los Banos, March.

Angeles, L. (1990). "Women's Roles and Statuses in the Philippines." In *Women's Springbook: Readings on Women and Society*, ed. M. Evasco, A. Javate de Dios, and F. Caagusan, 15–24. Quezon City: Fresan Press.

Angeles-Reyes, Edna. (1987). "The Structure of Rural Household Income and Its Implications on Rural Poverty in Bicol, Philippines." Staff Paper Series No. 87–05. Philippine Institute for Development Studies, Manila.

Apffel-Marglin, F., and S. Marglin, eds. (1990). *Dominating Knowledge: Development, Culture and Resistance*. Oxford: Clarendon Press.

Apffel-Marglin, F., and S. Simon (1994). "Feminist Orientalism and Development." In *Feminist Perspectives on Sustainable Development*, ed. W. Harcourt. London: Zed Books.

Arca-Alejar, R. (1988). "Profile of Rural Women in Pagkalinawan Jalajala, Rizal." Research Report. *Learning Site Series in Social Forestry No. 2*. Social Forestry Program, College of Forestry, University of the Philippines at Los Banos, Laguna.

Arellano-Carandang, M. L. (1979). "The Filipino Child in the Family." *Philippine Studies*, 27:469–82.

Aydin, Z. (1990). "Household Production and Capitalism: A Case of Southeastern Turkey." In *The Rural Middle East: Peasant Lives and Modes of Production*, ed. K. Glavanis and P. Glavanis, 163–82. London: Zed Books.

Ayiecho, O. Patrick. (1991). "The Role of Women in Agriculture: Siaya District." In *Women and Development in Kenya: Siaya District*, ed. Gideon Were et al., 44–53. Nairobi, Kenya: Institute of African Studies.

Azevedo, Mario, ed. (1993). *Kenya: The Land, the People and the Nation*. Durham: North Carolina Academic Press.

Balandier, Georges. (1993). "Postface, où il est question de modernité. In *Les nouveaux enjeux de l'anthropologie*, ed. Gabriel Gosselin, 295–302. Paris: L'Harmattan. Logiques sociales.

Balans, J. L. (1979). "Le système politique mauritanien." *Introduction à la Mauritanie*, 279–315. Centre de recherches et d'études sur les sociétés méditerranéennes, Centre d'études d'Afrique noire. Paris: Éditions du centre national de la recherche scientifique.

Barndt, D. (1980). *Education and Social Change: A Photographic Study of Peru.* Dubuque, Iowa: Kendall/Hunt.

Barth, F. (1972). *The Role of the Entrepreneur in Social Change in Northern Norway.* Bergen, Oslo, Tromso: Universitets Forlaget.

Bauer, J. (1985). "Sexuality and the Moral 'Construction' of Women in an Islamic Society." *Anthropological Quarterly*, 58(3): 120–29.

Bautista, Cynthia. (1987). "Impact of Changes in Farm Technology on Men and Women." In *Agricultural Change, Rural Women and Organizations: A Policy Dialogue*, 18–19. Kuala Lumpur: Asian and Pacific Development Centre (APDC).

Beneria, L., and G. Sen. (1981). "Accumulation, Reproduction and Women's Role in Economic Development: Boserup Revisited." *Signs: Journal of Women in Culture and Society*, 7(27).

Bennholdt-Thomsen, Veronika. (1984). "Subsistence Production and Extended Reproduction." In *Of Marriage and the Market. Women's Subordination Internationally and Its Lessons*, ed. Kate Young et al., 41–54. London: Routledge and Kegan Paul.

Bennholdt-Thomsen, Veronika, ed. (1994). *Juchitán—Stadt der Frauen. Von Leben im Matriarchat.* Reinbek: Rowohlt aktuell.

Berberoğlu, B. (1982). *Turkey in Crisis: From State Capitalism to Neo-Colonialism.* London: Zed Press.

Berger, M. (1989). "An Introduction." In *Women's Ventures: Assistance to the Informal Sector in Latin America*, ed. M. Berger and M. Buvinic, 1–8. West Hartford, Conn.: Kumarian Press.

Berger, M. (1989). "Giving Women Credit: The Strengths and Limitations of Credit as a Tool for Alleviating Poverty." *World Development*, 17(7):1017—32.

Berger, M., and M. Buviniv, eds. (1989). *Women's Ventures: Assistance to the Informal Sector in Latin America.* West Hartford, Conn.: Kumarian Press.

Bertaux, D. (1980). "L'approche biographique: sa validité méthodologique, ses potentialités." *Cahiers internationaux de Sociologie*, 49:197–225.

Bevis, P., M. Cohen, and G. Kendall. (1993). "Archaeologizing Genealogy: Michel Foucault and the Economy of Austerity." In *Foucault's New Domains*, ed. M. Gane and T. Johnson, 193–215. London: Routledge.

Bhatt, E. (1989). "Towards Empowerment." *World Development*, 17(7):1059–67.

"Bicol Express." (1988). *IBON Facts and Figures*, 9(1/15).

Bisilliat, J., and M. Fieloux. (1983). *Femmes du Tiers Monde.* Paris: Le Sycomore.

Boddy, J. (1991). "Anthropology, Feminism and the Postmodern Context." *Culture*, 11(1–2):125–33.

Bopp, M. (1985). *Developing Healthy Communities: Fundamental Strategies for Health Promotion.* Lethbridge, Alberta, Canada: Four Worlds Development Project.

Bopp, M. (1986). *Culture: The Ultimate Curriculum.* Lethbridge, Alberta, Canada: Four Worlds Development Project.

Boserup, E. (1970). *Women's Role in Economic Development.* London: George Allen and Unwin.

Boserup, E. (1983). "La femme face au développement économique." Paris: Presses Universitaires de France.

Boulding, E. (1983). "Measures of Women's Work in the Third World. Problems and Suggestions." In *Women and Poverty in the Third World*, ed. M. Buvinic, M. Lycette, and W. McGreevey, 286–316. Baltimore: Johns Hopkins University Press.

Boulton, G. (1983). *On Being a Mother: A Study of Women with Pre-School Children*. New York: Tavistock Publications.

Bourdieu, Pierre. (1979). *Entwurf einer Theorie der Praxis auf der ethnologischen Grundlage der kabylischen Gesellschaft*. Frankfurt: Surkamp.

Bourdieu, P. (1972). *Esquisses d'une théorie de la pratique*. Paris: Fayard.

Bourdieu, P. (1987). *Choses dites*. Paris: Les Editions de minuit.

Bouvier, P. (1989). "Le travail refaçonné." In *Le travail au quotidien*, 7–27. Paris: Presses Universitaires de France.

Braeckman, C. (1990). "Une des villes les plus mal loties du monde." *Le Soir* (5 décembre):1–2.

Briskin, L. (1990). *Feminist Pedagogy: Teaching and Learning Liberation*. Ottawa, Ont.: Canadian Research Institute for the Advancement of Women/Institut Canadienne de Recherches sur les Femmes.

Brookfield, S. (1987). *Developing Critical Thinkers: Challenging Adults to Explore Alternative Ways to Thinking and Acting*. Milton Keynes, U.K.: Open University Press.

Brookfield, S. (1990). *The Skillful Teacher*. San Francisco: Jossey-Bass.

Brunner, Otto. (1968). "Das 'ganze Hause' und die alteuropäische 'Ökonomik.' " In *Neue Wege der Verfassungs-und Sozialgeschichte*, ed. O. Brunner, 103–27. Göttingen: Vandenhoeck U. Ruprech.

Bulletin of the Philippine Development Assistance Program. (1991). "New Projects Approved." *Partnerships*, 5(2):19.

Butler, J. (1990). *Gender Trouble: Feminism and the Subversion of Identity*. London: Routledge.

Camagay, M. Luisa T. (1989). "Women Through Philippine History." In *The Filipino Women in Focus: A Book of Readings*, ed. Amaryllis Torres, 28–34. Bangkok: UNESCO.

Campbell, Howard, Leigh Binford, Miguel Bartolomé, and Alicia Barabas, eds. (1993). *Zapotec Struggles. Histories, Politics, and Representations from Juchitán, Oaxaca*. Washington and London: Smithsonian Institution Press.

Capelle, E. (1947). *La cité indigène de Léopoldville*. Léopoldville-Elisabethville: CESA et CEPSI.

Caratini, S. (1993). *Les enfants de nuages*. Paris: Éditions du Seuil.

Central Bank of Nigeria. (1991). *Annual Report and Statement of Accounts For the Year ended 31st December 1990*. Lagos.

Central Bank of Nigeria. (1992). *Annual Report and Statement of Accounts For the Year ended 31st December 1992*. Lagos.

Charmes, J. (1983). "Méthodes et résultats d'une meilleure évaluation des ressources humaines dans le secteur non structuré d'une économie en voie de développement." *Cahiers ORSTOM, Série Sciences humaines*, 19(1):93–106.

Chiñas, Beverly. (1973). *The Isthmus Zapotec: Women's Roles in Cultural Context*. New York: Holt, Rinehart, Winston.

*Code de la famille en République du Zaïre*. (1988). Kinshasa (Loi no. 87/010 du 1er août 1987), Service de documentation et d'études du conseil judiciaire.

Cole, S., and L. Phillips, eds. (1995). *Ethnographic Feminisms: Essays in Anthropology*. Ottawa: Carleton University Press.

Combes, Danièle, Anne-Marie Daune-Richard and Anne-Marie Devreux. (1991). "Mais à quoi sert une épistémologie des rapports sociaux de sexe?" In *Sexe et genre. De la hiérarchie des sexes*, ed. Marie-Claude Hurtig, Michèle Kail, and Hélène Rouch, 59–68. Paris: CNRS.

Comer, L. (1974). *Wedlocked Women*. Leeds: Feminist Books.

Comhaire-Sylvain, S. (1950). *Food and Leisure among the African Youth of Leopoldville*. Cape Town: N.p.

Comhaire-Sylvain, S. (1968). *Femmes de Kinshasa, hier et aujourd'hui*. Paris: Mouton et Co.

Coquery-Vidrovitch, C. (1985). *Afrique noire. Permanences et ruptures*. Paris: Payot.

Coquery-Vidrovitch, C. (1994). *Les Africaines: Histoire des femmes d'Afrique noire du 19e au 20e siècle*. Paris: Éditions Desjonquerres.

Coşar, F. (1978). "Women in Turkish Society." In *Women in the Muslim World*, ed. L. Beck and N. Keddie, 124–40. Cambridge, Mass.: Harvard University Press.

Côté, Jocelyne. (1993a). *Le travail et la vie quotidienne des enfants à Santa Teresita, La Cocha, Colombie*. Québec: Université Laval, Laboratoire d'anthropologie, coll. Rapports de recherches. Édition bilingue français-espagnol.

Côté, Jocelyne. (1993b). *Le travail de ceux qui aident: dynamique familiale et autorité dans la vie quotidienne des enfants des andes du sud de la Colombie*. Québec: Université Laval. Mémoire de maîtrise.

Couchard, F. (1994). *Le fantasme de séduction dans la culture musulmane. Mythes et représentations sociales*. Paris: Presses Universitaires de France, Sociologie d'aujourd'hui.

Covarrubias, Miguel. (1946). *Mexico South: The Isthmus of Tehuantepec*. New York: A. Knopf.

Crozier, M., and E. Friedberg. (1981). *L'acteur et le système*. Paris: Editions du Seuil.

Dally, A. (1982). *Inventing Motherhood: The Consequences of an Ideal*. London: Burnett Books.

Dandekar, H. (1986). *Men to Bombay, Women at Home: Urban Influences in a Sugao Village 1942–1982*. Ann Arbor: University of Michigan Press.

Daune-Richard, Anne-Marie, and Anne-Marie Devreux. (1985). "La construction sociale des catégories de sexe." *Bulletin d'information des études féministes (BIEF)*. "Sexes et catégories." Décembre, no. 17:39–53.

Daune-Richard, Anne-Marie, and Anne-Marie Devreux. (1992). "Rapports sociaux de sexe et conceptualisation sociologique." *Recherches féministes*, 5(2):7–30.

de Certeau, M. (1990). *L'invention du quotidien 1: Arts de faire*. Paris: Gallimard.

De Chassey, F. (1977). *L'étrier, la houe et le livre: "Sociétés traditionnelles" au Sahara et au Sahel occidental*. Paris: Éditions Anthropos.

De Chassey, F. (1984). *Mauritanie 1900–1975: facteurs économiques, politiques,*

*idéologiques et éducatifs dans la formation d'une société sous-développée.*
Paris: Éditions l'Harmattan.

Delaney, C. (1991). *The Seeds and the Soil: Gender and Cosmology in Turkish Village Society.* Berkeley: University of California Press.

Delaroziere, M. F. (1985). *Les perles de Mauritanie.* La Calade, Aix-en-Provence: EDisud.

Delphy, Christine. (1991). "Penser le genre: quels problèmes?" In *Sexe et genre. De la hiérarchie des sexes,* ed Marie-Claude Hurtig, Michèle Kail, and Hélène Rouch, 89–101. Paris: CNRS.

de Maximy, R. (1984). "Kinshasa, ville en suspens: Dynamique de la croissance et problème d'urbanisme. Approche socio-politique." Paris: ORSTROM, Travaux et documents, no. 176.

De Puigaudeau, O. (1992). *Pieds nus à travers la Mauritanie.* Paris: Plon, 1936. Nouvelle édition Phébus.

De Romana, A. L. (1989). "Une alternative sociale en émergence: l'économie autonome." *Inter-Culture,* 22(3), Cahier 104.

De Seve, M. (1982). "Les femmes et le développement: travailler plus pour gagner moins. Étude bibliographique." *Études internationales,* 4 (décembre):733–40.

Development Alternatives for Women in New Era (DAWN). (1985). *Development, Crises and Alternative Visions: Third World Women Perspectives.* Paris: Ct-Femmes Editions.

Diamond, I., and L. Quinby. (1988). "American Feminism and the Language of Control." In *Feminism and Foucault: Reflections on Resistance,* ed. I. Diamond and L. Quinby, 193–206. Boston: Northeastern University Press.

Domingo, M. F. (1977). "Child-Rearing Practices in Barrio Cruz-na-Ligas." *Phillippine Journal of Psychology,* 10:3–66.

Douglas, Mary. (1992). "Hiérarchie et voix de femmes (Angleterre-Afrique)." In *Philosophie et anthropologie,* 39–55. Paris: Éditions du Centre Pompidou.

Douma, W., H. Van den Hombergh, and A. Wieberdink. (1994). "The Politics of Research on Gender, Environment and Development." In *Feminist Perspectives on Sustainable Development,* ed. W. Harcourt. London: Zed.

Doutreloux, A. (1967). *A l'ombre des fétiches, Société et culture Yombe.* Louvain, Québec: Editions Nauwelearts, Les presses de l'université Laval.

Dreyfus, H., and P. Rabinow. (1984). *Michel Foucault: un parcours philosophique.* Paris: Gallimard.

Dumont, Louis. (1992). "Anthropologie, totalité et hiérarchie." In *Philosophie et anthropologie,* 11–24. Éditions du Centre Pompidou.

Edwards, William M. (1980). "Ten Issues in Carrying out Land Reform in Colombia." *Inter-American Economic Affairs,* 34(3):55–68.

Escobar, A. (1984). "Discourse and Power in Development: Michel Foucault and the Relevance of His Work to the Third World." *Alternatives,* 10(3):377–400.

Escobar, A. (1988). "Power and Invisibility: The Invention and Management of Development in the Third World." *Cultural Anthropology,* 3(4):428–43.

Escobar, A. (1992). "Imagining a Post-Development Era? Critical Thought, Development and Social Movements." *Social Text,* 10(2 and 3):20–56.

Esteva, G. (1987). "Development as a Threat: The Struggle for Rural Mexico." In *Peasants and Peasant Society*, ed. T. Shanin. London: Basil Blackwell.

Esteva, G. (1987). "Regenerating People's Space." *Alternatives*, 12:125–52.

Etounga-Manguelle, D. (1991). *L'Afrique a-t-elle besoin d'un programme d'ajustement culturel?* Ivry-sur-Seine: Éditions Nouvelles du Sud.

Evenson, Robert, Barry Popkin, and Elizabeth Quizon King. (1980). "Nutrition, Work and Demographic Behavior in Rural Philippine Households." In *Rural Household Studies in Asia*, ed. Hans Binswanger, Robert Evenson, Cecilia Florencio, and Benjamin White, 289–364. Singapore, Singapore: Singapore University Press.

Everett, J., and M. Savara. (1983). *Bank Credit to Women in the Informal Sector: A Case Study of DRI in Bombay City*. Bombay: SNDT Women's University.

Everett, J., and M. Savara. (1986). "Institutional Credit as a Strategy Towards Self-Reliance." In *Invisible Hands*. London: Safe Publications. Also published in 1991 in *Women, Development and Survival in the Third World*, ed. Afshar H. Harlow. Essex: Longman Group, UK.

Eviota, Elizabeth. (1992). *The Political Economy of Gender: Women and the Sexual Division of Labor in the Philippines*. London: Zed Books.

Ezumah, N. N. (1988). "Women in Agriculture: Neglect of Rural Women's Role." *African Notes*, Special No. 3 on Women in Agriculture, 9–15.

Fawole, A. J. (1994). "Women and Community Bank Credit in South-Western Nigeria." M.Sc. thesis, Obafemi Awolowo University, Ile-Ife, Nigeria.

Federal Office of Statistics (FOS). (1984). *National Integrated Survey of Households, The Nigerian Household, 1983–1984*. December.

Feldman, Rayadh. (1984). "Women's Groups and Women's Subordination: An Analysis of Policies Towards Rural Women in Kenya." *Review of African Political Economy*, February 27–28:67–85.

Ferber, Marianne A. (1982). "Women and Work: Issues of the 1980s." *Signs: Journal of Women in Culture and Society*, 8(2):273–95.

Ferchiou, S. (1989). "Pouvoir, contre-pouvoir et société en mutation: l'exemple tunisien." *Femmes et pouvoir, Peuples méditerranéens*. Revue trimestrielle, juillet-décembre.

Fessler, D. (1976). *Facilitating Community Change: A Basic Guide*. La Jolla, Calif.: University Associates.

Finas, L. (1977). "Michel Foucault: les rapports de pouvoir passent à l'intérieur des corps." *La quinzaine littéraire*, du 1er au 15.01.

Finkel, A., and N. Sirman, eds. (1990). *Turkish State, Turkish Society*. London: Routledge.

Flores, P. M., and I. Gomez. (1964). "Maternal Attitudes Toward Child Rearing." *Philippine Educational Forum*, 13:27–40.

Folbre, Nancy. (1984). "Household Production in the Philippines: A Non-neoclassical Approach." *Economic Development and Cultural Change*, 32(2):303–30.

Foucault, M. (1975). *Surveiller et punir*. Paris: Gallimard.

Foucault, M. (1976). *Volonté de savoir*. Paris: Gallimard.

Foucault, M. (1979). *Discipline and Punish: The Birth of the Prison*. New York: Vintage Books.

Foucault, M. (1980). *Power/Knowledge: Selected Interviews and Other Writings: 1972–1977*. New York: Collin Gordon Pantheon Books.

Foucault, M. (1983). "Afterward—The Subject and Power." In *Michel Foucault: Beyond Structuralism and Hermeneutics*, ed. H. L. Dreyfus and P. Rabinow, 208–26. Chicago: University of Chicago Press.

Fransella, Fay, and Kay Frost. (1977). *On Being A Woman: A Review of Research on How Women See Themselves*. London and New York: Tavistock Publications.

Fraser, N. (1989). *Unruly Practices: Power, Discourse, and Gender in Contemporary Social Theory*. Minneapolis: University of Minnesota Press.

Fraser, N. (1992). "The Uses and Abuses of French Discourse Theories for Feminist Politics." *Theory, Culture and Society*, 9(1):51–71.

Freire, P. (1970a). "Cultural Action and Conscientization." *Harvard Educational Review*: 40:452–77.

Freire, P. (1970b). *Pedagogy of the Oppressed*. Trans. M. B. Ramos. New York: Continuum.

Freire, P. (1973). *Education for Critical Consciousness*. Trans. M. B. Ramos. New York: Continuum Publishing. (Original work published 1969.)

Freire, P. (1977). "Guinea Bisseau: Record of an Ongoing Experience." *Convergence*, 10(4):11–27.

Galli, Rosemary. (1981). "Colombia: Rural Development as Social and Economic Control." In *The Political Economy of Rural Development. Peasants, International Development, and the State*, ed. R. E. Galli, 27–90. Albany: SUNY Press.

Gassert, T. (1985). *Health Hazards in Electronics: A Handbook*. Hong Kong: Asia Monitor Resource Centre.

Giebeler, Cornelia. (1994). "Politik ist Männersa che—Die COCEI und die Frauen." In *Juchitán—Stadt der Frauen. Von Leben im Matriarchat*, ed. V. Bennholdt-Thomsen, 89–108. Reinbek: Rowohlt aktuell.

Glenn, E. (1994). "Social Constructions of Mothering: A Thematic Overview." In *Mothering: Ideology, Experience, and Agency*, ed. E. N. Glenn, G. Chang, and L. R. Forcey, 1–29. New York: Routledge.

Goodno, James. (1991). *The Philippines: Land of Broken Promises*. London: Zed Press.

Gorz, J. (1968). "Limites de la rationalité économique." *Métamorphoses du travail: quête du sens*, 168–211. Paris: Galilée.

Government of India. (1986). *The Twenty Point Programme 1986: Perspectives and Strategies*. New Delhi: Ministry of Programme Implementation.

Government of India. (1989). *National Perspective Plan for Women 1988–2000*. New Delhi: Ministry of Urban Development.

Gros, Christian, and Yvon Le Bot. (1980). "Sauver la paysannerie du tiers-monde? La politique de la Banque mondiale à l'égard de la petite agriculture; le cas colombien." *Problèmes d'Amérique latine*, LVI, 31–61.

Grossman, R. et al. (1978). "Changing Role of SE Asian Women." Special issue of *Pacific Research*, IX(5). Mountain View, Calif.: Pacific Studies Center.

Guthrie, G. (1961). *The Filipino Child and Philippine Society*. Manila: Philippine Normal College.

Guthrie, G., and Jimenez Jacobs. (1966). *Child Rearing and Personality Development in the Philippines*. University Park: Pennsylvania State University.

Haicault, Monique. (1993). "La doxa de sexe, une approche du symbolique dans les rapports sociaux de sexe. *Recherches féministes*, 6(2):7–20.

Hall, Catherine. (1980). "The History of the Housewife." In *The Politics of Housework*, ed. E. Malos, 44–71. London: Allison and Busby.

Haraway, D. (1988). "Situated Knowledges: The Science Question in Feminism and the Privilege of the Partial Perspective." *Feminist Studies*, 14(3):573–99.

Hartsock, N. (1990). "Foucault on Power: A Theory for Women." In *Feminist/Postmodernism*, ed. Linda J. Nicholson. New York and London: Routledge.

Hay, Margaret Jean, and Sharon Stitcher. (1984). *African Women: South of the Sahara*. London and New York: Longman.

Hayes, D. (1987). "Making Chips with Dust-Free Poison." *Science as Culture*, 1: 89–104.

Hayes, D. (1989). *Behind the Silicon Curtain*. Boston: South End Press; London: Free Association Books.

Heinonen, Tuula. (1994). "Gender Differences in Household Approaches to Adult Illness in Rural Philippines." Doctor of Philosophy diss., Institute of Development Studies, University of Sussex, Brighton, U.K.

Hennessy, R. (1993). *Materialist Feminism and the Politics of Discourse*. New York: Routledge.

Heredero, J. M. (1978). *Rural Development and Social Change*. New Delhi, India: Manohar.

Heron, C., and R. Storey. (1986). "On the Job in Canada." In *On the Job: Confronting the Labor Process in Canada*, ed. C. Heron and R. Storey, 3–46. Kingston, Ont.: McGill–Queen's University Press.

Herz, B. (1989). "Bringing Women into the Economic Mainstream." *Finance and Development* (December): 22–25.

Hill Collins, P. (1994). "Shifting the Center: Race, Class and Feminist Theorizing about Motherhood." In *Mothering: Ideology, Experience, and Agency*, ed. E. N. Glenn, G. Chang, and L. R. Forcey, 45–65. New York: Routledge.

Hollnsteiner, M. R. (1984). "The Filipino Family Confronts the Modern World." In *Society, Culture, and the Filipino*, ed. M. R. Hollnsteiner, 95–102. Quezon City: Institute of Philippine Culture.

Holzer, Brigitte. (1994). "Mais: Tauschbeziehung zwischen Männern und Frauen." In *Juchitán—Stadt der Frauen. Von Leben im Matriarchat*, ed. V. Bennholdt-Thomsen, 140–51. Reinbek: Rowohlt aktuell.

Hope, A., and S. Timmel. (1984). *Training for Transformation: A Handbook for Community Workers*. Vols. 1–3. Gweru, Zimbabwe: Mambo Press.

Houyoux, J. (1986). *Kinshasa 1975*. Bruxelles: Institut d'études d'aménagement et d'urbanisme.

Hurtig, Marie-Claude, and Marie-France Pichevin. (1991). "Catégorisation de sexe et perception d'autrui." In *Sexe et genre. De la hiérarchie des sexes*, ed. Marie-Claude Hurtig, Michèle Kail, and Hélène Rouch, 169–80. Paris: CNRS.

Igben, M. (1980). "Socioeconomic Activities of Rural Women in Some Selected Nigerian Villages: Implications for Integrated Rural Development." In *Proceedings of the CENSER Conference on Integrated Rural Development and Women in Development, 11:950–62. Benin City.

Ilcan, S. M. (1993). "Masks of Domination: The Deployment of Morality in a Turkish Village." Ph.D. diss., Carleton University, Ottawa, Canada.

Ilcan, S. M. (1994a). "Magic and Social Domination in a Rural Turkish Community." Culture, 14(1):55–68.

Ilcan, S. M., (1994b). "Marriage Regulation and the Rhetoric of Alliance in Northwestern Turkey." Ethnology, 33(4):273–96.

Ilcan, S. M. (1994c). "Peasant Struggles and Social Change: Migration, Households, and Gender in a Rural Turkish Society." International Migration Review, 28(3):554–79.

Illich, I. (1992). "Needs." In The Development Dictionary, ed. W. Sachs. London: Zed.

Illo, Jeanne, and Jaime Polo. (1990). Fishers, Traders, Farmers, Wives: The Life Stories of Ten Women in a Fishing Village. Quezon City: Institute of Philippine Culture, Ateneo de Manila University.

Illo, Jeanne, and Cynthia Veneracion. (1988). Women and Men in Rainfed Farming Systems: Case Studies of Households in the Bicol Region. Manila: Institute of Philippine Culture, Ateneo de Manila University.

ILO. (1991). African Employment Report. Addis Ababa: JASPA.

ILO/UNDP/FDRD. (1987). Appropriate Technology for Rural Women in Nigeria. Home Economics Skills Training Unit, Lagos.

Infante, Teresita. (1975). The Woman in Early Philippines and among the Cultural Minorities. Manila: Unitas Publications.

Israel-Sobritchea, Carolyn. (1990). "The Ideology of Female Domesticity: Its Impact on the Status of Filipino Women." Review of Women's Studies, 1(1):26–41.

Jeune Afrique Press. (1993). January, no. 1672 (Paris).

Kandiyoti, D. (1984). "Rural Transformation in Turkey and Its Implications for Women's Status." In Women on the Move—Contemporary Changes in Family and Society, 17–29. Paris: UNESCO.

Kandiyoti, D. (1990). "Women and Household Production: The Impact of Rural Transformation in Turkey." In The Rural Middle East: Peasant Lives and Modes of Production, ed. K. Glavanis and P. Glavanis, 183–94. London: Zed Books.

Kandiyoti, D. (1991). "The End of the Empire: Islam, Nationalism and Women in Turkey." In Women, Islam and the State, ed. D. Kandiyoti, 22–47. Philadelphia: Temple University Press.

Karl, Marilee. (1984). "Women, Land and Food Production." In Women in Development: A Resource Guide for Organization and Action. ISIS: New Society Publishers.

Kelly, L., S. Burton, and L. Regan. (1994). "Researching Women's Lives or Studying Women's Oppression? Reflections on What Constitutes Feminist Research." In Researching Women's Lives from a Feminist Perspective, ed. M. Maynard and J. Purvis, 27–48. London: Taylor and Francis.

Keyder, C. (1987). State and Class in Turkey: A Study of Capitalist Development. London: Verso.

Keyder, C. (1989). "Social Structure and the Labor Market in Turkish Agriculture." International Labor Review, 128(6):731–44.

Kimani, Dagi. (1994). "Lifestyle." *Sunday Nation*, June 20, 4.

King, Elizabeth, and Robert Evenson. (1983). "Time Allocation and Home Production in Philippine Rural Households." In *Women and Poverty in the Third World*, ed. M. Buvinic, M. Lycette, and W. McGreevey, 35–61. Baltimore: Johns Hopkins University Press.

Knapp, Ulla. (1984). *Frauenarbeit in Deutschland*. 2 vols. München: Minerva Publikation.

Kocturk, T. (1992). *A Matter of Honour: Experiences of Turkish Women Immigrants*. London: Zed Books.

Koenig, M., and G. Foo. (1985). "Patriarchy and High Fertility in Rural India." Paper presented at the Rockefeller Foundation Workshop on Women's Status and Fertility, Mt. Kisco, New York.

Labrecque, Marie France. (1994a). *Femmes, hiérarchie et développement. Anthropologie des genres et des générations dans la région de La Cocha, Colombie*. Québec: Université Laval. Laboratoire de recherches anthropologiques. Collection "Rapports de recherche."

Labrecque, Marie France. (1994b). "Paysannerie, recherche et changement social. Analyse d'un processus en cours dans les Andes colombiennes." In *Entre tradition et universalisme*, ed. Françoise-Romaine Ouellette and Claude Bariteau, 345–64. Montréal: Institut québécois de recherche sur la culture.

Lapuz, L. V. (1977). *Filipino Marriages in Crisis*. Quezon City: New Day Publishers.

Lauby, Jennifer, and Oded Stark. (1987). "Individual Migration as a Family Strategy: Young Women in the Philippines." Discussion Paper Number 35, Migration and Development Program, Harvard University, Cambridge, Mass., December.

Lehmann, C. (1990). "Bread and Roses: Women Living Poverty and Popular Feminist Education in Santiago, Chile." Unpublished manuscript, University of Toronto, Department of Education.

Lewis, J. (1981). "Mothers, Daughters and Feminism." In *Common Differences: Conflicts in Black and White Feminist Perspectives*, ed. G. Joseph and J. Lewis, 127–48. New York: Anchor Press.

Licuanan, P. (1979). "Aspects of Child-Rearing in an Urban Low-Income Community." *Philippine Studies*, 27:453–68.

Longe, O. G. (1988). "The Role of Women in Food Production, Processing and Preservation in Nigeria." *African Notes*, Special Number 3, on Women in Agriculture, 27–35.

Lopez, M. E. (1991). *The Filipino Family as Home for the Aged*. Research Report No. 91-7, U.S. National Institute on Aging, the Comparative Study of the Elderly in Four Asian Countries.

Lopez Arellano, José. (1993). *Características sociales y economicas de una region andina del sur de Colombia*. Québec: Université Laval. Laboratoire de recherches anthropologiques. Collection "Rapports de recherche."

Lopez-Rodriguez, L. (1990). "Patriarchy and Women's Subordination in the Philippines." *Review of Women's Studies*, 1:15–25.

Lupungu, Kalambay. (1982). "Le nouveau droit foncier zaïrois." *Cahiers Economiques et Sociaux*, 19(1–2):100–110.

Lycette, M., and K. White. (1989). "Improving Women's Access to Credit in Latin

America and the Caribbean: Policy and Project Recommendations." In *Women's Ventures: Assistance to the Informal Sector in Latin America*, ed. M. Berger and M. Buvinic, 13–44. West Hartford, Conn.: Kumarian Press.

MacGaffey, J. (1987). *Entrepreneurs and Parasites: The Struggle for Indigenous Capitalism in Zaire*. Cambridge: Cambridge University Press.

MacGaffey, J. (1991). *The Real Economy of Zaire*. Philadelphia: University of Pennsylvania Press.

Machado, A. (1986). *Problemas Agrarios Colombianos*. Bogota: CEGA/SIGLO XXI editores.

Macy, J. (1985). *Dharma and Development: Religion as a Resource in the Sarvodaya Self-Help Movement*. West Hartford, Conn.: Kumarian Press.

Mahtre, S., S. Bhrame, and G. Kelhar. (1980). *Bank Credit to Women: A Study of Kanavals*. New Delhi: ICCSR.

Makil, Perla. (1989). "Philippine Studies of Women: A Review." In *The Filipino Women in Focus: A Book of Readings*, ed. Amaryllis Torres, 143–54. Bangkok: UNESCO.

Mananzan, Sr. Mary John. (1987). "The Filipino Woman: Before and After the Spanish Conquest of the Philippines." In *Essays on Women*, ed. Sr. Mary John Mananzan, 7–36. Manila: Women's Studies Program, St. Scholastica's College.

Marcus, J. (1992). *A World of Difference: Islam and Gender Hierarchy in Turkey*. London: Zed Books.

Maynard, M., and J. Purvis, eds. (1994). *Researching Women's Lives from a Feminist Perspective*. London: Taylor and Francis.

Mbemba, I. (1989). "Le secteur informel: Un aperçu des aspects conceptuels et méthodologiques. Quelques cas de l'Afrique sahélienne." *Série Dossiers*, no. 4. Centre Sahel, Université Laval.

Mbuyi, J., and G. Smal. (1973). *Femme africaine réveille-toi*. Paris: Le pensée universelle.

McKee, K. (1989). "Microlevel Strategies for Supporting Livelihoods, Employment and Income-generation of Poor Women in the Third World: The Challenge of Significance." *World Development*, 17(77):993–1006.

McNeil, M. (1993). "Dancing with Foucault: Feminism and Power-Knowledge." In *Up Against Foucault: Explorations of Some Tensions between Foucault and Feminism*, ed. C. Ramazanoğlu, 147–78. London: Routledge.

Mebrahtu, Saba. (1991). "Women, Work and Nutrition in Nigeria." In *Women and Health in Africa*, ed. Meredeth Turshen, 89–105. Trenton, N.J.: Africa World Press, Inc.

Medina, B. (1991). *The Filipino Family*. Quezon City: University of the Philippines.

Memmi, A. (1967). *The Colonizer and the Colonized*. Boston, Mass.: Beacon Press.

Ménard, Renée. (1993a). *Transfert technologique au féminin. Les cas de Santa Lucia et de Santa Isabel*. Québec: Université Laval. Laboratoire de recherches anthropologiques. Collection "Rapports de recherche," Édition bilingue français-espagnol.

Ménard, Renée. (1993b). *Travail des femmes et condition économique: une évidence? Étude de cas chez les petits producteurs andins de la région du Lac Guamuez, Nairo, Colombie*. Québec: Université Laval. Mémoire de maîtrise.

Mianda, G.D.M. (1996). *Femmes africaines et pouvoir: Les maraîchères de Kinshasa*. Paris: L'Harmattan, Collection Zaïre-Histoire et Société.

Michel, A. (1985). "Dix ans d'irruption des sciences humaines dans le domaine du travail des paysannes." *Revue Tiers Monde*, 26(102):261–71.

Mies, Maria. (1986). *Patriarchy and Accumulation on a World Scale: Women in the International Division of Labor*. London: Zed Books.

Mies, Maria, Veronika Bennholdt-Thomsen, and Claudia von Werlhof. (1988). *Women: The Last Colony*. London: Zed Books.

Mies, M., and V. Shiva. (1993). *Ecofeminism*. London: Zed Books.

Miller, N. Norman. (1984). *Kenya: The Quest for Prosperity*. Boulder, Colo.: Westview Press.

Minoza, A., C. Botor, and I. Tablante. (1984). *Mother-Child Relationships in Early Childhood*. Cebu: Cebu Star Press.

Minturn, L., and W. Lambert. (1964). *Mothers of Six Cultures: Antecedents of Child Rearing*. New York: Wiley.

Mitter, S. (1986). *Common Fate, Common Bond*. London: Pluto.

Mohanty, Chandra T. (1991). "Under Western Eyes: Feminist Scholarship and Colonial Discourse." In *Third World Women and the Politics of Feminism*, ed. Chandra T. Mohanty, Ann Russo, and Lourdes Torres. Bloomington: Indiana University Press.

Morvaridi, B. (1990). "Cash Crop Production and the Process of Transformation." *Development and Change*, 21:693–722.

Morvaridi, B. (1992). "Gender Relations in Agriculture: Women in Turkey." *Economic Development and Cultural Change*, 40:567–86.

Mulder, N. (1990–91). "Everyday Life in the Philippines: Close Family Ties and the Individual." *Review of Women's Studies*, 1:73–80.

Najmabadi, A. (1991). "Hazards of Modernity and Morality: Women, State and Ideology in Contemporary Iran." In *Women, Islam and the State*, ed. D. Kandiyoti, 48–76. Philadelphia: Temple University Press.

Nash, June. (1993). "Introduction: Traditional Arts and Changing Markets in Middle America." In *Crafts in the Global Market: The Impact of Global Exchange on Middle American Artisans*, ed. J. Nash, 1–22. Albany: SUNY Press.

National Centre for Economic Administration. (1991). "Women in Development." *NCEA National Workshop Report*.

National Commission on the Role of Filipino Women. (1985). *Women Workers in the Philippines*. Manila: National Commission on the Role of Filipino Women.

National Statistics Office. (1993). *La Mauritanie en chiffres. Mauritania*, no. 6.

Nelson, R. (1968). *The Philippines*. New York: Walker.

Njonjo, Apollo et al. (1984): *A Study of the Production and Marketing of Women's Groups in Kenya*. Nairobi: SIDA.

Nuqui, Wilfredo. (1991). *The Health Sector and Social Policy Reform in the Philippines Since 1985*. Innocenti Occasional Papers, Number 12, UNICEF International Child Development Centre, Florence.

Oakley, A. (1980). *Women Confined: Towards a Sociology of Childbirth*. New York: Schocken Books.

Okojie, C.E.E. (1983). "Women in the Rural Economy of Bendel State." Field Survey.

Okojie, C.E.E. (1985). "Women's Status and Fertility in Bendel State of Nigeria: A Comparative Study of Selected Communities." Field Survey.

Okojie, C.E.E. (1987). "Accelerated Human Resources Development for the Rural Sector: The Roles of ADPs and Local Governments in Human Resource Development with Special Reference to Women." Paper presented at the ARMTI Seminar on Human Resources Development in the Nigerian Agricultural and Rural Sectors, ARMTI, Ilorin, April 28–30.

Okojie, C.E.E. (1989). "Women in Agriculture in Bendel State." Manuscript.

Okojie, C.E.E. (1990a). "Enhancing the Access of Rural Women to Appropriate Technology in Food Production and Processing in Nigeria." Manuscript.

Okojie, C.E.E. (1990b). "Impact of Government Programmes on Conditions of Life of Rural Women." Manuscript.

Okojie, C.E.E. (1990c). "The Role of Women in the Development of the Rural Economy." NCEMA Workshop Report on Economic Management for Local Government Officers.

Okojie, C.E.E. (1991). "Achieving Self-Reliance in Food Production in Nigeria: Maximising the Contribution of Rural Women." Journal of Social Development in Africa, 6(2):33–52.

Okojie, C.E.E. (1992). "Women's Roles in the Rural Economy in Nigeria: Implications for Rural Development Programmes." Paper presented at the Tenth World Congress of the International Economic Association, Moscow, August 24–28.

Okojie, C.E.E. (1993). "Micro-Consequences of High Fertility in Nigeria." In Proceedings of the Population Council Seminar on Fertility, Family Size and Structure: Consequences for Families and Children, 77–116. New York: The Population Council.

Olayiwole, C. B. (1985). "Rural Women's Involvement in Food Production in Kaduna State, Seminar on Women in Development." Institute of African Studies, Ibadan, June.

Ong, A. (1987). Spirits of Resistance and Capitalist Discipline: Factory Women in Malaysia. Albany: SUNY.

Ongile, Grace. (1992). The Effects of Structural Adjustment Policies on Women's Access to Employment Opportunities. Working Paper No. 488. Institute for Development Studies. University of Nairobi.

Oppong, C. (1980). "A Synopsis of Seven Roles and Status of Women: An Outline of Conceptual and Methodological Approach." Working Paper No. 94. ILO, World Employment Programme Research, September.

Oppong, C., ed. (1987). Sex Roles, Population and Development in West Africa. London: Heinemann Educational Books, Inc.

Oshuntogun, A. (1976). "Rural Women in Agricultural Development: A Nigerian Study." Paper presented at the Conference on Nigerian Women and Development in Relation to Changing Family Structure, Ibadan, April.

Osteria, T. S., and P. Ramos-Jiminez. (1988). "Women in Health Development: Mobilization of Women for Health Care Delivery in a Philippine Community." Sojourn, 3(2):217–35.

Oswald, Ursula. (1994). *Juchitán: Los alimentos: un vehiculo de justicia social.* Cuernavaca: CRIM/UNAM.

Patel, A. U., and Q.B.O. Anthonio. (1973). *Farmers' Wives in Agricultural Development: The Nigerian Case.* Department of Agricultural Economics and Extension, University of Ibadan.

Paulus, J. P. (1959). *Droit public au Congo Belge.* Bruxelles: Université Libre de Bruxelles, Institut de sociologie, Solvay.

Peck, M. S. (1987). *The Different Drum: Community Making and Peace.* New York: Simon and Schuster.

Peebles, D. (1984). "Changing the Status of Women in Development." *CUSO Journal*, 9–13 (available from CUSO, Ottawa, Ontario, Canada).

Peristiany, Jean G., ed. (1966). *Honour and Shame. The Values of Mediterranean Society.* Chicago: University of Chicago Press.

Petek-Salom, G., and P. Hukum. (1986). "Women's Emancipation after the Ataturk Period." In *Women of the Mediterranean*, ed. M. Gadant, 92–109. London: Zed Books.

Peterson Royce, Anya. (1975). *Prestigio y afiliación en una comunidad urbana: Juchitán, Oax.* México City, México: Instituto Nacional Indigenista.

Phillips, L. (1987). "From Precarista to Cooperativista: Tomasa Munoz de Leon." In *The Human Tradition in Latin America: The Twentieth Century*, ed. W. Beezley and J. Ewell. Wilmington, Del.: Scholarly Resources.

Phillips, L. (1989). "Gender Dynamics and Rural Household Strategies." *Canadian Review of Sociology and Anthropology*, 26(2):294–310.

Phillips, L. (1990). "The Power of Representation: Agrarian Politics and Rural Women's Interpretations of the Household in Coastal Ecuador." *Dialectical Anthropology*, 15:271–83.

Phillips, L. (1993). "Cooperatives and Agrarian Transitions: Implications for Neoliberalism." *Canadian Review of Sociology and Anthropology*, 30(4):429–50.

Pineda-Ofreneo, Rosalinda. (1990). "Women and Work: Focus on Homework in the Philippines." *Review of Women's Studies*, 1(1):42–55.

PNUD (United Nations Development Program). (1991). *Coopération au développement: Mauritanie.* Rapport Mauritanie.

Pollert, Anna. (1983). "Women, Gender Relations and Wage Labor." In *Gender, Class and Work*, ed. Eva Gamarnikow et al., 97–114. London: Heinemann.

Popkin, Barry M. (1983). "Rural Women, Work and Child Welfare in the Philippines." In *Women and Poverty in the Third World*, ed. M. Buvinic, M. Lycette, and W. McGreevey, 157–76. Baltimore: Johns Hopkins University Press.

Rahnema, M. (1990). "Participatory Action Research: The 'Last Temptation of Saint' Development." *Alternatives*, 15(2):199–226.

Rassam, A. (1980). "Women and Domestic Power in Morocco." *International Journal of Middle Eastern Studies*, 12(2):171–79.

Republic of Kenya. (1972). *The Trade Licensing Act Chapter 497: Laws of Kenya.* Nairobi: Government Printer.

Republic of Kenya. (1991). *The Report of the Presidential Committee on Employment.* Nairobi, Kenya: Government Printer.

Republic of Kenya. (1992). *National Policy on Gender and Development.* Women's

Bureau, Ministry of Culture and Social Services with assistance from SIDA. Prepared by Eddah W. Gachukia.

Republic of Kenya. (1993a). *The 1989–1993 Development Plan*. Nairobi: Government Printer.

Republic of Kenya. (1993b). *Economic Survey 1993*. Office of the Vice-President and Ministry of Planning and National Development.

Republic of Kenya. (1993c). *Employment and Earnings in the Formal and Informal Sector: A Gender Analysis*. Women's Bureau/SIDA Project, Ministry of Culture and Social Services.

Republic of Kenya. (1993d). *National Women Group Census Report*. Women's Bureau, Ministry of Culture and Social Services.

Republic of Kenya. (1993e). *Participation in Community Development, Public Affairs, Politics and Decision-Making: A Gender Analysis*. Women's Bureau/ SIDA Project. Ministry of Culture and Social Services, Issue No. 7.

Republic of the Philippines, Regional Development Council, Region V, National Economic Development Agency (NEDA). (1986). *Medium-Term Bicol Region Development Plan 1987–1992*. Legaspi City: NEDA.

Republic of the Philippines and UNICEF. (1990). *Situation of Children and Women in the Philippines 1990*. Manila: Government of the Republic of the Philippines and UNICEF.

Rich, A. (1986). *Of Woman Born: Motherhood as Experience and Institution*. New York: W. W. Norton.

Roberts, H. (1979). *Community Development Learning and Action*. Toronto: University of Toronto Press.

Roces, A., and G. Roces. (1985). *Culture Shock! Philippines*. Singapore: Times Books International.

Rojas-Aleta, Isabel, Teresita Silva, and Christine Eleazar. (1977). *A Profile of Filipino Women: Their Status and Role*. Manila: Philippine Business for Social Progress.

Roseberry, William. (1988). "Political Economy." *Annual Review of Anthropology*, 17:161–85.

Rubin, G. (1975). "The Traffic in Women: Notes on the Political Economy of Sex." In *Toward an Anthropology of Women*, ed. Raynar Reiter, 157–210. New York and London: Monthly Review Press.

Rutten, Rosanne. (1990). *Artisans and Entrepreneurs in the Rural Philippines*. Amsterdam: VU University Press.

Sachs, W., ed. (1992). *The Development Dictionary*. London: Zed Books.

Sahlins, M. (1976). *Age de pierre, âge d'abondance: l'économie des sociétés primitives*. Paris: Éditions Gallimard, Bibliothèque des sciences humaines, 1972, 1976 (traduction).

Savara, M. (1987). *Women in Food-Processing Industry: A Study of Bombay and Pune Cities*. Bombay: Centre for Studies in Decentralized Industries.

Scott, J. (1985). *Weapons of the Weak: Everyday Forms of Peasant Resistance*. London: Yale University Press.

Scott, J. (1988a). *Gender and the Politics of History*. New York: Columbia University Press.

Scott, J. (1988b). "Genre: une catégorie utile d'analyse historique." *Les cahiers du GRIF*, Editions Tiercé, nos. 37–38, Printemps.

SDID. (1984). *Rapport de faisabilité*. Préparé par Claude Côté et Louis Roberge. Société de développement international Desjardins, Québec, Canada.

SEAD. (1984). *Electronics and Development*. Edinburgh: Scottish Education and Action for Development.

Secrétariat d'État à la Condition féminine. République Islamique de Mauritanie. (1995). *Rapport national pour la Quatrième Conférence des femmes: lutte pour l'égalité, le développement et la paix*. Pékin.

Sedghi, H. (1976). "Women in Iran." In *Women in the World: A Comparative Study*, ed. L. B. Iglitzin and R. Ross, 219–22. Santa Barbara: Clio Books.

Sen, A. K. (1990). "Gender and Cooperative Conflicts." In *Persistent Inequalities: Women and World Development*, ed. I. Tinker, 123–49. New York: Oxford University Press.

Sethuraman, S. V., ed. (1981). *The Urban Informal Sector in Developing Countries: Employment, Poverty and Environment*. Genève: International Labor Organisation.

Sevilla, J. (1983). *Research on the Filipino Family: Review and Prospects*. Manila: Development Academy of the Philippines.

Sevilla, J. (1989). "Filipino Women and the Family." In *The Filipino Women in Focus: A Book of Readings*, ed. Amaryllis Torres, 35–55. Bangkok: UNESCO.

SEWA. (1984). *Organizing Self-Employed Women: The SEWA Experience*. Ahmedabad: SEWA.

Sharamshakti, S. (1988). *A Report of the National Commission of Self-employed Women in the Informal Sector*. New Delhi: Government of India, Ministry of Social Welfare, Department of Women and Child Development.

Siegel, L. (1980). "Delicate Bands: The Global Microelectronics Industry." Special issue of *Pacific Research* 11(1). Mountain View, Calif.: Pacific Studies Center.

Silberschmidt, Margrethe. (1991). *Women's Position in the Household and Their Use of Family Planning and Antenatal Services: A Case Study from Kisii District, Kenya*. CDR Project Paper 91.4, Copenhagen, Denmark.

Simard, G. (1990). *Définition d'une composante Femmes et développement en Mauritanie*. Projet Santé-Population, ministère de la Santé et des Affaires sociales. République Islamique de Mauritanie.

Simard, G. (1994). "La filière de la beauté en milieu urbain, le cas des entrepreneurs maures de la République Islamique de Mauritanie." Ph.D. thesis, Department of Anthropology, University of Laval, Laval, Quebec, Canada.

Simmons, Emmy. (1975). "The Small-Scale Rural Food Processing Industry in Northern Nigeria." *Food Research Institute Studies*, 14(2):147–60.

Sirman, N. (1988). "Peasants and Family Farms: The Position of Households in Cotton Production in a Village of Western Turkey." Ph.D. diss., University College of London.

Sirman, N. (1990). "State, Village and Gender in Western Turkey." In *Turkish State, Turkish Society*, ed. A. Finkel and N. Sirman, 21–52. London: Routledge.

*Situation of Children and Women in the Philippines*. (1987). United Nations Children's Fund.

Sivanandan, A. (1979). "Imperialism and Disorganic Development in the Silicon Age." *Race and Class*, 21(2)(Autumn) 11:1–26.

Skeggs, B. (1994). "Situating the Production of Feminist Ethnography." In *Researching Women's Lives from a Feminist Perspective*, ed. M. Maynard and J. Purvis. London: Taylor and Francis.

*Solidaridad*. (1988). Vol. 12(1)(January-March).

Stamp, Patricia. (N.d.). *Kikuyu Women's Self Help Groups: Toward an Understanding of the Relation Between Sex-Gender System and Mode of Production in Africa*, 27–45.

Stamp, Patricia. (1991). "Buying Otieno: The Politics of Gender and Ethnicity in Kenya." *Signs: Journal of Women in Culture and Society*, 16(4).

Stark, Oded. (1991). "Migration in LDCs: Risk, Remittances and the Family." *Finance and Development* (International Bank for Reconstruction and Development) (December):39–41.

Suda, Collette A. (1994). "Gender Division of Labor and the Status of Women." In *Perspectives in Development: Voices from the South*, ed. M'hammed Sabour, 115–38. Joensuu, Finland: Joensuu University Press.

Sunder Rajan, R. (1993). *Real and Imagined Women: Gender, Culture and Postcolonialism*. London: Routledge.

Szanton, Christina Blanc. (1982). "Women and Men in Iloilo, Philippines: 1903–1970." In *Women of Southeast Asia*, ed. Penny Van Esterik, 124–75. Chicago: Center for Southeast Asian Studies, Northern Illinois University.

Talle, Aud. (1988). "Women at a Loss: Changes in Maasai Pastoralism and Their Effects on Gender Relations." *Stockholm Studies in Social Anthropology*. Department of Social Anthropology, Stockholm, Sweden.

Tanner, Nancy. (1974). "Matrifocality in Indonesia and Africa and Among Black Americans." In *Women, Culture and Society*, ed. M. Rosaldo and L. Lamphere. Stanford: Stanford University Press.

Tauzin, A. (1982). *Autour de la poésie amoureuse maure de la Mauritanie et du Mali*. Paris: Presses du CNRS.

Tauzin, A. (1988). "Excision et identité féminine: l'exemple mauritanien." *Anthropologie et sociétés*, 12(1):29–37.

Tcherkézoff, Serge. (1993). " 'L'individualisme' chez Louis Dumont et l'anthropologie des idéologies globales. Genèse du point de vue comparatif" (l'ère partie). *Anthropologie et sociétés*, 17(3):141–58.

Tekeli, Ş. (1990). "Women in the Changing Political Associations of the 1980's." In *Turkish State, Turkish Society*, ed. A. Finkel and N. Sirman, 259–88. London: Routledge.

Tewe, B. O. (1978). *The Role of Women in Farm Labor Supply: A Case of Okitipupa Division of Ondo State*. Department of Agricultural Economics, University of Ibadan.

Tidalgo, Rosa Linda. (1985). "The Integration of Women in Development and Philippine Development Planning." In *Missing Women: Development Planning in Asia and the Pacific*, ed. N. Heyzer, 354–419. Kuala Lumpur: Asian and Pacific Development Centre.

Tiglao-Torres, A. (1990). "Gender Imagery in Philippine Psychology." In *Women's Springbook: Readings on Women and Society*, ed. M. Evasco, A. de Dios, and F. Caagusan, 103–14. Quezon City: Fresan Press.

Tilakaratna, S. (1991). "Stimulation of Self-Reliant Initiatives by Sensitized Agents: Some Lessons from Practice." In *Action and Knowledge: Breaking the Monopoly with Participatory Research Action-Research*, ed. O. Fals-Borda and M. A. Rahman, 135–45. New York: Apex Press.

Tillion, G. (1966). *Le harem et les cousins*. Paris: Éditions du Seuil.

Tinker, I. (1985). *Utilizing the Street Food Trade in Development Programming*. Washington, D.C.: Equity Policy Center.

Tinker, I. (1987). "The Human Economy of Micro and Small Scale Entrepreneurs." *Women in Micro and Small Scale Enterprise Development*. International Seminar held in Ottawa-Hull, IDIC (Institut de développement international canadien), October 16–30.

Toprak, B. (1964). "Women and Fundamentalism: The Case of Turkey." In *Identity Politics and Women: Cultural Reassertions and Feminisms in International Perspective*, ed. V. M. Moghadam, 293–306. Boulder, Colo.: Westview Press.

Torres, A. (1989). "The Filipina Looks at Herself." In *The Filipino Women in Focus: A Book of Readings*, ed. Amaryllis A. Torres, 1–27. Bangkok: UNESCO.

Traore, A. (1979). "L'Islam en Mauritanie." *Introduction à la Mauritanie*, 155–67. Centre de recherches et d'études sur les sociétés méditerranéennes. Centre d'études d'Afrique noire. Paris: Éditions du Centre national de la recherche scientifique.

Tutino, John. (1993). "Ethnic Resistance: Juchitán in Mexican History." In *Zapotec Struggles*, ed. Howard Campbell et al., 41–61. Washington, D.C.: Smithsonian Institution Press.

United Nations. (1985). *The Nairobi Forward-Looking Strategies for the Advancement of Women*. Nairobi, Kenya.

United Nations. (1990). *Women 2000: Women in Decision-Making*. Centre for Social Development and Humanitarian Affairs, Vienna, Austria.

United Nations. (1992). *United Nations Focus: The Quest for Women's Rights*. UN Department of Public Information.

Valverde, M. (1994). "Moral Capital." *Canadian Journal of Law and Society*, 9(1): 213–32.

Valverde, M., and L. Weir. (1988). "The Struggle of the Immoral: Preliminary Remarks on Moral Regulation." *Resources for Feminist Research*, 18(3):31–34.

Vanacker, C. (1979). "La Mauritanie jusqu'au 20e siècle." *Introduction à la Mauritanie*, 45–65. Centre de recherches et d'études sur les sociétés méditerranéennes. Centre études d'Afrique noire. Paris: Éditions du Centre national de la recherche scientifique.

Vasquez, Noel. (1989). "Philippine Country Study on Rural Homeworkers." Paper presented at the Technical Meeting on the Rural Homeworkers Project, Bangkok, June.

Vergin, N. (1985). "Social Change and the Family in Turkey." *Current Anthropology*, 26(5):571–74.

Vyas, J. (1992). "Credit to Self-Employed Women: Problems and Possible Solutions." In *Self-Employed Women: Population and Human Resource Devel-

*opment*, ed. P. Visaria and J. Unni, 174–83. Ahmedabad: Gujrat Institute of Development Research.

Wamalwa, N. Betty. (1987). "Are Women's Groups Exploiting Women?" Draft discussion paper for Women's Networking Group. Public Law Institute, Nairobi, Kenya.

Whitehead, Harriet. (1981). "The Bow and the Burden Strap: A New Look at Institutionalized Homosexuality in Native North America." In *Sexual Meanings. The Cultural Construction of Gender and Sexuality*, ed. S. B. Ortner and H. Whitehead, 80–115. Cambridge: Cambridge University Press.

Williams, P., and L. Chrisman, eds. (1994). *Colonial Discourse and Post-Colonial Theory: A Reader*. New York: Columbia University Press.

Wolf-Graaf, Anke. (1981). *Frauenarbeit im Abseits*. München: Frauenoffensive.

Women Studies and Resource Center. (1988). *Peasant Women Study for Critical Consciousness and Self-Organization*. Davao City: Women Studies and Resource Center.

Women Working Worldwide. (1988). *Women Working Worldwide: The International Division of Labor in the Electronics, Clothing and Textile Industries*. London: War on Want.

Yates, B. (1982). "Colonisation, Education and Work: Social Differentiation in Colonial Zaire." In *Women and Work in Africa*, ed. E. Bay. Boulder, Colo.: Westview Press.

Ybanez, R. F., ed. (1992). *Valuing Women's Work*. Quezon City: Women Development and Technology Institute.

Young, G., V. Samarasinghe, and K. Kusterer, eds. (1993). *Women at the Center: Development Issues and Practices for the 1990s*. West Hartford, Conn.: Kumarian Press.

Youssef, N. (1976). "Women in the Muslim World." In *Women in the World: A Comparative Study*, ed. L. Iglitzin and R. Ross, 203–18. Santa Barbara, Calif.: Clio Books.

Yu, Elena, and William T. Liu. (1980). *Fertility and Kinship in the Philippines*. Notre Dame, Ind.: University of Notre Dame Press.

Zaide, Gregorio. (1957). *Philippine Political and Cultural History: The Philippines since Pre-Spanish Times*. Manila: Philippine Education Company.

# Index

# About the Editors and Contributors

DINA ABBOTT has a doctorate degree and is a lecturer in Development Studies at the University of Derby, England. Dr. Abbott has been a Visiting Fellow and part-time tutor-counselor at the Open University. She also taught industrial studies for the Trade Union Congress as well as for various trade unions. Her doctoral thesis was on women's poverty and home-based income generation in Bombay.

DELIA D. AGUILAR, Ph.D., has a joint appointment in Ethnic Studies and Women's Studies at Bowling Green State University in Ohio. She has been doing work with Filipino women and has written two books, *Filipino Housewives Speak* (1991) and *The Feminist Challenge* (1989), both of which were published in Manila. At present, she is interested in looking at the directions feminism is taking in the Philippines.

CLAIRE BÉLANGER is presently finishing her Ph.D. in Social Anthropology. Her thesis deals with the mobility of capital and labor in a rural area of Italy. Her interest lies in the analysis of class, gender, and the construction of women as subjects in a process of social change. She is also interested in rural women's issues in developing countries.

VERONIKA BENNHOLDT-THOMSEN, social anthropologist (Ph.D.) and sociologist (Ph.D.), has taught at universities in Germany, the Neth-

erlands, and Austria and has conducted empirical research in Mexico and
Germany on agrarian questions, peasant movements, and women's work.
One of the "mothers" of Women's Studies in Germany, she has contributed
to the development of feminist social theory and is the author of several
books and articles with translations into Spanish, English, Japanese, Swed-
ish, and Korean. She is currently director of the Institute for Theory and
Practice of Subsistence in Bielfeld, West Germany.

PARVIN GHORAYSHI, Ph.D., is Professor of Sociology at the University
of Winnipeg, Canada. She started her research career by studying agrarian
class structure in industrialized countries. Her research interests are in feminist theories and gender relations. She is the author of *Women and Work
in Developing Countries* (1995) and has published on agrarian issues and
on women in *Sociologia Ruralis* (1986); *The Canadian Review of Sociology
and Anthropology* (1989); and *The Political Economy of Manitoba*, ed.
Silver and Hull (1990); *Women and Politics* (1996). She is presently studying rural women in Iran.

ANGELA M. GILLIAM is a member of the faculty at The Evergreen State
College, Olympia, Washington, and has done research in Mexico, Brazil,
and Papua, New Guinea. Dr. Gilliam was a Fulbright Scholar in the grad-
uate program of the anthropology department at the University of Brasilia
in 1994–95 and is currently working on a book about women, work, and
race relations in Brazil.

TUULA HEINONEN, Ph.D., is interested in women and health, cross-
cultural social support features, social work in health care, and international perspectives on gender relations. Her research focuses on Filipino
women and her dissertation was entitled "Gender Differences in Household
Approaches to Adult Illness in Rural Philippines."

SUZAN M. ILCAN, Ph.D., teaches at the Department of Sociology and
Anthropology at the University of Windsor, Ontario. She has done extensive research in rural Turkey and has published in *Atlantis* (1986), *Ethnology* (1994), *Culture* (1994), and *International Migration Review* (1994).

MARIE FRANCE LABRECQUE has a Ph.D. from City University of New
York and is a Professor of Anthropology at Laval University in Quebec.
She has done research on Mexican peasant communities and has increasingly concentrated on women's issues. She is currently involved in research
projects both in Latin America and among native women in Quebec. Professor Labrecque has a number of publications and her most recent work
is a book entitled *L'égalité devant soi: sexes, rapports sociaux et développement international* (1994).

LES LEVIDOW holds a doctorate degree and is a Research Fellow at the Open University, Milton Keynes. He studies the safety regulations of agricultural biotechnology. He has been managing editor of *Science as Culture* since its inception in 1987 and of its predecessor, *The Radical Science Journal*. When he worked at Free Association Books, he coedited several books, including *Science, Technology and the Labor Process* (1981, 1985), *Anti-Racist Science Teaching* (1987), and *Cyborg Worlds: The Military Information Society* (1989).

GERTRUDE MIANDA has a Ph.D. in Sociology. Her thesis was entitled "Gender, Power and Development . . . Women's Strategies in the Production of Vegetables in Kinshasa, Zaire." She is interested in women's conditions and the construction of gender in the context of Africa and Zaire.

MARY MORGAN, M.A.Ed., is working in the area of social and economic development as an adult educator, developing curriculum that evolves from participants' experiences and ensures that educational process situates the context in the content. Her publications include *Creando Nuestro Futuro Hoy, Inciando Micro-Empresas y Participando en Fondos Reembosables* (1993) and *Creating our Future Today, Initiating Micro-Enterprises and Participating in Revolving Loan Funds* (1994).

CHRISTIANA E. E. OKOJIE obtained her Ph.D. from the University of Ibadan in Nigeria. She is now an Associate Professor in the Department of Economics and Statistics, University of Benin, Benin City, Nigeria. She has published several articles on women in development, labor market studies, and population issues. Her research projects have spanned topics such as women in rural and urban economics, women and health, the gender gap in education, and determinants of contraceptive use among men and women.

TIFFANY R. PATTERSON is Assistant Professor of History at Binghamton University in New York where she teaches courses on the African Diaspora with particular interest in the studies of race, gender, class, and culture within empire. Associate editor of the sixteen-volume series *Black Women in United States History*, edited by Darlene Clark Hine, she is currently working on a study of patronage and the politics of identity in African-American history.

LYNNE PHILLIPS, Ph.D., is an Associate Professor in the Department of Sociology and Anthropology at the University of Windsor in Ontario. Her research interests include feminist anthropology, comparative development, and medical discourse on/in the tropics. Her most recent articles are in *Alternatives, Canadian Review of Sociology and Anthropology, Latin*

*American Research Review*, and *Dialectical Anthropology*. She has co-edited a book with Sally Cole titled *Ethnographic Feminisms: Essays in Anthropology*.

GISÈLE SIMARD has a Ph.D. in Anthropology with specialization in Gender and Development. For the last fifteen years, Dr. Simard has been a consultant in international development; her mandates were concentrated mainly in French-speaking Africa in planning and evaluating programs aimed at improving the conditions of women. She is the author of *Animer, planifier et évaluer l'action: La methode du "Focus group"* (1989), contextualized for Africa and tailored to capture the voice of women.

COLLETTE SUDA, Ph.D., is a Senior Research Fellow at the Institute of African Studies, University of Nairobi, Kenya. She is a rural sociologist and her research interests are in the areas of gender and development, rural development, child rights, and family studies. She has done extensive research and published widely on diverse issues within her areas of interest. She has also lectured and consulted for various groups and organizations within and outside Kenya.

ISBN 0-313-29797-5

90000>

EAN

9 780313 297977

HARDCOVER BAR CODE